SYSTEMIC CORRUPTION

Systemic Corruption

CONSTITUTIONAL IDEAS FOR AN ANTI-OLIGARCHIC REPUBLIC

CAMILA VERGARA

PRINCETON UNIVERSITY PRESS

PRINCETON & OXFORD

Copyright © 2020 by Princeton University Press

Requests for permission to reproduce material from this work
should be sent to permissions@press.princeton.edu

Published by Princeton University Press
41 William Street, Princeton, New Jersey 08540
6 Oxford Street, Woodstock, Oxfordshire OX20 1TR

press.princeton.edu

All Rights Reserved

First paperback printing, 2022
Paperback ISBN 978-0-691-21156-5
Cloth ISBN 978-0-691-20753-7
ISBN (e-book) 978-0-691-20873-2

British Library Cataloging-in-Publication Data is available

Editorial: Matt Rohal
Production Editorial: Brigitte Pelner
Production: Erin Suydam
Publicity: Kate Hensley (US) and Amy Stewart (UK)
Copyeditor: Kathleen Kageff

This book has been composed in Arno

To plebeians, in solidarity

CONTENTS

ILLUSTRATIONS

ACKNOWLEDGMENTS

THIS IS A BOOK written against the grain that recovers a lost plebeian tradition and seeks to radically transform constitutional democracy to empower common people against the powerful few who today control most of the financial resources and keep political elites on their payrolls. When I began researching and writing about radical reform, I encountered plenty of conservative thinkers who had no hesitation in calling the project of institutionalizing popular power simply ridiculous, and others who were drawn to critically engage with it from opposing theoretical banks. In many ways this book has been shaped, for the better, by conflict. Here I want to acknowledge the few who supported my outlandish ideas as well as those who constructively opposed them for years, helping me to strengthen my arguments to satisfy criticism and respond to incredulity.

I began working on this project while a doctoral student in political theory at The New School for Social Research, where I found a stimulating academic community that nurtured my growth as a critical theory scholar. I want to recognize Andrew Arato, sociologist of law and one of the most formidable and generous intellectual sparring partners I had during these formative years. Even though he was not formally my adviser, I met with Andrew regularly to discuss constitutions, constituent processes, and revolutionary rules in theory and practice throughout the years. Even if he could not get himself to decisively support the institutional proposal I develop in the last chapter of the book, I am eternally grateful for the time he dedicated to our conversations over several shots of espresso at the local Joe's Coffee, and the material and emotional support he so selflessly offered me in times of need. Similarly, I want to thank the philosopher Richard Bernstein for reading several drafts of the chapter on Hannah Arendt and encouraging me to develop a novel interpretation of her work on the council system. He was also a fundamental source of moral and intellectual support, to which I have returned several times since leaving The New School.

Perhaps the person who did the most to help me succeed is Nadia Urbinati, who offered me a place at Columbia University after I had to leave The New School because of a lack of institutional funding. Despite our sometimes unbridgeable theoretico-political differences, she never doubted my capacity to make a significant contribution to the multiple fields this book speaks to. Among the many disagreements we had over the years, the most fruitful was her challenge to the need for radical reform. She pushed me to find the strongest justification to fundamentally change our representative political systems, which I found in the deplorable corruption levels in virtually every democracy around the world, and in the neglected *systemic* nature of political corruption, which came to frame the whole project, ultimately becoming the title for the book. It was also my analysis of systemic corruption that caught the attention of my editor Matt Rohal, who "discovered" my paper abstract at the annual meeting of the American Political Science Association in the summer of 2018. Even if he initially wanted me to write a whole book on systemic corruption, he became even more interested in the project when I told him what he'd seen was only chapter 1. I am grateful for his constructive and creative engagement with my work as well as for his unwavering support throughout the process.

I want also to recognize the crucial role played by David Johnston, who, in addition to his generous commenting on my work, became my emotional rock during the highest moments of pushback and self-doubt, giving me the necessary stability to navigate the treacherous waters of dissertation writing. Even if we were not always in agreement, he recognized the value of the project from the first time we met in the summer of 2012. His support was instrumental for trespassing the intellectual gatekeeping I encountered, and it allowed the project to move from "ridiculous" to "timely," and to be ultimately awarded with "distinction" in a unanimous vote by the dissertation committee.

The first staunch academic supporter of this project centered on plebeian responses to oligarchic domination was John McCormick, whom I met in 2013 in the conference on Machiavelli that Nadia, David, and I organized to celebrate the five-hundred-year anniversary of the publication of *The Prince* at Columbia University. In addition to his supportive comments on my interpretation of the Florentine secretary's work over the years, like a good Machiavellian John became my consigliere, giving me realist guidance in moving about the academic field without too many scars. I am grateful for his generous advice and friendship. Two other Machiavelli scholars, Jérémie Barthas and Giovanni Giorgini, whom I also met at that symposium, gave me much needed support over the years, kindly sharing their knowledge and giving me constructive critique. Finally, I want to thank Jeremy Kessler and Bernard Harcourt, two legal scholars whose help proved vital during the last stages of writing. While Jeremy gave me substantive feedback both on the chapter on material constitutionalism, and on the enforcement provisions in the juridical scheme for a plebeian branch, Bernard was the first to recognize the value of my institutional proposal and to wholeheartedly support my research on plebeian politics and philosophy, which now I continue as a postdoctoral research scholar at the Eric H. Holder Initiative for Civil and Political Rights at Columbia Law School.

In addition to the intellectuals who have engaged with this ambitious project of rethinking the republic, I want to thank the women in my life who gave me indispensable material and emotional support for raising my children while I completed my doctoral studies, taught seminars, advised students, traveled the world to present my work, and wrote this book. I am most grateful for the unconditional support and encouragement of Ann Scobie, Marissa Wilhelm, and my mother, Verónica González, who despite our ideological differences never doubted my capacity to deliver a book that would better diagnose our current political maladies, propose creative solutions, and inspire others to think outside the constitutional box and engage in political action. I also want to thank my father, Pedro Pablo Vergara, who patiently listened, for over a decade, to my ideas about institutionalizing popular power to change the world. And lastly, I want to thank my resilient and compassionate children, Ulysses and Aquarela, to whom I gave birth in the midst of it all and who had to endure with patience and empathy years of an overworked, sleep-deprived mother, but nevertheless cheered for me all the way to the finish line.

SYSTEMIC CORRUPTION

Introduction

CRISIS OF THE REPRESENTATIVE REPUBLIC

TODAY THE IDEA that democracy is failing, not only in the United States but around the world, has become ubiquitous.[1] Even if it was only after the 2016 presidential election that the "crisis of democracy" narrative went mainstream,[2] this particular cycle of political decay in our constitutional regimes appears to have begun in the 1970s and 1980s with the first neoliberal experiments led by General Augusto Pinochet in Chile, Margaret Thatcher in the United Kingdom, and Ronald Reagan in the United States.[3] Increasing income inequality and immiseration of the working classes were effectively depoliticized and naturalized to the point that today it is considered legitimate that three individuals in the United States own more wealth than the bottom 50 percent; that while the wealth of the superrich has grown 6,000 percent since 1982, median

---

1. The rise of far-right supremacist parties in many European countries, which are forming alliances at the supranational level; a government in India that is building concentration camps for religious minorities; and a government in Chile that represses mass protests, violating human rights, to protect a neoliberal model imposed in dictatorship: all show that democracies are malfunctioning. On the totalitarian experiments in India, see Jeffrey Gettleman and Hari Kumar, "India Plans Big Detention Camps for Migrants. Muslims Are Afraid," *New York Times*, August 17, 2019, https://www.nytimes.com/2019/08/17/world/asia/india-muslims-narendra -modi.html. On the popular uprising in Chile, see my article "The Meaning of Chile's Explosion," *Jacobin*, October 29, 2019, https://www.jacobinmag.com/2019/10/chile-protests -sebastian-pinera-constitution-neoliberalism.

2. For an elitist republican interpretation on the crisis of democracy, in which elites are the culprits of decay, see Levitsky and Ziblatt, *How Democracies Die*.

3. For a partial historical account of neoliberalism, see Slobodian, *Globalists*. A Euro-centric viewpoint prevents Slobodian from taking into account the illiberal origins of neoliberalism, first implemented in Chile under Pinochet with the help of the so-called Chicago Boys, trained in the United States in the 1960s.

household wealth has gone down 3 percent over the same period; and that one out of five children currently lives in poverty in the richest country in the world.[4]

Because patterns of accumulation of wealth at the top, in which corporations pay zero taxes despite high profits while their employees have to rely on public assistance to make ends meet,[5] are far from natural—but rather enabled by existing rules and institutions—part of what this book sets out to accomplish is to extend the horizon of analysis so we can better appreciate our political regime as an experiment that has led to acute inequality and a dangerous oligarchization of power, and therefore in need of structural reform. Representative democracy is an artificial political infrastructure that we have designed for ourselves, and that, as it was first established, it can similarly be overhauled. Structural innovations to political systems, even those considered radical or extreme, have been achieved in the past, and there is no reason to believe they cannot be attained in our lifetime.[6]

I theorize the crisis of democracy from a structural point of view, arguing that liberal representative governments suffer from *systemic corruption*, a form of political decay that manifests itself as an oligarchization of power in society. I trace and analyze the concept of political corruption in Plato, Aristotle, Polybius, Cicero, and Machiavelli and then offer a critique of our current juridical and individual understanding of corruption. I argue that we need to move away from the "bad apples" approach, the view that corruption exists only because there are corrupt people in office, and look at the structure in which these corrupt elites are embedded. We must entertain the possibility that if a tree consistently produces "bad apples," it might be a "bad tree." Systemic corruption refers to the inner functioning of the system as a whole, independent of who occupies the places of power. A democracy is a political regime in which an electoral majority rules, and therefore it makes sense to think that "good" democratic government would benefit (or at least not hurt) the interests of the majority. When the social wealth that is collectively created is consistently and increasingly accumulated by a small minority against the material interests of the majority, then it means that the rules of the game and

---

4. Chuck Collins, "The Wealth of America's Three Richest Families Grew by 6,000% since 1982," *The Guardian*, October 31, 2018, https://www.theguardian.com/commentisfree/2018/oct/31/us-wealthiest-families-dynasties-governed-by-rich.

5. Louise Matsakis, "The Truth About Amazon, Food Stamps, and Tax Breaks," *Wired*, September 6, 2018, https://www.wired.com/story/truth-about-amazon-food-stamps-tax-breaks/.

6. My viewpoint originates in a deep-seated constitutional skepticism rooted in the experience of having lived in Chile, under an illegitimate constitution that entrenched a neoliberal economic model and a small, subsidiary state as well as religious and patriarchal social norms.

how they are being used and abused are benefiting the powerful *few* instead of the *many*. This trend of oligarchization of power within a general respect for the rule of law, regardless of who controls the government, is what I conceive as systemic corruption in representative democracy.

As a response to this political diagnosis, in which the crisis of democracy is due to an overgrowth of oligarchic power, I propose to retrieve the constitutional wisdom of past republican experiences with oligarchic domination to find an institutional solution to structural decay.[7] Based on an in-depth analysis of institutional, procedural, and normative innovations proposed by Niccolò Machiavelli, Nicolas de Condorcet, Rosa Luxemburg, and Hannah Arendt, I propose to institutionalize popular collective power in a mixed constitution as the most effective way to deal with systemic corruption and oligarchic domination.

A mixed constitution necessarily entails opposing institutional powers for the few and the many. From the realist and material perspective of the republicanism of Machiavelli, society is seen as divided between the powerful few and the common people, and therefore the political order needs to include institutions both to allow a selected elite to rule within limits and to enable the common people to push back against the inevitable domination that eventually comes from the government by few. Recognizing this oligarchic tendency and the asymmetry of power between the few and the many, mixed constitutions set up *plebeian* institutions to resist the overreach of the few. Constitutional frameworks today have nothing of the sort and therefore have left the many vulnerable to oligarchic domination. Democracies contain only institutions through which representatives govern and check each other (e.g., Congress, the president) and elite institutions supposed to censure their decisions (e.g., the Supreme Court), effectively leaving the elites to police themselves. Common people do not have an exclusive political institution through which they can veto oppressive measures coming from representative government or directly censor their representatives. We thus have much to learn from ancient and modern republics about the kind of plebeian institutions—empowering the common people who do not rule—that are necessary to effectively counter the relentless oligarchization of political power.

---

7. I approach the decay of constitutional democracies and possible institutional solutions from the perspective of radical republican thought, and therefore I will not engage with other diagnoses and solutions offered from within democratic theory—most prominently coming out of participatory and deliberative democratic theory—but rather focus only on the republican tradition and its model of mixed constitution.

I take therefore as a given that representative democracies are not mixed orders but *monocratic* regimes with separation of functions:[8] a form of government in which the selected few, authorized by the people, exert ruling power through different institutions, and the collective power of the many is not institutionalized. While legislative, executive, and judicial powers are the virtual monopoly of the selected few[9]—who exert legitimate power based on citizens' consent—the many—common citizens who do not effectively govern—do not have a collective institutional role in the political decision-making process,[10] and therefore there is no effective counterpower to an increasingly corrupt and oligarchic representative government. The many are today atomized, and their power has been reduced to selecting representatives and sometimes proposing and voting referenda through the aggregation of individual preferences. The high degree of political corruption in most representative systems evidences that elections are not an effective means to control public officials who write corrupt laws or support policies that benefit powerful corporations to the detriment of the common welfare.

Political power is today de facto oligarchic. Materially, the people who get to decide on policy, law, and the degree of protection of individual rights—the president, members of Congress, and Supreme Court justices—are part of the richest 2 percent and therefore tend to have the same interests and worldview of the powerful few who benefit most from the status quo.[11] Moreover, the control of special interests over politics via campaign finance has allowed money to influence lawmaking and public policy, which has in turn allowed the building of legal and material structures that disproportionally benefit the wealthy at the detriment of the majority. In the United States, the richest 1 percent currently owns 40 percent of the country's wealth—more than the

---

8. Pasquino, "Classifying Constitutions."

9. All modern constitutions today lack a popular institution in which citizens can collectively participate in the decision-making process by proposing, deliberating, and deciding on law, except for the Swiss "cantonal assembly" system (*Landsgemeinde*), one of the oldest surviving forms of *direct* democracy, which is practiced in only two of the twenty-five Swiss cantons. They are nevertheless subject to Swiss federal law.

10. Elections, recalls, referenda, and citizen initiatives are powers of the individual, not the many as collective subject. In addition to being weak, in my view, these political instruments (or "methods" as Machiavelli calls them) have already been (ab)used as weapons of domination by the better-organized parts of civil society. See, for example, Proposition 8 in California banning same-sex marriage.

11. This material structural analysis of elite institutions does not exclude, of course, the few social justice advocates, such as Justice Ruth Bader Ginsburg, who, despite sharing material conditions with the rest of the elite, has ruled consistently in favor of the *many*.

bottom 90 percent combined.[12] This pernicious inequality enables billionaires and their CEOs to live the life of feudal lords in mansions, surrounded by servants, having the power to hire and fire legions of workers who struggle to maintain a precarious standard of living in a society in which most basic services have been privatized and the minimum wage is not enough to cover basic housing, food, health-care, and education costs. To tackle this problem of systemic corruption, in which the structure consistently works to enrich the few and oppress the many, I argue we need to go beyond legal reform and partial fixes—especially in countries where oligarchy has become too powerful to allow for meaningful legislative change—and establish a new plebeian institutional counterweight strong enough to keep elites in check.

The plebeian branch I propose to add to current constitutional orders would be autonomous and aimed not at achieving self-government or direct democracy, but rather at serving anti-oligarchic ends: to judge and censor elites who rule. The plebeian branch, which is designed to be incorporated into already existing democratic regimes, is composed of a decentralized network of radically inclusive local assemblies, empowered to initiate and veto legislation as well as to exercise periodic constituent power, and a delegate surveillance office able to enforce decisions reached in the assemblies and to impeach public officials. The establishment of local assemblies not only would allow ordinary people to push back against oligarchic domination through the political system but also inaugurates an institutional conception of the people as the many assembled locally: a collectivity that is not a homogeneous, bounded subject but rather a political agent that operates as a network of political judgment in permanent flow. The *people-as-network* would be a political subject with as many brains as assemblies, in which collective learning, reaction against domination, and social change occurs organically and independently from representative government and political parties.

I begin by providing in chapter 1 a diagnosis for the crisis of democracy based on systemic corruption. After reconstructing from the works of Plato, Aristotle, Polybius, and Machiavelli a notion of systemic political corruption particular to popular governments, I then engage with recent neorepublican and institutionalist attempts at redefining political corruption within our current political regimes. I argue that we still lack a proper conception of systemic corruption comparable in sophistication to the one offered by ancient and modern philosophers because we are as yet unable to account for the role that procedures and institutions play in fostering corruption through their normal functioning. The chapter concludes by proposing a definition of systemic

---

12. Wolff, "Household Wealth Trends in the United States."

corruption as the oligarchization of power transpiring within a general respect for the rule of law. This conception of corruption appears as intrinsically connected to increasing socioeconomic inequality, which enables inequality of political influence and the drift toward oligarchic democracy: a regime in which the many empower, through their ballots, the powerful few, who enable the dispossession and oppression of those many.

The recognition of systemic corruption as a relentless process of political decay prompted ancient and modern political thinkers to study existing constitutions and engage in efforts to design the perfect regime: a political order immune to the degradation of its institutions and procedures, and thus insulated from social decay and regime decline. Chapter 2 traces the intellectual history and institutional iterations of the theory of the mixed constitution, which originated as a critique of pure, monocratic constitutions and offered a realist redress for systemic corruption based on the institutionalization of different forms of social power. I offer a genealogy of two main strands of interpretation: (1) an *elitist-proceduralist* strand commenced by Polybius and Cicero, reinterpreted by Montesquieu, constitutionalized by Madison, and recently brought perhaps to its highest level of philosophical sophistication by Philip Pettit; and (2) a *plebeian-materialist* strand originating in the political experience of the plebs within the ancient Roman republic and continuing in Machiavelli's interpretation of this experience in light of the political praxis of the *popolo* during the Florentine republic. I make the distinction between elitist and plebeian constitutions based on who has final decision-making power in a given framework: the selected few or the common people. Throughout the book I provide a visual representation of constitutional orders based on this basic distinction between the few and the many, to allow for a better spatial understanding of the distribution of powers in any given constitution as well as for a comparison between different models of republics.

To rethink the republic from a structural perspective implies not only the need to theorize the crisis of democracy at the systemic level, and to find adequate institutional solutions, but also the necessity of approaching constitutionalism from a point of view that allows us to acknowledge ever-expanding systemic corruption and oligarchic domination. Chapter 3 proposes a novel methodological approach to the study of constitutions that goes beyond the written text and jurisprudence, to incorporate the material structure of society. This material interpretation originates in the factual organization and exercise of power that is allowed and enabled by foundational institutions, rules, and procedures—or lack thereof. What I term *material constitutionalism* is premised on the idea that the organization of political power cannot be analyzed without taking into account political and socioeconomic power structures, and it therefore establishes a constitutional ideology that stands opposed to

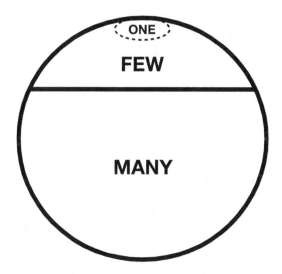

FIGURE I.1. The material constitution. Basic structure of spatial representation of the constitution as distribution of power.

legal positivism, formalism, and proceduralism. The chapter begins by putting forward this material approach, which I trace back to Machiavelli, and distinguishing two strands: one *institutionalist*, developed by Condorcet, Thomas Jefferson, and Arendt, and more recently by John McCormick and Lawrence Hamilton, and another, *critical*, developed by Karl Marx, Evgeny Pashukanis, and Antonio Negri, and more recently by Marco Goldoni and Michael Wilkinson. Within this taxonomy, Rosa Luxemburg's materialist critique of law and her proposal for institutionalizing workers' councils are a bridge between the critical and institutionalist traditions.

I dedicate the second part of the book to reviewing the constitutional thought of those who dared propose the institutionalization of popular power and endowed it with supreme authority to protect political liberty: Machiavelli, Condorcet, Luxemburg, and Arendt. These thinkers have all suffered reactionary backlashes, and therefore their work has consistently been misunderstood, instrumentalized, demonized, or neglected. Consequently, part of what I want to accomplish is to offer a serious engagement with their ideas and proposals using a plebeian interpretative lens under which they fit together, as part of a plebeian constitutional tradition. This sort of "B side" of constitutionalism is therefore composed of those who support the institutionalization of the power of the many as the only way to achieve liberty for all, misfits in an elitist tradition dominated by the impulse to suppress conflict in favor of harmony, stability, and security.

I begin chapter 4 by presenting Machiavelli's constitutional thought as the foundation of a type of constitutionalism that is material in its analysis of law and procedures, and anti-oligarchic in its institutional design. Recognizing the influence that socioeconomic inequalities exert over political power, Machiavelli embraces conflict as the effective cause of free government and strives to empower and channel emancipatory, plebeian energies through the constitutional order. The chapter focuses on Machiavelli's most important contribution to materialist constitutionalism: the plebeian nature of constituent power. I argue that the constituent power in Machiavelli serves not as a bridge between basic principles and politics, but rather as the power exerted to resist oppression and establish plebeian and anti-oligarchic institutions. While in democratic theory the constituent power has been conceived as the *autopoietic* power of the community, a republican theory of constituent power is defined functionally, determined by the goal of achieving liberty as nondomination. Because for Machiavelli liberty demands the productive channeling of the plebeian desire not to be dominated, the preservative power of free government is the power the people have to periodically redraw the boundaries of what is considered permissible and what is deemed oppressive. Only the many—who desire not to be oppressed and do not partake in ruling—are the guardians of liberty. I analyze Machiavelli's proposal for reforming Florence through his theory of institutional renewal aimed at redeeming corrupt republics, focusing on his proposal to normalize instances of constituent creation and punishment in ten-year intervals as an antidote for systemic corruption.

Chapter 5 is devoted to the constitutional thought of Nicolas de Condorcet, the challenge of representing the sovereign demos, and his proposal for considering the people in its institutional character rather than as an atomized collective subject that can never be made fully present and therefore properly represented. As an alternative to the liberal constitution established in the American colonies, Condorcet proposed a republican framework in which the ruling power of making laws and decisions about administration is concentrated in a representative assembly, which is legally responsive to an institutionalized popular power—a network of primary assemblies—aimed at checking its laws, policies, and abuses. The chapter presents an in-depth analysis of the 1793 constitutional plan for the French republic proposed by Condorcet, read through the lens of his egalitarian tracts on education, slavery, and the rights of women.

While Condorcet was writing at the birth of modern representative government and was concerned with preserving the revolutionary spirit to protect the republic from corruption, Rosa Luxemburg proposes to embrace workers' councils as a political infrastructure of emancipation at a moment when the modern party system had begun to consolidate. It is when the Social

Democratic Party—a party in support of the interests of the working class—had gained partial control of the German government that she realized that the liberty of the working class demanded a different political infrastructure. The betrayal of the revolutionary party proved to her the truth of Marx's argument that the "working class cannot simply lay hold of the ready-made state machinery and wield it for its own purposes,"[13] and therefore she proposed to alter "the foundation and base of the social constitution"[14] from below by institutionalizing workers', soldiers', and peasant councils and establishing a national council of workers as part of a revolutionary constitutional political order.

The final chapter in this section analyzes Hannah Arendt's intellectual relation with Luxemburg's work, her critique of the American founding, and her proposal for establishing a council system. According to Arendt, the moment the founders focused on representation and neglected "to incorporate the township and the town-hall meeting into the Constitution," the revolutionary spirit was lost, and government became mere administration.[15] Arendt embraces the council system as an alternative form of government aimed at the continual reintroduction of freedom as action in a public realm dominated by administration. I argue that we should understand Arendt's proposal as a novel interpretation of the mixed constitution, one in which the division between the few and the many is replaced by that of *parties* dedicated to administration, and *councils* dedicated to political judgment.

In the third and final part of the book I survey the development of plebeian thought in the twenty-first century, its philosophical foundations and institutional proposals. In chapter 8 I analyze plebeianism as a political philosophy in the works of Martin Breaugh and Jeffrey Green and then provide and in-depth analysis of two recent attempts at retrieving the mixed constitution and proposing institutional innovations by John McCormick and Lawrence Hamilton. I first engage with McCormick's proposals to revive the office of the Tribunate of the Plebs and bring back plebeian power to exert extraordinary punishment against agents of corruption, and I argue that his radical republican interpretation of Machiavelli places class struggle, the threat of plutocracy, and the need for popular institutions to control the rich at the center of material constitutionalism. I then problematize the illiberal nature of his proposals and the legitimacy problems arising from lottery as mode of selection. The chapter then analyzes Hamilton's proposal to combine consulting

13. Marx, "Manifesto of the Communist Party" in *Marx and Engels Reader*, 470.
14. Luxemburg, "The Socialization of Labor," in *Rosa Luxemburg Reader*, 343.
15. Arendt, *On Revolution*, 224.

participatory institutions with an "updated tribune of the plebs" and a plebe-ian electoral procedure and discusses the challenge of proliferating sites of popular participation and competing authorities arising in such a scheme.

Finally, in chapter 9 I make my own contribution to plebeian constitutional theory by proposing to constitutionalize popular power in a "plebeian branch" that is thought through Arendt's model of parties and councils, incorporating features from the proposals establishing plebeian institutions analyzed in the previous sections. I first lay out a way to separate the few from the many that would in principle conform to the current liberal constitutional framework, and then I describe the two institutions that would make up the proposed plebeian branch: a network of primary assemblies with the power to initiate and veto or repeal any law, public policy, judicial decision, and appointment as well as to update the constitution, and a Tribunate office aimed at enforcing mandates coming out of the network of assemblies and fighting political cor-ruption. To close this final chapter I offer a tentative juridical framework for this plebeian branch, which is meant to be incorporated into any existing rep-resentative democratic regime and is aimed at empowering plebeians— common people who enjoy only second-class citizenship within the current constitutional structure—as a more enduring solution to the systemic corrup-tion of representative systems and the oligarchic domination that inevitably comes with it.

I close the book with an epilogue discussing possible scenarios in which plebeian power could be institutionalized from the point of view of revolution-ary politics, and I argue that if—following Machiavelli, Condorcet, Luxem-burg, and Arendt—the aim of revolution is liberty, which demands self-emancipatory political action, then revolutionary change—aimed at building the legal and material infrastructure for plebeian political power—could be achieved without the need of an outright revolution. The redistribution of political power could be done by revolutionary reformers within the bound-aries of the Constitution or by the people themselves, claiming collective power and authority by disrupting the ordinary administration of power with their extraordinary political action in local assemblies.

PART I

Systemic Corruption and the Material Constitution

1

Corruption as Political Decay

I BEGIN this book from the premise that liberal democracy, as any other political regime throughout history, is flawed and perfectible, a product of fallible human thinking. Of the many deficiencies of our current regime form, perhaps the most problematic is its inability to effectively combat corruption. According to Transparency International, corruption is a serious problem. In 2016 only two countries—Denmark and New Zealand—out of 176 states surveyed scored above percentile 90 (equivalent to an A in political cleanliness), and over two-thirds scored below 50 percent, which indicates that the majority of representative governments[1] suffer from "endemic corruption," a kind of "systemic grand corruption [that] violates human rights, prevents sustainable development and fuels social exclusion."[2] Even if the Corruption Perceptions Index attempts to explicitly account for *systemic* corruption—as opposed to mere cash for votes, quid pro quo corruption—the current definition of political corruption does not yet allow for an accurate measurement of its structural layer because it remains blind to the role procedures and political institutions play in fostering corruption through their normal functioning. In this chapter I argue that we are working with an imperfect, reductionist explanation of political corruption that, even if it allows for quantitative research and generalizations based on discreet observable variables, does not capture the broader, more intractable and pernicious form of systemic corruption that ancient and modern political thinkers wanted to avoid.

The predominant definition of corruption as "illegal actions concerning public officials" is narrower and departs in significant ways from the meaning that was attached to corruption in earlier periods of Western thought.[3] Our

---

1. According to the *Democracy Index*, 69 percent of the 167 countries surveyed are considered a type of democracy (full, flawed, or hybrid).

2. *Corruption Perceptions Report 2016.*

3. Barcham, Hindess, and Larmour, *Corruption*, 8.

current understanding of political corruption is positivist and individualistic, which has served well the research model that became hegemonic in the social sciences in the 1990s, which demanded the development of concepts that could be easily measured and plugged into large N models. Corruption has thus been conveniently reduced to its most visible and clear expressions: illegal acts involving public officials (e.g., bribery, fraud, nepotism). But even if the reduction of political corruption to a discreet set of expressions serves the reliable measurement of the phenomenon, this account can be only partial since it is clear that political corruption is a slow-moving process, where meaningful change in the dependent and independent variables occurs only over the long run, tending then, in practice, to fall off the radar within this type of quantitative methodology.[4]

Despite a recent renewed empirical interest in systemic corruption and the most effective ways to counter it,[5] the concept is yet to be adequately defined and understood. The bulk of research on corruption is policy oriented, aimed at ameliorating the negative economic consequences associated with corruption, especially in the developing world.[6] "Corruption is thus presented as if it were a matter of misconduct on the part of public officials who are seen, especially in poor countries, as pursuing their own private interests and likely to act corruptly in return for money and other favours, thereby undermining economic development."[7]

In conformity with the individualistic model that undergirds the current conception of corruption but acknowledging the limitations of analyzing corruption only through its narrow definition, the different organisms aimed at combating corruption have relied on individuals' *perception* of corruption as a way to complement the tallying of individual illegal acts as a proxy for the rate of corruption in society. This is of course very problematic. If there is no working definition of corruption beyond the legal, on what evidence are respondents of these surveys basing their perceptions? Corruption conceived in this way is guilty of moral relativism and legal positivism because it does not consider an independent standard to judge the law and thus could even end up legalizing the most prominent means of corruption (e.g., campaign finance, donations, lobby).[8] In our current juridical conception of corruption, for example, there is no way to account for *legal* corruption, for laws and

---

4. Pierson, "Big, Slow-Moving, and . . . Invisible."

5. Johnston, *Syndromes of Corruption*; Mungiu-Pippidi, *Quest for Good Governance*.

6. Rose-Ackerman and Palifka, *Corruption and Government*.

7. Barcham, Hindess, and Larmour, *Corruption*, 3.

8. While lobbying was illegal for much of US history, today it dominates politics. For a historical account, see Teachout, *Corruption in America*.

policies that promote the interests of a few against the common good, what the ancients would understand as the gradual decay of good government.

The few attempts at engaging with the concept at a theoretical level fall short of fully conceiving the fundamentally systemic nature of political corruption,[9] or adequately grounding it on intellectual history and its contexts,[10] and thus these attempts are potentially liable to anachronism through what Quentin Skinner has identified as "mythologies of doctrines."[11] This chapter contributes to this emerging literature by providing a contextualized theoretical analysis of a type of political corruption that seems a systemic feature of all constitutional popular governments. Systemic corruption, which encompasses structural forms of corruption such as legal and institutional corruption, not only is different from the actor-based meanings of the term— the bending and breaking of the law by a clan or class for their own benefit, or the buying of political influences by private interest[12]—but also differs from definitions of corruption as the undermining of the rule of law.[13] Systemic corruption is a term that seems to directly address the nature of the superstructure itself, and not the manipulation or dismantling of a structure that is seen as the normative ground for neutrality.

Systemic Political Corruption in Ancient Thought

Even though today we associate corruption with illegal action, the etymological origin of the word has a far more complex meaning. The Greek ancestor of the word *corruption* has been traced to *phthora* (φθορά), which meant destruction, decay, and "passing away" as correlative to genesis—the beginning of a process.[14] While in early pre-Socratic texts the word was used only to denote

---

9. DeLeon, *Thinking about Political Corruption*; Heywood, *Political Corruption*; Thompson, *Ethics in Congress*.

10. See Patrick Dobel's gathering of "scattered insights" by Thucydides, Plato, Aristotle, Machiavelli, and Rousseau in "Corruption of a State." A notable exception is *An Intellectual History of Political Corruption*, edited by Lisa Hill and Bruce Buchan, even if it centers on tracing the current individual, juridical concept of corruption, devoting only a few pages to systemic corruption.

11. Coherence, prolepsis, and parochialism. Skinner, "Meaning and Understanding in the History of Ideas."

12. In his taxonomy of corruption Michael Johnston identified the corruption of "influence markets," in which private interests seek political influence, as the most pervasive in advanced market democracies. *Syndromes of Corruption*.

13. See for example Rothstein, *Quality of Government*.

14. Peters, *Greek Philosophical Terms*, 158.

the moral degradation of women and youth, and the ruining of crops from bad weather, the concept appears to acquire a decisively abstract meaning in the sixth century BC. The theoretical conception of phthora was first developed, according to Aristotle, by Thales of Miletus, the founder of the school of philosophy that studies unchangeable elements in nature, principles that are "neither generated nor destroyed, but persist eternally."[15] The Physicists—as Aristotle called this school of thought—attempted to understand how plurality in the cosmos could be generated from matter as a "single underlying substance." Anaximander argued matter was governed by a "diversifying antithesis" in which matter is constantly being generated through "condensation and rarefication," and that phthora was the natural process through which things returned to the original, indefinite principle.[16] Empedocles and Anaxagoras assigned a direction to this *poietic* process of generation. While for Empedocles generation of matter was circular, always coming back to its starting point, for Anaxagoras this movement was spiral, never repeating itself.[17]

The concept of corruption acquired a political meaning when it was first attached to the constitution of the state by Plato, and then furthered analyzed by Aristotle in the *Politics*—work explicitly dedicated to the analysis of the corruption (φθορά) and preservation of constitutions. I would argue both authors developed their conception of corruption responding to their own sociopolitical context, and thus we should analyze their ideas on political corruption as inherently tied to a stable democratic regime in a diminished, postimperial Athens. Through a contextual analysis of their ideas, in what follows I show that while for Plato the source of corruption in democracy was the constitutive principle of liberty, which gradually eroded hierarchies and rule, for Aristotle corruption sprang from the full realization of the principle of equal share in government.

Since the series of constitutional reforms begun by Cleisthenes (508/7 BC) based on the principle of *isonomia* (ἰσονομία), right up to Pericles's prodemocratic policies, the popular sectors in ancient Athens were gradually empowered until acquiring preeminence. By the fourth century almost all magistrates were selected by lottery from a broad pool of citizens[18] who enjoyed *isegoria* (ἰσηγορία)—the equal right to speak to the assembly—and were paid by the

---

15. Air, water, earth, and fire. Aristotle, *Metaphysics*, 984a.

16. Simplicius, *Commentary on Aristotle's Physics*, 24.13–21.

17. Aristotle, *Physics*, I.IV, 187a.

18. Even wage laborers, *thêtes*, could become officeholders. Aristotle, "On the Constitution of Athens," 7.4. See also Ober, *Mass and Elite*, 80.

state to exercise political power.[19] The empowerment of nonelite citizens came hand in hand with Athens's increased naval power and state revenue, and with the diminishing of the elite's institutional power. While during the golden years of Athens the increased participation of the masses in political power was financed through colonial tributes and high production of state silver mines, after Athens lost its empire and the production of mines begun to decrease, equal share in government was mostly financed through direct taxation on the leisured classes, whose political influence decreased especially after the aristocratic Areopagus was stripped of its veto power.[20]

An Athenian citizen of high status, Plato came of age in the midst of the Peloponnesian War (431–404 BC), in which Athens was ultimately defeated, and the longtime-brewing 411 oligarchic coup.[21] He also witnessed the execution of his mentor, Socrates, condemned to death by the Athenian assembly for corrupting the youth and religion. Pay for assembly goers and jurors, and the establishment of the *nomothetai* (νομοθέται) selected by lot,[22] had effectively made the popular sectors the judges of behavior and the interpreters of law, and in Plato's eyes the death of Socrates came to evidence the hubris the multitude was capable of when drunk with liberty. *Dēmokratiā* was certainly not a perfect form of government, and its consolidation (or radicalization) was seen by Plato as only one more phase in the relentless decay of political organizations. In *The Republic* he envisioned the best form of government as that of the philosopher-kings, an aristocracy of the guardians of virtue, who are able to organize society in the best way possible because they lack a stake in it; in *Kallipolis* guardians would live communally, separated from other classes and barred from owning property. However, even this seemly perfect constitution maintained by the most virtuous elite would not be able to escape corruption, because "*phthora* (φθορά) awaits everything that has come to be, [and] even a foundation of this kind will not survive for the whole of time."[23]

Even if in later writings Plato further explores phthora only as a process of degradation that is proper to *physis*, since there is no strict separation between the natural and the political in his thought, this process of decay would also

---

19. Citizens were paid for exercising all three functions of state power: judging, lawmaking, and making and executing decisions. Ober, *Mass and Elite*, 53–103.

20. Ephialtes's reforms in 462 undermined the elite's power to preserve the status quo through vetoing "unconstitutional" decisions by the Assembly. Ober, *Mass and Elite*, 77.

21. Thucydides, *History of the Peloponnesian War*, 8.45–98.

22. A sort of popular constitutional tribunal aimed at protecting democracy. Hansen, *Athenian Democracy*, chapter 7.

23. Plato, *Republic*, 546a; Plato, *Laws*, 894a.

rule the political realm created by men.[24] In *Timaeus* Plato puts forward a basic intuition about the decay of bodies, which would later be validated by the discovery of the second law of thermodynamics[25] as revealing an inherent process of degradation through the transfer of energy:

> For when any one element suffers a change of condition that is contrary to nature, all its particles that formerly were being cooled become heated, and the dry presently become moist, and the light heavy, and they undergo every variety of change in every respect. For, as we maintain, it is only the addition or subtraction of the same substance from the same substance in the same order and in the same manner and in due proportion which will allow the latter to remain safe and sound in its sameness with itself. But whatsoever oversteps any of these conditions in its going out or its coming in will produce alterations of every variety and countless diseases and corruptions.[26]

What Plato depicts as the extremely difficult process to preserve the nature of things is what the second law of thermodynamics explains as the inevitable transfer of heat energy and the resulting increase of entropy (disorder) in closed systems. Degradation occurs because internal energy is transferred within different bodies in a given system, and in this inevitable transfer process, energy is transformed and wasted until the process ends at a certain temperature in which there is no difference of heat between the inside and outside of a body. The only way to reverse this process of decay is by applying "work" through an *external* energy source. So, if the system is for instance an ice cube with tight molecules, the natural process according to the second law is for these molecules to move more and more, and for energy to be transferred from the warmer parts to the colder ones, until the molecules have separated and spread out and the cube has completely melted. The only way to preserve the ice cube is to artificially keep the molecules tight by creating an environment below freezing level through the use of external energy.

The same way that an ice cube will inevitably melt at room temperature and cease to be an ice cube and become water, the constitution of a given state would be completely ruined by the entropy inevitably produced by its normal functioning, and turn into a different political order. From the utopian aristocracy of *Kallipolis*, according to Plato political forms would gradually

---

24. Aristotle further develops the relation between *physis* and politics, arguing that political virtue also requires *ethos* and *logos*. See Ward, "Two Conceptions of *Physis*."

25. Discovered by Robert Clausius in 1850.

26. *Timaeus*, 82a–b.

degrade first into the lesser form of timocracy (the regime by the honorable), then into oligarchy (rule by the wealthy), then into democracy (based on equal share in political power and liberty), and finally into tyranny, the worst form of government that imposes "the harshest and most complete slavery."[27] Tyranny is for him an order that is the complete opposite of the virtuous aristocracy of the guardians, in which all citizens are virtuous and contribute in their particular roles to the harmony of the polis. Tyranny is for Plato anarchy, the transgression of natural hierarchies and the absence of rule.

When developing his idea of political decay Plato's target was the democracy of his own time. While he recognizes that liberty is the principle of democracy, he argues that liberty is itself a liability, a source of disorder because it results in individuals living according to "their own constitution," having their own rules, pursuing only their own interests, and respecting no other authority but their own will.[28] For Plato, corruption in a democracy would be the inevitable result of the equal distribution of liberty, which allows for the pursuit of individual interest and the consequent increase of entropy, as it were, within the constitutional framework. In other words, liberty as constitutive to the democratic regime is for Plato a liability that contaminates the public realm, weakening the possibility of *arche* and virtue, permanently undermining hierarchies, tradition, and rules, and making government prone to *hubris* and destined to injustice and tyranny.[29]

Departing from Plato's linear pattern of corruption as a gradual process of decay from aristocracy to tyranny, Aristotle argues for a typology of regimes based on the fundamental "diversifying antithesis" of genesis and corruption that exists in everything. Since "all things that come into existence in the course of nature are either opposites themselves or are compounded of opposites," corruption can be analyzed as a movement "along the determined line between the terms of contrast; or (if we start from some intermediate state) the movement towards one of the extremes."[30] On this premise of the generative nature of opposites Aristotle bases one of his most original observations, with far-reaching political implications: that change comes about through the corruption of nature, that "change (μεταβολή) is primarily a 'passing away' (φθορᾶς)."[31] Phthora, therefore, is an inevitable, natural force driving change in the physical world, working within bounded spheres determined

---

27. Plato, *Republic*, 564a.
28. Ibid., 557b–e.
29. Ibid., VIII, 558a.
30. Aristotle, *Physics*, I.v, 188b.
31. Ibid., IV.xiii, 222.b.

by the opposition implied in the "coming into being" of a thing; each thing has a principle (or mixture of them), and it is its realization that brings about corruption. Everything begins to corrupt the moment it is fully realized, and *metabole* occurs when that realization is fully negated.

Since "all things arose out of what existed, and so must be there already,"[32] according to Aristotle every political constitution would have constitutive principles that would become fully realized, enabling its demise. The degree of corruption of constitutions would relate to the movement within its extremes. Following this idea, Aristotle conceived of three good constitutions (kingship, aristocracy, and *politeia*) based on the nature of the sovereign (one, few, or many) and their final cause (ruling for the common interest, *eudaimonia*), and their corresponding perverted forms brought about by corruption (tyranny, oligarchy, and democracy) aimed not at advancing the common good but at satisfying the personal interests of the rulers.[33] There is much debate about the fundamental feature of the ideal politeia in Aristotle's thought. While some define politeia as a combination of democracy and oligarchy, and thus a mixed government in which the interest of the few and the many keep each other in check,[34] others emphasize its "constitutional" character given that the ultimate authority would reside on fundamental law and not on the will of the majority.[35] I would argue these interpretations are not mutually exclusive.

As Aristotle described in "On the Constitution of Athens" and the *Politics*, Athenian democracy during his time corresponded to the most extreme and corrupt form of democracy—the absolute rule of the many for their own benefit. In his classification of regimes, he identified four types of democracy based on the social basis of the sovereign, the degree of participation in government, and the supremacy of the law. The first three types of democracy, in which the masses share equally in constitutional rights but are unable, because of material constraints, to actually exercise their sovereign power, the rule of law is supreme and thus Aristotle considered them "good," constitutional forms of government. The fourth type of democracy, however, which he identifies with the Athenian democracy of his time, is inherently corrupt since the "mass of the poor," thanks to a system of state-payment for attending the assembly, are "the sovereign power instead of the law."[36] This extreme form of

32. Ibid., I.iv, 187b.
33. Aristotle, *Politics*, III. vii, §2.
34. Pasquino, "Classifying Constitutions."
35. Castiglione, "Political Theory of the Constitution."
36. Aristotle, *Politics*, IV.vi §§2–6.

democracy, as it were, is brought about by "leaders of the demagogue type," who arrive precisely because decrees and not laws are sovereign, enabling the transformation of the sovereign *demos* into a type of despotic autocrat.[37] This form of government has no proper constitution, since the people are sovereign in all matters,[38] and are easily influenced by demagogues who have no official position other than the one conferred by the contingent favor of the masses. Demagogues educate the poor on how to advance their own interests, increasing their power[39] and thus are the agents of corruption, enabling interest to be made into law. The full realization of an equal share in government appears then to inevitably produce regime change since such a system, in which "everything is managed merely by decrees, is not even a democracy."[40]

In Aristotle's particular account of the history of Athens, demagoguery had plagued the state since the rise of Pericles, who not only "took powers away from the Areopagites" but also "impelled the state toward naval power [and] as a result of this power it befell that the masses took confidence and began in greater degree to draw the whole constitution into their hands."[41] Thus, departing from Thucydides's account of Athenian history, which puts total control of government in the masses *after* Pericles's death in 429 BC, Aristotle argues that the extreme form of democracy had begun three decades earlier with the reforms of the Areopagus, which enabled a regime change (*metabole*).[42] While the absolute liberty the assembly gained after the last aristocratic constraints were removed would mark the beginning of regime change, the complete realization of democracy occurs only when the principle of equal access to political power is fully materialized.

Even though a corrupt state implies for Aristotle a loss of virtue by both rulers and common citizens, he is very clear that virtue depends on the appropriate legal structure to thrive. Because virtue is not natural to human beings, but needs to be acquired by habit and action, the degree of virtue and corruption in the polis is determined by the law and its effects on the members

---

37. Ibid., IV.vi §§25–31.

38. Aristotle's argument stands against the codification of law at the turn of the century and the establishment of the *nomothetai* as a constitutional tribunal. See Hansen, *Athenian Democracy*.

39. Aristotle, *Politics*, IV.iv §§26–30.

40. Ibid., IV.iv §§30.

41. Aristotle, "On the Constitution of Athens," 27.1.

42. This interpretation appears based not on de jure modifications, but on de facto changes, evidencing for Aristotle a change in the spirit of democracy. Day and Chambers, *Aristotle's History of Athenian Democracy*, 140.

of the state.[43] In Aristotle's account, good character—desire in accord with right reason—cannot exist without habituation. Moral virtue is difficult to acquire because it is concerned with pleasures and pains, the discipline of the appetites, and the internalization of social norms. Therefore, the right habituation must be learned from others and exercised constantly to create a sort of second, moral nature:

> For pleasure causes us to do base actions, and pain causes us to abstain from fine ones. That is why we need to have had the appropriate upbringing—right from early youth, as Plato says—to make us find enjoyment or pain in the right things; for this is the correct education.[44]

At the political level, it is the legislator who, grasping the principles of the common good, creates a constitution that can make "the citizens good by habituating them."[45] Good laws make good citizens by providing them with the principles of virtuous action, the form to which they should shape their character; the legal framework materializes the universal principles guiding action toward the common good, providing both the limits and the opportunities to engage in virtuous action. The same can be said for corrupt action (preferring individual/sectional interest against that of the polis), as being enabled by the legal structure, with the crucial difference that corruption is a natural tendency that will exist regardless of laws. Therefore, each regime needs to habituate its citizens appropriately through good laws aimed at fostering moral and civic virtue against relentless, unavoidable corruption. If a regime fails to do this and laws become inadequate, allowing and even fostering greed and the thirst for domination in the sovereign, citizens become habituated in this way, and the polis inevitably becomes a corrupt state. Democracy as absolute, unconstrained rule by the people, a form of government effectively lacking a constitution as higher law, is thus for Aristotle inherently corrupt.

Despite their different theories of constitutions, both Plato and Aristotle agree that political corruption occurs in pure regimes because of a loss of virtue in the sovereign body when personal interests take the place of the common good as the final cause of government. If viewed from the second law of thermodynamics, the process of political corruption as *phthora* could be conceived as the natural increase of entropy generated by the pursuit of individual/sectional interest against the common good within a given constitutional framework. This loss of virtue in the ruling body would mark the beginning of

---

43. Aristotle, *Nicomachean Ethics*, II.1.
44. Ibid., II.3.
45. Ibid., II.1.

the end of a given good constitution, if no constant or episodic external "work" is applied to it to counteract the thrust of actions aimed at the satisfaction of partial interests. Moreover, because corruption and the increase of entropy inevitably produce a change of nature and thus an effective modification of the constitution of the state, the quest for virtue is connected to the idea of *preservation against corruption.*

Aristotle aims at counteracting corruption by proposing as the best form of government one based on a mixture of natures and principles, in which both the few and the many share in government, and the majority of citizens are part of the middle classes. Aristotle's politeia is a constitutional direct democracy in which "the masses govern the state with a view to the common interest,"[46] and the masses are composed mainly of the middle classes, who possess "moderate and adequate property."[47] This best "practicable" constitution—an intermediate regime between the extremes of oligarchy and democracy—would successfully combine qualifications of wealth and legal equality because the middle classes—the majority after the exclusion of the poor—would effectively control government.

The politeia being a mixture of constitutions and thus in an intermediate position, one could argue that, following Aristotle's ideas on corruption, the politeia as an ideal type could become corrupt by tending either to oligarchy or to democracy. However, like Plato, he entertains only a corrupting tendency toward democracy, even if from his ideas of the nature of things it is clear that things that are in intermediate positions inevitably drift toward either of the extremes that define them. The same way a politeia would suffer metabole if the principle of equal share in government were fully realized, were the principle of oligarchy—inequality based on wealth, status, knowledge—to become predominant and driven to its extreme—with a handful of people owning most of the property—the politeia would inevitably undergo a regime change into a oligarchy, a regime "analogous to the last form of democracy" in which the sovereign is unbound to seek its own advantage, "closely akin to the personal rule of a monarch."[48]

Extending Aristotle's taxonomy of good and deviant constitutions, and combining it with Empedocles's cosmological theory of cyclical change,[49] the Greek historian Polybius, who documented the rise of the Roman republic from 264 to 146 BC, articulated a "cycle of political revolution, the course

46. Aristotle, *Politics*, III.vii §3.
47. Ibid., IV.xi §§10–1.
48. Ibid., IV.vi §§7–11.
49. See Tromp, *Idea of Historical Recurrence in Western Thought.*

appointed by nature in which constitutions change, disappear, and finally return to the point from which they started."[50] According to his *anacyclosis*, pure
regimes, starting from the best one—kinship then aristocracy and finally
democracy—are bound to degenerate into their deviant forms, until the tyranny of the many establishes the rule of violence, and the people "degenerate
again into perfect savages and find once more a master and monarch."[51] For
Polybius corruption is inevitable in pure regime forms,

> just as rust in the case of iron and wood-worms and ship-worms in the case
> of timber are inbred pests, and these substances, even though they escape
> all external injury, fall a prey to the evils engendered in them, so each con-
> stitution has a vice engendered in it and inseparable from it.[52]

Following Aristotle, he argues that only mixture can stave off corruption.
However, instead of combining the worse two regime types as Aristotle did,
following the example of the Spartan lawgiver Lycurgus, Polybius argues
that we must regard as the best constitution a combination of the three best
forms of government—kinship, aristocracy, and democracy—which he
conceived as forms of *limited* government. While the king's actions were
bounded by rational principles, and aristocratic rule was limited by the
morality and wisdom of the few selected to administrate public affairs, democracy was the regime in which majority decision prevailed within a tra-
ditional framework of popular obedience to the dictates of religion, elders,
and civil laws.[53]

The Roman constitution was of a mixed nature because it institutionalized
these three sources of authority, which shared "in the control of the Roman
state."[54] While the consuls exercised authority in Rome over all public affairs,
the Senate exerted control over the republic's finances and public works, in
addition to dispatching embassies and declaring war, and giving advice to magistrates.[55] The people, on the other hand, through the Plebeian Council[56] and
the Tribunate, had the "right to confer honors and inflict punishment," especially on individuals who had held public office, and the power of approving
or rejecting laws and ratifying issues related to war and peace.[57] These three

---

50. Polybius, *Histories*, VI.9.
51. Ibid.
52. Ibid., VI.10.
53. Ibid., VI.4.
54. Ibid., VI.2 and 5.
55. Advice that was generally followed. Ibid., VI.12–13.
56. Concilium Plebis.
57. Ibid., VI.14.

Roman Republic

Three sources of authority

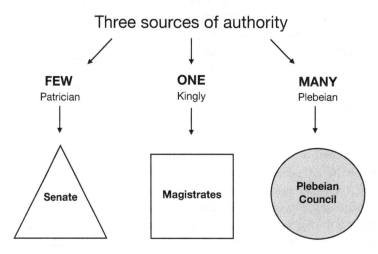

FIGURE 1.1. Sources of authority in the Roman republic.

forms of authority and institutional power were, moreover, in permanent dynamic balance in a system in which "none of the principles should grow unduly and be perverted into its allied evil, but that, the force of each being neutralized by that of the others, neither of them should prevail and outbalance another."[58] Corruption in this mixed regime, which Polybius associates with the Roman republic, is not the full realization of an *antithesis*, but the result of an *imbalance* of political power in the constitution, which allows for the domination of one of the principles or factions over the others. However, Polybius does not acknowledge the corruption slowly unraveling at the moment he was writing the *Histories*.

Even if by the late republic the Plebeian Tribunate appeared as a strong institution able not only to give protection to individuals against the consuls, but also to obstruct the Senate and initiate legislation, it was unable to ultimately thwart the overgrowth of the power of the nobility. The republic kept progressively drifting into oligarchy mainly because of the cooptation of plebeian tribunes into patrician ranks and the Senate's disregard of the legislative authority of the Plebeian Council. The tumults that resulted from this disregard of plebeian authority plagued the late Roman republic and served as a catalyst for regime change and the birth of imperial authority.

58. Ibid., VI.10.

Individual Corruption and the Machiavellian Challenge

The translation of *phthora* into the Latin root *corruptus* kept its abstract meaning of destruction and decay at the systemic level[59] alongside a substantive, moral meaning related to individual political actions: to bribe, falsify, seduce, or pervert.[60] It was mainly Cicero who used the word *corruptus* in a political sense to refer to the decay of mores and the "depravity of evil custom"[61] as the culprit of the decline of Rome. Following closely Plato's analysis of the corruption of democracy, Cicero blames the decay of the republic to the success of the "extreme liberty" that inevitably reaches everything in a commonwealth in which everyone is free and "all sense of shame is lost."[62] This individual moral meaning of *corruptus* was further developed during medieval times, pivoting on the sinful nature of human beings. Following closely the Ciceronian legacy, Augustine famously argued all earthly governments are inherently corrupt, because rooted in the original sin, and veered the focus of analysis to civic stability as the highest attainable political good. This approach spawned more than ten centuries of "mirror of princes" texts centered on the moral virtue of rulers as a form of achieving stability and good rule.

After the reintroduction of Aristotle to philosophical inquiry in the thirteenth century, political analyses of virtue and corruption shifted once more from the moral qualities of individual rulers toward the institutional merits of political regimes. Within scholastic thought, Aquinas fused moral values to the Aristotelian conception of "right reason" producing a new political meaning of virtue and corruption associated with the *res publica christiana*.[63] Political corruption was once again associated with the preference for individual interest against the common good[64] but remained pegged to Christian morality and the Augustinian framework that conceived of civic stability as the highest political goal, and of civic discord as a sign of corruption. Scholastic thought had a significant impact on the new humanist strand that developed in early quattrocento Florence, which attempted to defend the republican experiment in scholastic terms based primarily on virtue ethics.[65] It is in this

---

59. The meaning of "damaged or spoiled," closer to the original *phthora*, was predominant in ancient Rome. Perseus Digital Library Project.

60. The Romans had a specific word for "electoral bribery," a common vice: *ambitus*. Hill and Buchan, *Intellectual History*, 27–29.

61. Cicero, *On the Laws*, in *"On the Commonwealth" and "On the Laws,"* I.

62. Cicero, *On the Commonwealth*, in *"On the Commonwealth" and "On the Laws,"* I. 67.

63. Aquinas, *Summa Theologica*, I.CIII, 3 resp.

64. Ibid., I–II.XC, 2.

65. Skinner, *Foundations*, 145.

Ciceronian-scholastic humanist legacy—according to which political corruption is reduced to individual vicious actions—that our current juridical conception of corruption is grounded.[66]

A crucial challenge to the scholastic view of political corruption centered on individual virtue came from a "civic" strand of humanist thinkers from the Italian city-states being threatened by papacy and empire in the fourteenth and fifteenth centuries. Reintroducing ancient Roman political values, this humanist tradition brought to the fore the political concept of liberty as connected to civic virtue and good, popular government,[67] and it put corruption as an evil in need of permanent contention in their proposed constitutional designs. Even if Machiavelli was not the first thinker of the Renaissance to focus on the role of corruption in politics, according to Skinner he reveals a "heightened awareness of the problem, and devote[s] an unprecedented amount of attention to the investigation of its causes."[68] By challenging humanists' virtue ethics and their support for the rule by an educated elite as the best form of government, Machiavelli proposes a structural understanding of corruption that puts the burden of good government on institutions, laws, and procedures rather than individual actions by the ruling elite. While "virtue-ethics" humanists saw virtue in the ruling class as the key to good government,[69] for Machiavelli, republican liberty was the result of good laws, which are themselves the product of the institutional conflict between the few and the many.[70]

Machiavelli's preoccupation with political corruption was embedded in the extraordinary democratic experiment of the republic of Florence, which began in 1494 with the establishment of the Great Council, a form of direct democracy that allowed for extensive citizen participation in legislative, electoral, and judicial authority within the republic. Despite the extensive powers of the Council, the republic remained effectively dependent on the financial oligarchy because of its reliance on mercenary armies that were paid by an extraordinary system of public debt. According to Jérémie Barthas, as secretary and second chancellor of the republic, Machiavelli saw as his central task to liberate the republic from the grip of the financial oligarchy through the introduction of a project of mass conscription, an "ordinary and socialized mode of defense" that would establish the autonomy of the republic of Florence from the

---

66. Hill and Buchan, *Intellectual History*. I disagree fundamentally with their interpretation of Machiavelli's approach to corruption.

67. Skinner, *Foundations*, 6–12.

68. Ibid., 166.

69. Hankins, "Machiavelli, Civic Humanism, and the Humanist Politics of Virtue," 102.

70. Machiavelli, *The Prince*, IX; *Discourses*, I.4, in *Machiavelli Chief Works*.

financial power of the *grandi*.[71] I argue Machiavelli's conception of corruption needs to be understood as connected to this constant threat of oligarchic power, and thus his constitutional proposals should be analyzed as socialized modes of defense against the relentless force of political decay.

Following the Aristotelian definition of political corruption as the favoring of individual interests instead of the common good, in *Florentine Histories* Machiavelli defines a corrupt state as the one in which "laws and ordinances, peace, wars, and treaties are adopted and pursued, not for the public good, not for the common glory of the state, but for the convenience or advantage of a few individuals."[72] Since for Machiavelli men are by nature wicked and fickle, prone to breaking the rules "at every chance for their own profit,"[73] every form of government has a natural tendency toward corruption. Even though a good foundation can counteract this egotistic inclination, it does not eliminate it, so the degeneration of political rule is a constant threat that needs to be averted through extraordinary measures.[74]

In his analysis of corruption, Machiavelli distinguishes three interrelated elements: matter, form, and method. In a city the matter is constituted by the citizens, the form by the laws, and the methods by the rules and procedures for selecting magistrates and making laws.[75] Even if Machiavelli certainly denounces "gifts" and "promises" as frequent means to corrupt individuals,[76] and agrees with Cicero that a corrupt government necessarily entails corrupt mores, his conception of corruption is decisively institutional, and his analysis thus focuses on the rules and procedures that enable citizens to exert domination. For Machiavelli the corrupting process does not begin in the *matter* (governed in part by the unavoidable egoistic tendencies of individuals) but on the *form* restraining individual interest and the *methods* by which rulers are selected. Individual interest is a force permanently trying to unduly influence government but succeeding, and thus effectively corrupting the republic, only if laws and methods are flawed and liberty's scaffolding is already being slowly dismantled from within. According to Machiavelli, "an evil-disposed citizen cannot effect any changes for the worse in a republic, unless it be already corrupt."[77]

---

71. Barthas, "Machiavelli, the Republic, and the Financial Crisis," 273.

72. Machiavelli, *Florentine Histories*, IV.6, in *Machiavelli Chief Works*.

73. Machiavelli, *The Prince*, XVI.

74. For Machiavelli on dictatorship as the ordinary method to deal with extraordinary circumstances, see Geuna, "Extraordinary Accidents."

75. Machiavelli, *Discourses*, I.18.

76. Ibid., I.40; Machiavelli, *The Description*, in *Machiavelli Chief Works*.

77. Machiavelli, *Discourses*, III.8.

For Machiavelli good laws promote civic virtue, and bad laws enable general corruption. Throughout his writings he identifies two types of corrupting norms promoting two forms of evil: license and socioeconomic inequality. Referring to the case of Scipio—"that most excellent man, not only of his own times but within the memory of man, against whom, nevertheless, his army rebelled in Spain"[78]—Machiavelli makes the case that norms allowing for increased license bring ruin even to the most glorious men and institutions. Scipio was called "the corrupter of the Roman soldiery" because he was too lenient and "gave his soldiers more license than is consistent with military discipline,"[79] which encouraged them to become unruly.[80] And the same way that good, disciplined soldiers became bad and rowdy through the lifting of restraints to their behavior, the general corruption of mores is allowed to begin when "the laws that restrained the citizens . . . were changed according as the citizens from one day to another became more and more corrupt."[81]

In addition to promoting moral license and undermining virtue, laws play a key role in allowing for inequality, which ultimately makes the protection of liberty and the republican project impossible. Because republics need relative equality to exist—great inequality produces princedom, relative equality is conducive to republican rule[82]—if laws allow for accumulation of wealth in the hands of a few and the destitution of the majority, the gradual transition from good government into a corrupt one is inevitable. Because Machiavelli sees the republic as a type of political organization that is inherently tied to the socioeconomic structure of society, republican liberty demands that citizens live in *relative* equality, in a correspondence based on individual labor and frugality. For him lords (*gentiloumini*) "who without working live in luxury on the returns from their landed possessions" are dangerous for any republic; they are the beginners of "corruption and the causes of all evil."[83]

But even if Machiavelli strongly denounces wealthy elites and their great influence as "the cause of states being reduced to servitude,"[84] he also acknowledges that a "republic that has no distinguished citizens cannot be well governed"[85] and that it is the job of the institutions of the state to adequately

---

78. Machiavelli, *The Prince*, XVII.

79. Ibid., XVII.

80. For further analysis on Scipio, see McCormick, "Machiavelli's Inglorious Tyrants."

81. Machiavelli, *Discourses*, III.18.

82. Ibid., I.55. For further analysis of the relation between inequality and constitutions in Machiavelli, see McCormick, "'Keep the Public Rich, but the Citizens Poor.'"

83. Machiavelli, *Discourses*, I.55.

84. Ibid., I.55; III.18.

85. Ibid., III.28.

channel individual interest for the benefit of the republic. Bad laws enable undue influence on government from "fatal families" and the division of society into factions that "will strive by every means of corruption to secure friends and supporters" in order to satisfy their interests.[86] Good laws, on the other hand, establish necessity and duty to create virtuous citizens and make sure the influence of wealth "is kept within proper limits"[87] by prohibiting the legal ability to command enormous fortunes, castles, and subjects.[88] Anticorruption laws putting limits to the command of wealth and patronage are thus essential to preserving a good constitutional form.

Even though in Machiavelli's theory fundamental laws make good citizens[89] by establishing appropriate limits, rights, and duties, it is for him on the *methods* that the burden of the maintenance of the constitution and the virtue of the citizens appears to be finally placed. Because human affairs are in constant flux, and the matter is not homogenous but composed of two opposing humors (the desire to oppress and to be left alone), there is a dynamic relation between form and matter, laws and men. Therefore, the methods regulating the creation of law and the exercise of power, the procedures allowing for the institutional balance between the elite and the people, are crucial. Good laws are not enough to shape good citizens and keep corruption at bay; an appropriate method of allocating political power and the management of state rule—good procedures aimed at nondomination—is also necessary. It is at this point in his analysis that Machiavelli criticizes, as vehicles for corruption, what are the two most fundamental elements of our current liberal representative systems: elections and free speech.

Using as an example the Roman republic, Machiavelli describes how corruption derived from inequality at the political level ultimately undermined the constitutional order. The procedures for the selection of magistrates, based on voluntary candidacy, and the right to propose legislation and speak in the assembly, even though they were in the beginning good, allowing for the most able to become magistrates and for "each one who thinks of something of benefit to the public" to have the right to propose it,[90] were the means through which corruption crept into the political system, undermining liberty:

86. Ibid., III.27.

87. Ibid., I.1.

88. Even though Machiavelli refers to the German citizens, who if they get gentlemen "into their hands, they put them to death," he does not want to bring equality by murdering the rich, but by adopting laws to curb inequality. *Discourses*, I.55.

89. Machiavelli, *Discourses*, I.3.

90. Ibid., I.18.

Such a basic custom became bad, because only the powerful proposed laws, not for the common liberty but for their own power, and for fear of such men no one dared to speak against those laws. Thus the people were either deceived or forced into decreeing their own ruin.[91]

While the procedure of election, based on the political equality to compete for office, brought corruption through the self-selection of candidates, the right to speak in the assembly, what for Athenian democracy constituted the fundamental principle of *isegoria*, became the vehicle through which the powerful imposed their values and ideas on the many, forcing their consent. The rights to election and political speech, at least as they were originally conceived, were thus the mediums through which corruption through hegemony[92] was imposed, creating a state in which the many chose and decreed their own ruin, undermined their actual power, and destroyed the republic. Consequently, for Machiavelli it is when the grandi dominate the popolo based on their own (forced) consent, by creating through deed and speech a narrative of their worldview that is gradually accepted as legitimate, that the matter is corrupted and laws are not enough to maintain liberty. In other words, when socioeconomic inequalities permeate the political process and laws are consistently being made (or not approved) for the interest of the few, amid generalized complacency, universal corruption ends up transforming the republic into a tyrannical government. This gradual corruption of the republic into oligarchy happens then not despite institutions and procedures but enabled by them.

At least two lessons are to be learned from what Machiavelli discovered in the examples of the ancients: that neither the matter nor the form is inherently virtuous, and that even if the matter has been made good through an original virtuous form, the form is not enough to keep citizens good when corruption has been introduced through legitimate political methods and has become pervasive. Moreover, when the matter is corrupt, the form and the methods do *nothing more* than foster corruption, and republics increasingly drift into an oligarchy of consent through the natural functioning of their methods.

Institutional Corruption and Corrupting Dependence

As seen from a *longue durée* perspective, it is clear that the concept of political corruption was meant to account for a systemic phenomenon, a layer of great explanatory value that was almost entirely dropped from theoretical analysis

---

91. Ibid.

92. "The ideas of the ruling class are in every epoch the ruling ideas . . . nothing more than the ideal expression of the dominant material relationships." Marx, "German Ideology," 172.

after the eighteenth century, when corruption was reduced to its current juridical form. While the ancients thought of corruption as inherent to everything, and thus inescapable for political forms, Machiavelli was perhaps the only modern thinker to engage, at length, with the problem of universal corruption as a constitutional challenge. I argue we need to pick up this lost thread of thinking that conceptualized political corruption as systemic and draw the contours of this structural form of political corruption for our present time. This alternative meaning of corruption should be seen as complementing, instead of replacing, political corruption as individual acts of misconduct by public officials, since particular instances of corruption are expressions of a universal phenomenon that cannot be reduced to their aggregation. This attempt at rethinking political corruption from a republican approach is meant to contribute to an emerging literature that has been assertive in criticizing the neorepublican interpretation of corruption (for not being different enough from the liberal conception) but not propositive enough.

The most prominent scholars to dedicate attention to corruption in republican thought are J.G.A. Pocock, Quentin Skinner, and Philip Pettit. Despite their invaluable contributions in bringing republican thought to the forefront during the last four decades, I would argue their misreading of Machiavelli makes them unable to grasp the systemic nature of political corruption. This misreading is of course not rooted in their lack of knowledge about Machiavelli, but rather on their own fierce commitment to liberal democracy. To question the constitutional structure of a regime that was progressively becoming "the only game in town" in the last stages of the Cold War would have been perhaps ludicrous, especially after legal positivism and a minimalist procedural conception of democracy had become hegemonic in the social sciences.[93] But it is precisely the consolidation of liberal democracies—when, according to Adam Przeworski, the regime "becomes self-reinforcing" and "no one can imagine acting outside the democratic institutions"[94]—that for Aristotle would prompt metabole, allowing for systemic corruption to begin taking hold of institutions, relentlessly moving the regime into oligarchy. This drift was missed by mainstream academia, oblivious of rising inequality and its effects on the political system,[95] dedicated to studying the institutional framework instead of appraising it, and thus unable to recognize systemic

93. Przeworski famously defended the minimalist definition, arguing that the ability to change governments through popular vote made democracy inherently valuable because it avoided bloodshed. "Minimalist Conception of Democracy."

94. Przeworski, *Democracy and the Market*, 26.

95. For a critique of the obscuring of inequality and its effects on American democracy, see Stepan and Linz, "Comparative Perspectives on Inequality."

corruption and articulate a structural critique of liberal democracy. Republican theory was no exception to this blind spot.

In his civic humanist reading of the Florentine secretary, Pocock famously identifies in Machiavelli the emergence of contingency as an "irruption of temporality in political discourse," which positioned republican thought as a radically immanent approach to theorizing the political.[96] Nevertheless he understood Machiavellism as a mode of thought that pursued "universal values in transitory form,"[97] which minimized both the role of institutional conflict to produce good laws and the radical creative force of *virtù* during republican refoundings. In his recent critique of Pocock, Robert Sparling argues that this Aristotelian reading of Machiavelli coupled with Pocock's attempt to construct a conceptual continuous tradition of corruption from the early Renaissance to the late eighteenth century resulted in a misleading interpretation of political corruption and the pessimistic outlook derived from it. If corruption is connected to universal values that cannot be fully realized in any given institutional form, then corruption is perennial and liberty at most only partial. What Sparling misses in his critique is that Pocock chooses principles as the source of normativity because he neglects the pivotal role institutional conflict between the few and the many plays in Machiavelli's theory of republican liberty. It is not constitutionalized principles that for Machiavelli keep the republic free from corruption, but rather political conflict and periodic renewals of fundamental laws and institutions. Pocock's hopelessness of effectively counteracting corruption in an era determined by commerce and self-interest also seems to run against Machiavelli's account of virtù as an inherently contingent force, grounded on necessity and effectual truth (*verità effetuale*), capable of bringing republics back to their beginnings even in the case of universal corruption.

Machiavelli's project in the *Discourses* was to figure out how to reestablish liberty and then keep it. In his theory of foundings, Machiavelli argues that refounding a republic is the most glorious action because it is the most difficult—because of the strength with which individuals benefiting from corruption will defend the status quo—and thus we should not only admire the actions of extraordinary leaders such as Romulus, Lycurgus, and Solon but also imitate them.[98] As Sparling argues, in Pocock's *The Machiavellian Moment* the language of corruption is one of "rhetorical excess and of moral absolutes,"

96. Palti, "On the Thesis of the Essential Contestability of Concepts," 123; Althusser, *Machiavelli and Us.*

97. Pocock, *Machiavellian Moment*, 333.

98. Machiavelli, *Discourses*, I. Preface.

which is neither coherent with the radical immanence of Machiavelli's thought nor conducive to a republican critique of corruption in liberal democracies, serving more as "dynamite than foundation"[99] for reformers aimed at addressing the threat of oligarchy.

Even if in Pocock's interpretation of Machiavelli political corruption is an "irreversible, one-way process"[100] of moral decay, and thus it is the degeneration of customs and mores that renders the constitutional framework ineffective to reactivate civic virtue, it is Skinner who decisively positions corruption within the current liberal, juridical paradigm. As Amanda Maher shows in her critique of Skinner's interpretation of Machiavelli, his humanist reading of the Florentine secretary coupled with his project to combine civic participation and negative liberty obscured the "sociological foundations of political corruption in Machiavelli's republicanism."[101] Skinner reduces corruption to a sinful disposition, to being unable "to devote one's energies to the common good,"[102] "a failure of rationality"[103] that can be best counteracted by promoting civic virtue and a sense of patriotism in the citizenry. Even if he acknowledges both the role of institutions in fostering virtue through participation and the connection between corruption and the capture of the state by oligarchs, like Cicero, Skinner puts the burden of liberty on the virtue of individual citizens instead of on institutions, procedures, and material conditions. Because he detaches this "ineptitude for a free way of life"[104] from its fundamental cause—inequality—in his analysis Skinner is unable to account for the structural conditions that determine individuals' public spirit incompetence.

Systematizing Skinner's interpretation of Machiavelli, Philip Pettit put forward a theory of republicanism based on the conceptualization of republican liberty as the lack of arbitrary interference. Despite Pettit's important contribution to the decoupling of domination from interference—broadening the conception of negative liberty to account for domination even in the absence of interference—his conception of corruption is even further removed from Machiavelli's than those of Pocock and Skinner are. In reducing domination to arbitrary power, Pettit is unable to escape laws and procedures as parameters for arbitrariness and legitimacy, and thus his theory of liberty as nondomination creates a problem of endogeneity with respect to corruption. If domination is defined by arbitrary power, and what is considered arbitrary is

99. Sparling, "Concept of Corruption," 170.

100. Pocock, *Machiavellian Moment*, 211.

101. Maher, "What Skinner Misses," 1005.

102. Skinner, *Foundations*, 164.

103. Skinner, "Republican Ideal of Political Liberty," 304.

104. Skinner, *Foundations*, 166.

determined by the legal regime, then there is no external referent to judge laws and procedures in terms of their potential corrupting tendencies.

Even if Pettit conceives interference as being nonarbitrary if it "track[s] the interests and ideas of those who suffer the interference,"[105] this surely can apply only to interference coming from the state, leaving interpersonal relations of domination largely unaccounted for. One could not reasonably expect that individual contracts must track equally the interests and ideas of all the parties involved—at least not in our capitalist societies in which relations of production are necessarily unequal. Moreover, because for Pettit liberty as nondomination is advanced "through a legal regime stopping people from dominating one another without itself dominating anyone in turn," the burden of keeping this basic constitutional structure free from corruption relies on citizens' "virtuous vigilance" and their effective contestation through institutional mechanisms.[106] However, while citizen's civic judgment might be "clouded by uncivic inclinations born of radical material inequalities,"[107] institutional mechanisms might be too corrupt to allow for meaningful input and reform.

In Pettit's framework, if a citizen suffers domination, he or she has the civic duty to contest it through a process that on the ground tends to be time-consuming and frustrating. From a collective action perspective, to expect aggrieved citizens to stand up for their interests, given the high costs involved in claim procedures, is wishful thinking.[108] To put the burden of keeping corruption at bay on individual agency is thus a recipe for disaster because it allows for the silent, gradual, apparently consented-to slip into oligarchy. Pettit is unable to see that material conditions determine the possibility of civic virtue—there is no vigilance when mere survival is at stake, and one does not need to be in abject poverty to be overwhelmed enough to remain passive instead of seeking redress when wronged. In addition to being time-consuming, dealing with bureaucracy and the courts is not a particularly pleasant experience, and thus placing the struggle against domination in the hands of individual citizens seems, from a realist point of view, not very different from leaving institutions to their own devices.

Recognizing the institutional corruption that the neorepublican conception of corruption neglects, in the mid-1990s there were increasing attempts in the fields of ethics to challenge the prevailing positivist, individualist

---

105. Pettit, *Republicanism*, 55.
106. Ibid., 250.
107. Sparling, "Political Corruption," 638.
108. See Olson, *Logic of Collective Action*.

approach to political corruption, which pushed the focus of corruption studies toward the political structure. Dennis Thompson was the first to identify a type of corruption that is institutional, "usually built into the routines and practices of organizations," that pertains to actions that tend to undermine institutions' normal processes, frustrating their primary purposes.[109] Corruption is for him the "condition in which private interests distort public purposes by influencing the government in disregard of the democratic process."[110] He highlights the case of democratic elections in which laws allowing for private financing of campaigns and lobby generate institutional corruption by enabling the distortion of public purposes by private interests.

Building on this perspective, Lawrence Lessig argues that institutional corruption is the outmost threat to democracy because it promotes "dependence corruption"[111] based on material relations of subordination, which undermines citizens' trust in democratic institutions. According to Lessig, corruption should be understood as

> a systemic and strategic influence which is legal, or even currently ethical, that undermines the institution's effectiveness by diverting it from its purpose or weakening its ability to achieve its purpose, including, to the extent relevant to its purpose, weakening either the public's trust in that institution or the institution's inherent trustworthiness.[112]

Corruption occurs when institutions deviate from their "intended dependence," what Lessig deems their "magnetic north," because of a competing dependence that skews institutions' public compass. Seen from this perspective, campaign finance laws would enable institutional corruption not only because they facilitate the distortion of public purposes but, more importantly, because they normalize and foster the dependence of elected representatives on their financiers rather than on voters.

Despite the important contribution of the institutionalist approach to corruption, which allows us to see more clearly the corrupting dependence fostered by electoral rules in the normal functioning of representative institutions, its functionalist definition leaves open the problem of determining the proper objective of government, and therefore it is unable to provide a systemic account of corruption beyond the direct link between financiers and elected representatives. Moreover, it has been argued that corruption might

109. Thompson, *Ethics in Congress*; Thompson, "Two Concepts of Corruption."
110. Thompson, "Two Concepts of Corruption," 1037.
111. Lessig, *Republic, Lost*, chapter 12.
112. Lessig, "Foreword: 'Institutional Corruption' Defined," 553.

even be functional to the primary purpose of institutions since some forms of clientelism may result in a more *efficient* delivery of goods and services, depending on the relative weakness of the state; if an institution is inefficient and unable to fulfill its task, patron-client relations may increase its efficiency, allowing it to fulfill its goal.[113] Finally, because it does not provide for criteria for the "magnetic north" of government, institutional corruption seems to be applicable only to particular institutions in relation to the political structure, taking basic institutional and procedural arrangements as a given.[114]

Perhaps as a way of salvaging the neorepublican tradition, Sparling suggests republican thought should incorporate this institutionalist conception of corruption by conceiving domination as a form of dependence. Since liberal democracies have eradicated "dominating dependence," Sparling argues republican theory should focus on analyzing and averting "corrupting dependence," which is the dependence "at issue in systemic corruption."[115] Even if I agree that republican thought needs a new theory of freedom to account for this type of systemic corruption, and that it is necessary to identify socioeconomic inequality and an "unbalanced regime"[116] form as the structural origins of corruption, Sparling's attempt to reduce corruption to a form of dependence seems to me misguided. First, because dependence is not inherently corrupting, the need for a substantive agreement on what kind of dependence would be considered corrupting would still be needed. Second, if corruption is the opposite of civic virtue, it has more to do with the prevalence of interest against the common good rather than directly with dependence—corrupting dependence being the result of corruption. And finally, reducing corruption to dependence does not allow us to escape interpersonal relations as the locus of corruption, leaving us unable to properly define systemic corruption structurally.

Systemic Corruption and the Oligarchization of Power

In his essay analyzing the problems associated with developing an encompassing definition of political corruption, Mark Philp argued that the main challenge any such definition encounters is that it presupposes a notion of an ideal,

---

113. Efficiency in fulfilling an institution's primary purpose through clientelism would nevertheless damage the institution in the long run. Philp, "Defining Political Corruption"; Heidenheimer, *Political Corruption*, pt. 4, "Corruption and Modernization," 477–578.

114. For a liberal critique of institutional corruption, see Ceva and Ferrett "Political Corruption."

115. Sparling, "Political Corruption," 620.

116. Ibid., 639.

uncorrupted form of political rule.[117] Whether democracy should be understood as a procedural,[118] deliberative,[119] or radical[120] political form is in itself a controversial issue. I do not wish to contribute to this debate but simply to identify a minimal condition of good popular government.

Following Aristotle's logic, representative government could be conceived both as a compound ideal type defined by its terms of contrast, and as an intermediate political regime that moves toward one of its extremes. Ideal liberal democracy being a hybrid regime composed of the principles of democracy and liberalism, a minimal definition of it would be a regime that fully realizes its democratic and liberal ends: to accurately represent the interests of the majority within the limits imposed by individual rights and separation of powers. The complete opposite of this ideal type would be an unrepresentative illiberal government, in which neither the interests of the majority nor basic norms are respected. This corrupt government would fall within the ancient definition of tyranny, in which those in power benefit themselves without any limitations on their will but their own power of coercion.

From the perspective not of principles but of the regime's ruling element, given that representative government is factually a collection of individuals elected by citizens to make law and policy decisions, this minimalist conception of an ideal type of liberal democracy would be akin to a constitutional electoral aristocracy: a government by the few (the best, wisest, most representative) chosen by the majority to rule within established constitutional limitations. Seen through a republican lens, the corrupt form that completely negates liberal democracy would be then an illiberal oligarchy: a government by few, for the benefit of few, without constitutional constraints. Even if everyone would agree that a government that does not represent the majority and does not respect rights is no longer a democracy, this analysis is not helpful for developing a definition for systemic corruption, which thrives within highly guarded constitutional frameworks.

If we conceive this ideal type as an intermediate regime that corrupts by moving toward either of its extremes, liberal democracy would corrupt by becoming either unrepresentative of the majority, or illiberal, depending on what principle is being undermined or realized. Therefore, a liberal democracy could corrupt and become either (1) an *oligarchic democracy*, a nonrepresentative liberal government in which individual rights and separation of powers

117. Philp, "Defining Political Corruption," 21.

118. Saffon and Urbinati, "Procedural Democracy."

119. J. Cohen, "Deliberative Democracy."

120. Abensour, "Savage Democracy," 703.

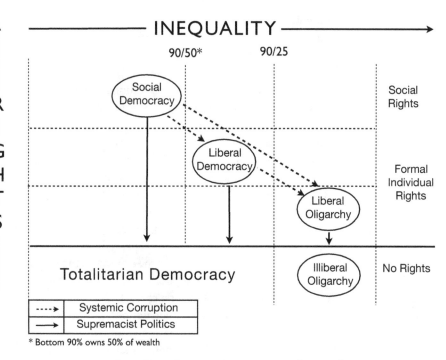

FIGURE 1.2. Inequality, rights, systemic corruption, and regime change.

are upheld but the interests of the majority are consistently not represented, or (2) an *illiberal democracy*, a representative but illiberal government in which the majority's interests trump the rights of minorities. While an oligarchic democracy is still a democracy in which there are "free and fair" elections and formal individual rights are protected, an illiberal democracy is a totalitarian form of government in which human rights of minorities are systematically violated.

Even if certainly there have been examples of these three corrupt forms of government—illiberal oligarchy, oligarchic democracy, and illiberal democracy—the type of systemic corruption republican thinkers were most concerned about, and that is ubiquitous today, is the gradual decay of "representativeness" and the increasing oligarchization of government and society within a general respect for the rule of law. A conception of systemic corruption thus needs to be connected to increasing socioeconomic inequality, which enables inequality of political influence and the drift into oligarchic democracy, a regime in which citizens empower, through their ballots, those who enable those very citizens' own dispossession and oppression.

Perhaps the first contour we need to draw to accurately define systemic corruption is its political nature. Currently, political corruption relates to

fraudulent action involving public office, which puts the focus on the corrupt
nexus between public and private. Given the complex relation between corruption and the law, a definition that focuses mainly on the agents of corruption and their exchanges seems inappropriate to conceptualize the systemic
layer of political corruption. The conception of institutional corruption, even
if a step in the right direction—away from the mainly juridical conception—is
also unable to appropriately track the oligarchic component of systemic corruption given its ungrounded functionalism that avoids substantive definitions of primary purposes. I would argue systemic corruption in liberal democracies should be understood as a long-term, slow-moving process of
oligarchization of society's political structure, and thus it should be analyzed
at the macro level. Instead of looking at the *inputs* of political corruption
(undue influence, which is hard to prove and thus prosecute), we should focus
rather on its *outputs*, as anything pertaining to rules, procedures, and institutions that has the *effect* of benefiting the wealthy at the expense of the majority.
We need to move away from *intention* and toward the *consequences* of political
corruption to identify and measure its structural character.

Following the ancients' insights on systemic corruption as an inevitable and
progressive process, the first major implication of this alternative meaning of
political corruption would be that our liberal democracies would not be ex-
empt from this degenerative movement because of the individual liberty they
guarantee. This awareness would make us not only recognize the folly and
presumptuousness of the modern and contemporary men who believed their
institutional creations were close to perfection, but, more importantly,
acknowledge that our constitutional systems are inherently flawed and in need
of immediate and periodic repair owing to the high degree of "entropy" they
allow for.

The second implication, which was so evident to the ancients, as it was also
to modern republican thinkers like Machiavelli, is that the law is not necessarily a source of virtue, and that not all constitutional forms are virtuous enough
to counteract natural and relentless corrupting tendencies. Consequently,
what is legal is not necessarily virtuous, and what is corrupt is not necessarily
illegal. Campaign finance and lobbying regulations, which legalized forms of
bribery and undue influence, are an example of this. If we take as a premise
that all constitutions and the laws they produce could tend to foster corruption, the relativity of the *rule of law*, which both neorepublican and neoliberal
thinkers argue is the mark of liberty, becomes evident. As we saw in Machiavelli's work, corruption is the vehicle for oppression, and it originates not only
in individuals but also in laws, and thus the rule of law must not be necessarily
understood as a source of liberty. Because laws can be manipulated and used
as tools for oppression, the rule of law appears not only as an inadequate

measure of liberty, but also as an extremely problematic one since it could actually tend to uphold and sustain domination instead of combating it.

A third implication comes from qualifying political corruption as pertaining to rules, procedures, and institutions that affect the sociopolitical realm: there is an inevitable enlargement of the scope of the phenomenon. If the mark of political corruption is the advancement of individual or sectional interests against those of the majority, then we could think corrupt not only those laws and policies *actively* favoring the wealthy, and consider corrupting those ideologies that have this consequence when implemented, but also the negligence of lawmakers and policy makers to counteract oligarchic outcomes, *passively* letting the wealthy keep further enriching themselves. Because conceiving political corruption in terms of its systemic effects allows us to separate corruption from individual immoral disposition and its immediate, tangible actions, ideologies such as neoliberalism—which has the effect of increasing socioeconomic inequality and thus the power of the wealthy[121]—and governmental inaction, such as the lack of proper regulation in the financial system—which ultimately enabled the most recent global economic crisis and the transfer of wealth from the many to the few[122]—could be conceived as forms of political corruption because they enable the further oligarchization of liberal democracy.

In terms of how we could attempt to measure systemic corruption, the only way to account for the drift into oligarchy would be to take into account the effects that the legal structure and governmental action have on society. And thus the Corruption Index should include, in addition to anticorruption laws, number of prosecutions, and opinion polls, variables relating to the outputs of law and policy such as the degree of inequality, the gap between capital and labor, allocation of GDP among social classes, and regressive versus progressive taxation schemes. This data not only is already available but also seems better suited for undertaking a comparison among countries than is solely relying on laws, court records, and individual perceptions of corruption, which are in themselves conditioned by the legal political culture.

121. An example of the implementation of neoliberalism at the constitutional level is Chile, which has the highest rate of inequality in the OECD and is among the fifteen most unequal countries in the world.

122. Between 2009 and 2012, the top 1 percent of US households captured 95 percent of total income gains, while the bottom 90 percent of households saw their income fall by 16 percent. Saez and Piketty, "Income Inequality in the United States." Individuals and institutions on Wall Street that contributed directly to this upward redistribution of wealth still remain unpunished.

If one agrees that the minimal normative expectation of liberal democracies is that governments should advance the interests of the majority within constitutional safeguards, increasing income inequality and the relative immiseration of the majority of citizens would be a sign of corruption. However, this insight is yet to be properly analyzed since our juridical, individualist conception of corruption prevents us from fully capturing its systemic nature and its effects on the exercise of individual liberties. Following Machiavelli's analysis, if corruption is reduced to individual illegal actions, the relentless process of political degradation and loss of liberty is obscured. Individual pursuit of interest is an inevitable feature in a free state, and so is the degradation of the constitutional constraints on undue influence on government. While the former cannot be eliminated, the latter must be acknowledged and remedied to keep corruption at bay.

2

Elitist Interpretations
of the Republic

AS THE PREVIOUS chapter argues, systemic political corruption should be
conceived as an inescapable phenomenon, a constant threat to liberty that is
endemic to all forms of government. The recognition of this relentless process
of political decay prompted ancient and modern political thinkers to study
existing constitutions and engage in perhaps the impossible task of designing
the perfect regime: a political order that would be immune to the degradation
of its institutions and procedures, and thus perennial, severed from the inevitable fate of decay and regime change. The theory of the mixed constitution—
which can be traced back to Aristotle's politeia, a mixture of oligarchy and
democracy[1]—originated as a critique of pure, monoarchic constitutions,
and it proposed a realist cure for systemic corruption based on the institutionalization of different forms of power that are in constant expansion and limitation, checking each other following their own expansionary tendencies rather
than purely out of virtue or legal obligation.

In this chapter and the following I will show that there are two main interpretations of the theory of the mixed constitution, which are determined by
the degree of institutionalization of the powers of the few and the many, and
by the hierarchy given to each within the constitutional structure: (1) an *elitist*
interpretation, developed from the vantage point of elites and thus conservative of the existing socioeconomic hierarchies, arguing the few (a) should
rule—authorized and checked by the people—and (b) have final decision-
making power; and (2) a *plebeian* interpretation, developed from the experience of resistance of the common people against oligarchic domination, arguing the people (a) should effectively control the few who govern by *actively*
participating in politics through plebeian institutions and (b) should have final

---

1. Aristotle, *Politics*, IV.8 1293b; Pasquino, "Machiavelli and Aristotle."

decision-making power. By setting apart *elitist* and *plebeian* interpretations of the mixed constitution, I am not only questioning the rather neat continuity that J.G.A. Pocock saw in modern republican thought from Machiavelli to the American Founders[2] but also proposing there can be a sharp distinction between schools of interpretation if we take as the point of departure the position and role of the "popular" element in the constitutional structure.[3] Thus, instead of conceiving republican thought as exclusively divided between ancients and moderns,[4] I argue the parting should be done, at least in terms of constitutional thought, between elitist and plebeian approaches to the constitution.[5]

Plebeian interpretations of the mixed constitution, which would place the ultimate political judgment on the common people as guardians of liberty, have yielded only a handful of constitutional models with variations stemming from the different ways of institutionalizing popular authority.[6] Elitist interpretations of the mixed constitution, on the other hand, have produced a range of constitutional models:[7] from political orders having a highly institutionalized, but subordinate "popular power" such as the one in James Harrington's *The Commonwealth of Oceana* (1656), to constitutional frameworks like the ones we have today, completely lacking a popular institution but incorporating instead neutral, countermajoritarian, unelected elite bodies to play the "democratic" role of checking on government.[8]

2. Even if Pocock recognized the different emphasis of Machiavellian, Harringtonian, and post-Puritan republicanism, there is no sharp distinction between elitist and popular strands of republican thought in Pocock, *Machiavellian Moment*.

3. The distinction springs from John McCormick's distinction between Machiavelli's assembly-based model and Guicciardini's electoral, senatorial model. McCormick, *Machiavellian Democracy*, 9.

4. See, for example, Rahe, *Republics Ancient and Modern*.

5. I propose to make the distinction based on who should have final political decision-making power in a given constitution—the selected few or the common people. Perhaps this division is as arbitrary as one based on a historical epoch, but it is clear-cut and not based on a convention, but rather on a constitutional rule, which could help better distinguish different strands in the republican tradition of thought.

6. Machiavelli, *A Discourse on Remodeling the Government of Florence* (1520) in *Machiavelli Chief Works*, vol. 1; *Discourses*.

7. Perhaps this is because the elitist interpretation of the mixed constitution was the only one preserved from the ancients. Almost all written sources preserved from the ancients were authored by members of the elite, and thus we have been analyzing democracy and the republic from the point of view of the critics of democratic and plebeian power.

8. See Rosanvallon, *Counter-democracy*.

	Elitist Republicanism		Plebeian Republicanism	
	Material	Procedural/ Liberal	Revolutionary Reformers	Critical
Plebeian Institutions	Polybius Cicero Guiccardini		Machiavelli Condorcet Jefferson Luxemburg Arendt McCormick Hamilton	Marx
No Plebeian Institution	Harrington	Montesquieu Madison Pettit		Negri Rancière Green

FIGURE 2.1. Varieties of republicanism.

My objective in this chapter is to present a compelling reading of the predominant elitist strand of interpretation of the mixed constitution by offering an analysis of what Pocock called Atlantic republican thought. I trace the ideas, proposals, and philosophical justifications that yielded the current elitist-proceduralist interpretation of the republican constitution. I argue this interpretation is not only blind to forms of domination occurring within and through legal structures, but also complicit in their reproduction because of its uncritical engagement with the socioeconomic hierarchies embedded in the status quo. The *elitism* of this strand of thought refers simply to the endorsement of elites—those who are distinct from the common people by either birth, wealth, knowledge, popularity, or technical expertise—as being better suited to rule and have final decision-making power. The particular *procedural* bent of this elitist strand comes from the justification of elitism: the belief that a set of procedural mechanisms and constraints are *sufficient* institutional conditions for the rule of law to guarantee and promote liberty for plebeian citizens.[9] This proceduralist approach to the rule of law is unable to account for the slow progression of systemic corruption and oligarchic power within the constitutional structure because it focuses on formal rules and delegation of powers instead of on how political decision making is actually done, on modes of selection instead of on the special interests behind candidates, and on equal constitutional rights instead of on the evident structural gender and racial oppressions existing alongside formal protections.

9. I follow Jeffrey Green's plebeian interpretation of liberal democracy in which ordinary citizenship is second-class citizenship. I will discuss his plebeian description of the liberal democratic experience in chapter 8. Green, *Shadow of Unfairness*.

Through a plebeian lens that sharpens the difference between procedural and material, formal and factual forms of power, in what follows I analyze the infrastructure of power that the constitution establishes for the common people, paying close attention to (1) the degree of institutionalization and the role of the few and the many within the power structure, as well as (2) the antidemocratic arguments and elitist justifications that served as normative premises for the establishment of elitist republics and liberal democracies.

Foundations of Elitist Constitutionalism:
Polybius and Cicero

Republican political thought has been commonly traced back to the Roman republic of the second century BC, originating within a mixed constitution that combined three forms of government: kinship, aristocracy, and democracy. Different from other great states such as Sparta, Rome had a constitution that was not set up by one virtuous man, but became a mixed constitution in an evolutionary manner, through the struggle between patricians and plebeians over debt and war.[10] The Roman constitution was not a document, but rather a tradition that incorporated fundamental institutions as well as written and unwritten norms (*ius*) and evolving practices (*mos*).[11] To understand the extent of the power wielded by patricians and plebeians within the constitutional structure, it is thus necessary to analyze formal power through the actual practices of different forms of power in society.

Even if not the first to theorize about the mixed constitution,[12] Polybius was the first to attempt a conjunctural narrative of the Roman constitution, putting for the first time "Roman political behavior in a conceptual framework."[13] In his description, written during a period of great expansion and conquest, Polybius accounted for formal and material aspects of political power and elaborated a model of Rome's evolutionary constitutional tradition aimed at justifying the superiority of the republic as mixed constitution. I argue that this aim made him gloss over the "very considerable shifts of power" that occurred during the period in which the republic supposedly was in balance.[14]

---

10. Lintott, *Constitution of the Roman Republic*, 32–38.

11. Ibid., 4–7.

12. Dicaearchus of Messene, disciple of Aristotle, would have written *Tripoliticus*, a tract about the best constitution as a mixture of monarchy, aristocracy, and democracy, one and a half centuries before Polybius. Fritz, *Theory of the Mixed Constitution in Antiquity*, 82.

13. Lintott, *Constitution of the Roman Republic*, 8.

14. Fritz, *Theory of the Mixed Constitution in Antiquity*, x.

According to Polybius, institutions giving legal authority to the one, the few, and the many shared "in the control of the Roman state,"[15] allowing for a balance of power that gave stability and endurance to the republic. For Polybius, Rome's mixed constitution made its republic superior to the democracies and oligarchies in the Greek world because of its ability to prevent the overgrowth of power and the corruption stemming from it. However, as we saw in the previous chapter, his account of Rome's political evolution was unable to grasp the oligarchization process unfolding underneath the formal structure of laws and procedures—perhaps because his aim was to explain the greatness of the Roman system of government, not its incipient decadence.

If we analyze the evolution of the Roman republic through a plebeian lens, the trajectories of plebeian formal and material power within the constitutional framework do not appear to track each other after plebeians were successful in occupying the highest spaces of political power. Since the establishment of the Tribunes of the Plebs in 494 BC,[16] the increase in formal plebeian power through the middle and late republic was progressive. While at the beginning resolutions passed in the Plebeian Council bound only the plebs, and plebeian leadership was limited to obstructing political acts (*intercessio*) and protecting individuals from magistrates (*auxilium*), by mid-fourth century plebeian leaders were allowed to become dictators, censors, and consuls, and plebeian resolutions were binding for all citizens.[17] By the late republic plebeians could elect magistrates and become elected to the highest offices,[18] decide on war, peace, and alliances, enact and reject laws, create colonies and distribute public land, inflict the death penalty, and even control admission to Roman citizenship.[19] Plebeians appear wielding great institutional power— certainly much more than the institutional power citizens enjoy today.

This broad institutional power of plebeians stands in contrast to the rather narrow institutional prerogative of the Senate, which appears as an advisory body with no institutional power other than its control over finance. However, the power over the public budget made the magistrates effectively dependent on the Senate. The Senate decided on the budget for lucrative contracts, had

15. Polybius, *Histories*, VI.2 and 5.

16. After plebeian soldiers refused to march against the enemy, and instead seceded to the Aventine Hill, leaving the city to its fate, patricians conceded by allowing plebeians their own exclusive leaders.

17. *Lex Hortensia*, 287 BC.

18. The last offices to be opened to plebeians were religious. *Lex Ogulnia* (300 BC) opened access to the priesthood, and in 254 BC Tiberius Coruncanius was selected as the first plebeian pontifex maximus.

19. Lintott, *Constitution of the Roman Republic*, 200.

a say in all matters involving the treasury, even having veto power over withdraws from public coffers.[20] Even if the Senate did not have formal power over magistrates, being unable to legally punish them if they did not follow its directions, magistrates needed to justify their requests for money and their decisions to the Senate. The incentive for magistrates to follow the Senate's directions was strong since deviation from senatorial advice would likely bring future denial of funding.[21]

The Senate's control over the budget, however, does not account for all the power patricians had over plebeians. At least formally, the Tribunate was the only office that was not under the purview of the Senate; plebeian tribunes were dependent only on the Plebeian Council and aimed at *obstructing* patrician institutional power.[22] Polybius's class-based explanation for the Senate's power over the people shifts the focus to socioeconomic dependence.[23] In addition to widespread patronage, which gave the nobles control over their dependent individuals, Polybius points to the people's general deference toward the aristocracy, which was connected with the control nobles had over public religion. Priestly power was supreme, and the "interpretation of the requirements of the gods remained an aristocratic prerogative and the ensuing decisions took priority over, and could render void, even resolutions of the assemblies."[24] Patricians retained the ultimate veto power over plebeian institutions via the interpretation of divine auguries, to which the *populus Romanus* was deeply devoted.[25]

In addition to socioeconomic dependence, aristocratic authority, and religion, the Senate had control over the office of the dictator, who wielded absolute power in cases of emergency. The magistracy of dictator was set up by a three-step procedure in which the Senate requested a dictator, who was then selected by a consul,[26] and then ratified by the Comitia Curiata, an assembly organized based on Rome's patrician clans in which plebeians were not

20. Except for the consuls who had free access to the treasury. *Histories*, VI.13. However, Polybius states at the beginning of book VI that magistrates can withdraw from the treasury at their own discretion. For an analysis of the contradictions in Polybius's account of distribution of power in Rome, see Fritz, *Theory of the Mixed Constitution in Antiquity*, ch. 7.

21. Polybius, *Histories*, VI.13.

22. Cicero, *On the Commonwealth*, II.58.

23. Polybius, *Histories*, VI.17; Lintott, *Constitution of the Roman Republic*, 198.

24. Lintott, *Constitution of the Roman Republic*, 198.

25. For an analysis of Roman pagan religion, see Merrill, "Attitude of Ancient Rome toward Religion and Religious Cults."

26. The first dictator, Tituts Larcius, was a consul nominated by the other consul, Cloelius, who, after, "abdicated the consulship himself." Dionysius, *Roman Antiquities*, V.72.

allowed to vote. Given the weight of the Senate's authority, this procedure gave elites the control over the republic's emergency power institution, effectively excluding the people from influencing the nomination.

Another source of elite control over plebeians came paradoxically from the success of the plebeian political struggle. Parallel to the progressive institutional empowerment of plebeians, there was an increasing cooptation of plebeian leadership into patrician ranks, which ended up consolidating a new "patricio-plebeian aristocratic consensus."[27] According to Livy the plebeian struggles of the mid-fourth century BC were mainly led by wealthy, politically ambitious plebeians who wanted to "clear for themselves the way to all the other distinctions."[28] After *leges Liciniae Sextiae* (367 BC), which gave plebeians access to the consulship,[29] and *lex Hortensia* (287 BC), which eliminated the Senate's approval of legislation, plebeian institutional power appears to have been systematically blunted and disarmed. Plebeian colonization of patrician governing structures not only brought patrician and plebeian elites together, creating a new sociopolitical bond, but also made plebeian elites the beneficiaries of a status quo they now wanted to preserve instead of challenge.[30] Consequently, as soon as plebeians gained full formal access to the governing structure, the so-called Struggle of the Orders ended, and plebeian representatives began to serve the structure of power instead of contesting it, becoming "slaves to the nobility."[31]

This new form of politico-institutional dependence that resulted in the oligarchization[32] of plebeian leadership appeared to have been manifested primarily through negligence and inaction. Despite the broad range of powers that the Plebeian Council had acquired, if we look at the exercise of these powers, it becomes clear that by the late republic plebeians saw a de facto retrenchment of their political prerogatives. Even if traditionally plebeians had the power to declare war and peace, and ratify treaties, the Senate appears to

27. Lintott, *Constitution of the Roman Republic*, 194; Vishnia, *State, Society, and Popular Leaders*.

28. Livy, *History of Rome*, 6.35.2.

29. Rachel Vishnia argues for a new periodization of Roman history in which the *leges Liciniae Sextiae* would be the origin of the patricio-plebeian consensus. *State, Society, and Popular Leaders*, 7.

30. After the initial patrician rejection of sharing the consulship with plebeians, the integration seems to have been rather smooth owing mainly to the increased economic benefits resulting from Roman expansion. See Harris, *War and Imperialism in Republican Rome*, 74–77.

31. Livy, *History of Rome*, 10.37.11.

32. For the general process of detachment of leadership from the grassroots, see Michels, *Political Parties*.

have monopolized these decisions in the late republic.[33] And even what Polybius argues is the fundamental prerogative of the people—to allocate honors and penalties, which served the function of protecting the republic against tyrannies of the one or the few[34]—appears to have been substantially weakened by the time he was writing. Even if there is evidence of trials being held in the assembly, there are no capital punishment cases resulting in conviction during the late republic, "which calls into question their effectiveness as a popular weapon against the aristocracy."[35]

Despite the plebeian formal infrastructure of power, plebeian authority was overridden through negligence, usurpation, contempt, and open violence. Since enforcement of laws was part of the executive function, which was informally under the authority of the Senate, even if plebeians could formally pass laws, the Senate and magistrates could choose to disregard the legislative authority of the Plebeian Council. A little over a decade after Polybius's *Histories* ends, the Roman republic experienced a constitutional crisis that ended in the assassination of the tribune Tiberius Gracchus in 133 BC over land redistribution. According to Plutarch, Tiberius's "zeal and determination" in pursuing an agrarian law was "honorable and just" because it did not come from his own desire to advance his office or his name, but was instead kindled by the people themselves, who set up "writings upon the porches, walls, and monuments, calling upon him to reinstate the poor citizens in their former possessions."[36] Despite commanding a majority in the Plebeian Council—which would have meant a favorable plebiscite and the consequent establishment of the Agrarian Law—the tribune Marcus Octavius opposed the law, vetoing the motion. Plutarch states that Octavius's opposition was prompted by "the prayers and supplications of many influential men," and since Tiberius could not pass the law in any other way, he was forced to do something "illegal and unseemly": to eject Octavius from his office. Tiberius justifies this illegal motion by arguing that a plebeian representative that maims or annuls the people's power is not only a "bad tribune" but "no tribune at all."[37] While the refusal of the Senate to recognize and enable the reforms to the Agrarian Law disregarded the legislative prerogative of the Plebeian Council, the murdering of Tiberius directly violated the foundation of plebeian power: the sacrosanctity of tribunes.[38] This constitutional crisis was brewing when Polybius elaborated his

---

33. Polybius, *Histories*, VI.13; Lintott, *Constitution of the Roman Republic*, 197.

34. Polybius, *Histories*, VI.14.

35. Lintott, *Constitution of the Roman Republic*, 201–2.

36. Plutarch, "Life of Tiberius," §8.

37. Ibid., §9.

38. For a description of the powers of the tribunate stemming from its sacrosanctity, see Lintott, *Constitution of the Roman Republic*, 33.

interpretation of the Roman republican experience, and despite evident signs of oligarchic overgrowth, he insisted on the adequate "balance" of the powers within the constitutional structure.

While Polybius's analytical description of the Roman republic focused on Rome's apogee, before the first constitutional crisis, Cicero wrote under a crumbling system, rife with violence and corruption. In *On the Commonwealth* he laments the decay of the republic:

> And so, before our time, ancestral morality provided outstanding men, and great men preserved the morality of old and the institutions of our ances-tors. But our own time, having inherited the commonwealth like a wonder-ful picture that had faded over time, not only has failed to renew its original colors but has not even taken the trouble to preserve at least its shapes and outline.[39]

While Polybius was unable to account for the increasing oligarchic domina-tion growing parallel to an expansion of formal plebeian power, Cicero ac-knowledged the corruption of the constitution, but his solution was to regain virtue by reasserting the dominance of the ruling elite. He explained the cor-ruption of the republic as due to the loss of "ancestral morality" and "outstand-ing men,"[40] and so the way out of crisis was for him to reestablish morality through good leadership: "whatever moral alteration takes place in the leaders soon follows among the people."[41] In the voice of Scipio, Cicero states that a good leader, by strengthening the sense of shame among the people, keeps citizens seeking "the praise and respect of the best man."[42] Cicero not only shifted the focus of analysis away from institutions and toward morality and individual behavior as the source of corruption and erosion of the republic, but he also gave preeminence to the aristocracy as source of normativity. The best commonwealth is for him the one "controlled by its best citizens," in which the liberty of the plebs corresponds only to the "power of honorably pleasing respectable citizens."[43] Even if Cicero recognized not only the need for a balanced form of government—in which "some things [are] set aside for the judgment and wishes of the people," to avoid giving the plebs reasons to revolt[44]—but also the positive role played by plebeian tribunes in protecting

39. Cicero, *On the Commonwealth*, V. 2a.
40. Ibid.
41. Cicero, *On the Laws*, III §31.
42. Cicero, *On the Commonwealth*, V. 6.
43. Ibid., III. 38.
44. Ibid., III. 69.

liberty by checking the ambition of elites, what ultimately produces good government for him is the virtue of the ruling class.

Cicero follows closely Plato's ideas on the damaging effects of extreme equal liberty in democracies, which seems endemic to the "equal share in the constitution and public office."[45] For Plato the desire for "pure, unmixed freedom" in democracies produces anarchy:[46] in the family children do not respect their parents, "immigrants are put on a par with citizens," "pupils have an equal contempt for their teachers and their attendants," slavery is abolished, and even "horses and donkeys are in the habit of wandering the streets with total freedom."[47] Cicero reproduces Plato's argument, saying that in a democratic commonwealth "private homes have no master and this evil extends even to animals"; "fathers fear their sons," "pupils scorn their teachers," and even "women have the same rights as their husbands."[48]

Even if Cicero's antidemocratic position is fragmentary, the thrust of his argument indicates that to avoid democratic tyranny the aristocratic element must be supreme within the power-sharing structure of the republic. Cicero's is not a controversial argument since, unlike Athens, the Roman republic was effectively governed by elites. Cicero's philosophical support for the dominance of elites was thus a normative description of his political reality. According to him, mixed constitution, "this combined and moderately blended form of commonwealth," is more solid than a pure regime that easily corrupts and also tends to maintain the social hierarchies. "There is no reason for revolutions when each person is firmly set in his own rank, without the possibility of sudden collapse."[49] Cicero argued the ballot is "a badge of liberty" that should be used to please the "best and most respectable citizens"; having the right to vote is enough satisfaction for the people, who then tend to follow the lead of elites.[50]

Cicero attempts not only to justify the current constitutional framework but also to innovate by proposing to broaden the legal prerogatives of the ruling class. He reduced the liberty of the people to choosing the worthiest of the few and acting in a harmonious political process in which plebeians would confirm what the Senate decided, and the magistrates executed. This shift in the scale in favor of elites did not mean however directly attacking the power of the Tribunate. Even if among Cicero's circle "everyone agrees" the power of

45. Plato, *Republic*, 8.557e–566.

46. For the relation between democracy and anarchy, see Gourgouris, *Perils of the One*.

47. Plato, *Republic*, 8.562c–564.

48. Cicero, *On the Commonwealth*, I.67.

49. Ibid., I. 69.

50. Cicero, *On the Laws*, III §38.

the tribunes was "excessive," Cicero defended the office of the Tribunate as necessary.[51]

While he considered it of benefit for the republic that the popular sectors have representation in an exclusively popular institution, Cicero considered popular authority subordinated to aristocratic authority. According to him, the unbound people-as-crowd is more dangerous than their political representatives, who moderate their own behavior out of self-interest, rapidly becoming systemic actors. Even if the Gracchi tribunes had caused much conflict and violence, the unrepresented crowd would be much worse. And even if in some instances, tribunes could have made things worse, it would be dangerous to abolish the plebeian office because it could cause a new civil war:

> When the senate yielded this power [of representation] to the plebeians, the weapons were put down, the sedition was calmed, moderation was discovered, which allowed the lesser people to think that they were made equal to the leaders; and that was the single source of salvation for the state.[52]

While he had "no quarrels with the Tribunate" and thus his ideal regime would preserve the office intact (to the strong disapproval of his interlocutors), Cicero proposed to reassert the dominance of elites, on the one hand by giving magistrates the indirect power to obstruct the Plebeian Council by "taking the auspices," and on the other by strengthening the authority of the Senate in the making of the law. In his ideal commonwealth magistrates would have "the right to take the auspices and give judgment," which would establish a way to "obstruct many useless but appealing initiatives."[53] Since the "immortal gods" have usually "suppressed unjust impulses of the people," giving the right to magistrates to take the auspices would neutralize undesirable plebeian motions without causing conflict. Even if you had a Tiberius Gracchus, willing to risk his life for land redistribution, his initiative could be suppressed if the auspices were unfavorable, without any bloodshed. There was no need to abolish the Tribunate to reassert the subordination of the plebeians to aristocratic authority. If controversial motions could be vetoed by the priests as a religious upper chamber, then the power of the Tribunate would be neutralized, becoming an institution reproducing the lead of the ruling class instead of challenging it, unable to counteract the oligarchic tendencies of the few.

---

51. Ibid., III §23.
52. Ibid., III §23–24.
53. Ibid., III §27.

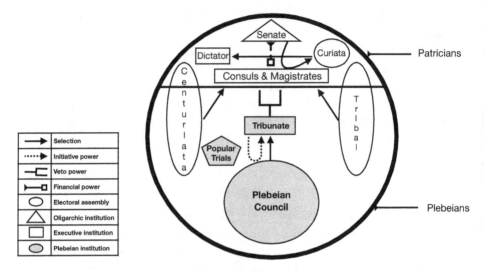

FIGURE 2.2. Roman republic before *leges Liciniae Sextiae* (367 BC).

In addition to placing an indirect limit on plebeian decisions, Cicero wanted the Senate to dominate the legislative process, giving the nobles the power to decree, and the people the power to ratify:

> For it works out that if the senate is in charge of public deliberation, and if the remaining orders are willing to have the commonwealth guided by the deliberation of the leading order, then it is possible through the blending of rights, since the people have power and the senate authority, that that moderate and harmonious order of the state be maintained, especially if the following law is obeyed; for what follows is: "Let the senatorial order be free from fault; let it be a model to others."[54]

Cicero envisioned a mixed constitution in which the senatorial order was dominant and the power of plebeians was only formal. His elitist model uses institutions and procedures as a way of taming popular power, satisfying and neutralizing the people so to avoid violence. Like Plato's, Cicero's ideal model is aimed at harmony, a politics of cooperation that is not achieved by directly disempowering the plebeians from their institutional power, but by giving the people a power that is formal and subordinate: "my law gives the appearance of liberty while keeping the authority of the respectable and eliminating an occasion for dispute."[55]

54. Ibid., III §28.
55. Ibid., III §38.

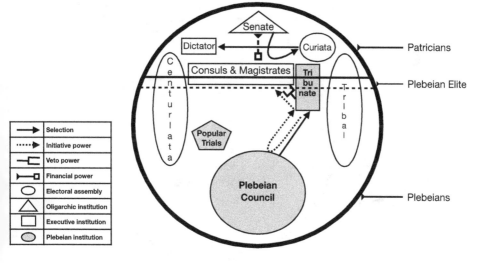

FIGURE 2.3. Roman republic after the patricio-plebeian consensus.

The English Republican Tradition
of Harrington and Montesquieu

Even if Cicero's ideas on the commonwealth were never implemented, his elitist interpretation of the mixed constitution was preserved and later reproduced in medieval Europe mainly through Augustine's citations.[56] In England the mixed constitution began to be discussed in relation to the English commonwealth in the mid-1500s, becoming the "dominant political theory" in the seventeenth century.[57] In 1642, at the verge of civil war, King Charles I declared in his *Answer to the Nineteen Propositions* that England was a mixed government in which the "laws are jointly made by a king, by a house of peers, and by a house of commons chosen by the people, all having free votes and particular privileges."[58] This declaration was a preemptive strategy by the king to define the political future on his own terms. While a "regulated monarchy" would govern according to the laws, the House of Commons ("an excellent Conserver of Libertie, but never intended for any share in Government")

56. For an account of the tradition of the mixed constitution in the Middle Ages through the study of Aristotle, see Blythe, *Ideal Government*.

57. Vile, *Constitutionalism and the Separation of Powers*, 41.

58. Charles I, *His Majesties Answer to the Nineteen Propositions*. For a full sociopolitical context of this royal proposal going back to the Middle Ages, see Mendle, *Dangerous Positions*.

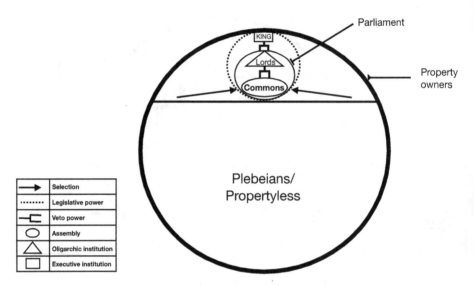

FIGURE 2.4. England's mixed monarchy, 17th century.

would have the power only to levy money and impeach public officials. The Lords would wield "judicatory power,"[59] which was later interpreted as the power to arbitrate, "to trim the balance, to act as a supreme court of constitutional law."[60]

While in the English mixed government of the *Answer* the indirect power of the people through their elected representatives was supposed to be narrow, specific to taxation and impeachment, this was the opposite of what was happening on the ground. Despite the English Parliament being a temporary advisory body that did not wield formal institutional power, the House of Commons had been successful in the previous decades in getting legislation passed against the king's wishes and was "close to claiming the right to issue ordinances without his consent."[61] Similar to the Roman Senate, which was an advisory body with de facto power over the executive function through its control over the budget, the House of Commons was gradually becoming the dominant institution, abrogating the power to legislate and make policy.

According to M.J.C. Vile, because the mixed constitution was seen as a tool to defend a limited monarchy, the tradition of the mixed constitution incorporated the nascent doctrine of separation of powers, allowing for their later

59. Charles I, *His Majesties Answer to the Nineteen Propositions*.
60. Pocock, *Machiavellian Moment*, 361.
61. Ibid., 364.

confusion.[62] A year after the *Answer*, Philip Hunton in his *Treatise of Monarchy* aimed at giving supremacy to the law as opposed to the arbitrary will of the monarch by arguing that while the legislative function was to be shared, the king's executive role was his sole prerogative. According to Hunton, the English form of government was a "mixed monarchy" rather than a mixed constitution, because the predominant element—which in this case was the monarch with his monopoly over executive power—"gives the denomination to the whole."[63] Vile argues that Hunton's arguments regarding the separation of functions as determining the nature of the regime became one of the basic elements of the dominant constitutional theory after the revolution of 1688, which tended to confuse the checks and balances produced by institutional powers grounded in social orders with the mechanistic separation of functions of government.[64]

After the king's death one of the first actions by the Rump Parliament (1649–53) was to declare England a commonwealth that was to be governed "without any king or house of Lords."[65] However, kingly and aristocratic power would shortly be reinstated. After the civil wars and the establishment of the Protectorate under Lord Oliver Cromwell, the doctrine of separation of powers was deployed to justify the 1653 *Instrument of Government*, England's first written constitution.[66] Part of what was finally incorporated into this constitutional framework came out of the Putney Debates, in which the Grandees—the conservative faction of the New Model Army—presented their *Heads of Proposals* in opposition to the Levellers' *Agreement of the People*, which proposed expanding suffrage. The elitist interpretation of the mixed constitution prevailed. The *Instrument of Government* established three political institutions: the advisory Council of State, an elected Lord Protector with monopoly over the executive power, and the Parliament, in charge of legislation, meeting every three years. A property requirement to have the right to elect a representative to Parliament effectively excluded the masses from the "Commons."[67] The

62. Vile, *Constitutionalism and the Separation of Powers*, 37.

63. Philip Hunton, *A Treatise of Monarchy* (London: Thoemmes Continuum, 1643), 5. Quoted in Vile, *Constitutionalism and the Separation of Powers*, 45.

64. Vile, *Constitutionalism and the Separation of Powers*, 37–38.

65. Gardiner, *Constitutional Documents of the Puritan Revolution*, 338, cited in Worden, "Republicanism, Regicide and Republic," 315. Despite the dismantling of monarchic and aristocratic institutions, Richard Tuck refers to this political period as being governed by "boards of oligarchs." *Philosophy and Government*, 222.

66. Vile, *Constitutionalism and the Separation of Powers*, 52.

67. This exclusionary understanding of citizenship is pervasive in aristocratic republicanism, which in the early sixteenth century restricted active citizenship to the gentry, excluding yeomen and burgesses. Peltonen, "Citizenship and Republicanism," 95.

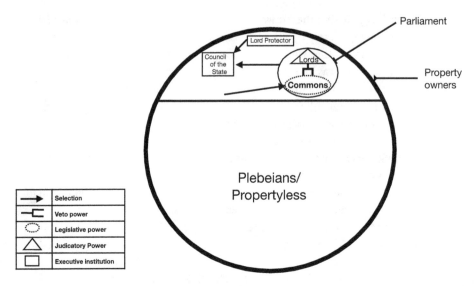

FIGURE 2.5. England under the Protectorate.

arguments against the broadening of the suffrage hinged on property being a proxy for independence, and "if there be anything at all that is a foundation of liberty it is this, that those who shall choose the law-making shall be men freed from dependence upon others."[68] Property owners were independent and therefore would not be servile to the interests of others, but only to those of the commonwealth. After four years this constitution was replaced by the *Humble Petition and Advice* (1657), which originated in a remonstrance to the Lord Protector by the Grandees. The original document not only rehashed the elitist interpretation of the mixed constitution put forward in the *Answer* and the *Instrument of Government* but also proposed to convert the office of the Protectorate into a hereditary monarchy.[69] Cromwell refused and eliminated the clause of kinship. He also introduced a second chamber similar to the House of Lords to avoid the Commons abrogating judiciary powers.[70]

A few months before Cromwell signed the new power arrangement, James Harrington had published his powerful materialist critique of the procedural

68. Commissary-General Henry Ireton, extract from the debates at Putney, in *English Levellers*, 129.

69. Pocock, *Machiavellian Moment*, 384.

70. The case of James Naylor, who was judged and harshly punished by the House of Commons on the crime of blasphemy, prompted Cromwell to reinstate the House of Lords.

interpretation of the mixed constitution in *The Commonwealth of Oceana*. For Harrington all commonwealths are a form of "domestic empire" that stand on the principles of "good of fortunes" or riches. Because all "domestic empire is founded upon dominion," and dominion is property, then who holds the property should be what determines the nature of the regime. "If one man is the sole landlord of the territory" the regime is an absolute monarchy; if the few are the landlords or "overbalance the people unto the like proportion," it is a "mixed monarchy"; and if the whole people are landlords, it is a commonwealth.[71] Because political power is grounded on property, a constitution that does not take due account of the distribution of property would not last for long uncorrupted. Harrington attributes the collapse of the Roman republic to increased dispossession of the masses and the inability of the constitution to properly address this problem in time:

> Whence by the time of Tiberius Gracchus the nobility had almost eaten the people quite out of their lands, which they held in the occupation of tenants and servants; whereupon the remedy being too late and too vehemently applied, the commonwealth was ruined.[72]

Writing during the breakdown of monarchical authority, Harrington proposes an alternative constitutional arrangement for Oceana, a commonwealth that the same as England and Venice also would exist in an island. According to Pocock, Harrington's purpose was to argue against going back to the "ancient" English constitutional tradition based on common law and fixed social hierarchies, and bridge the gap between the Grandees' property requirements for active citizenship and the Levellers' expansion of suffrage to independent citizens.[73] For Harrington a proper commonwealth is possible only when the few are not able to disproportionally concentrate wealth and overbalance the people. Therefore, in *Oceana* all people should be landlords, "or hold the land so divided among them" or "the balance of treasure [that] may be equal unto that of land"; only relative material equality would allow for political equality.

Despite his materialist approach to constitutional thought and strong support for land redistribution and strict laws regulating property, Harrington's constitutional proposal is closer to those of Plato and Cicero than to that of

---

71. Harrington, *Oceana*, "The Preliminaries," in *"Commonwealth of Oceana" and "A System of Politics,"* 11–12.

72. Harrington, *Oceana*, "The Preliminaries," 37.

73. Pocock, *Machiavellian Moment*, 385. The Levellers were fine with excluding apprentices, servants, and beggars "because they depend upon the will of other men and should be afraid to displease them." *English Levellers*, 130.

Machiavelli, who he claims to be most indebted to.[74] Harrington's ideal constitution endorses an elitist version of the mixed constitution with the few as the dominant element, having the power to set the legislative agenda, and the people having the power to elect the ruling elite and decide only when prompted. Taking Polybius's "balanced" mixed constitution and Cicero's elitist position in which the republic needs to be "controlled by its best citizens," Harrington's *Oceana* endorsed the separation of functions, with "the senate proposing, the people resolving, and the magistracy executing."[75] Harrington was aiming not so much at a plebeian type of mixed constitution, but rather, as Pocock argues, at trying to "rehabilitate aristocracy in the wake of what he saw as the collapse of feudal oligarchy":[76]

> I agree with Machiavel that a nobility or gentry, overbalancing a popular government, is the utter bane and destruction of it; so I shall show in another that a nobility or gentry in a popular government, not overbalancing it, is the very life and soul of it.[77]

Unlike Machiavelli, who chose the agonistic Roman republic as his model, Harrington's preferred model was Venice,[78] a hereditary oligarchic republic that he praises as "the most equal in the constitution,"[79] equal both in "the balance or foundation and in the superstructures, that is to say in her agrarian law and in her rotation."[80] In addition to being the most equal commonwealth—given that all citizens were property owners, sharing in the wealth of trade, and public offices were held in turns through election—Venice was for Harrington also the most democratic republic because even "though she do[es] not take in the people, never excluded them."[81] Of course the common people were actually excluded, but in a manner different from the exclusion of the popular sectors in other republics. Venice was founded on an original legal border between citizens, who were all rich merchants, and the rest. This original legal division

74. Pocock argues the contrary, taking Harrington's praise of Machiavelli as an endorsement of Machiavellism. Harrington, *Oceana*, xv. Jonathan Scott argues, on the contrary, that Harrington's use of Greek and Roman moral philosophy sets him apart from Machiavelli. "Classical Republicanism," 66–69.

75. Harrington, *Oceana*, "The Preliminaries," 25.

76. Pocock, "Classical Theory of Deference," 518.

77. Harrington, *Oceana*, 15.

78. For an analysis of the influence of the Venetian model on Harrington, see Fink, "Venice and English Political Thought."

79. Harrington, *Oceana*, 33.

80. Ibid., 33.

81. Ibid., 17.

happened in the late thirteenth century when "the codification of a list of families authorized to sit in the Great Council marked the formal separation of the nobles from the rest of the population,"[82] securing for these families a monopoly over citizenship and political power.

The Venetian constitution completely excluded the *popolani*—those who "we might otherwise call plebeians; those who practice the lowliest arts to support themselves, and have no status (grado) in the city,"[83] who were the great majority of the population.[84] The popolani were never formally excluded from political power but were "defined rather by what they were not and by what they did not have."[85] The total exclusion of the majority of the population from political power kept Venice "undisturbed," having constant civil peace according to Harrington because its "body consists of one order, and her senate is like a rolling stone," with rotation disabling "divided or ambitious interests."[86] The rotation of the ruling class from a pool of property owners assured that political leaders would serve the commonwealth. This was for Harrington the great discovery of Venice: election and rotation as the basis for a stable republic.

Despite the relative material equality of citizens, the organization of power of the Venetian constitution was decisively elitist. As portrayed by Donato Giannotti, "the most excellent describer of the commonwealth of Venice,"[87] the republic of Venice had a pyramidal structure of power with the Great Council of three thousand men at the bottom having mainly an electoral function; the Senate of 335 men in the lower half dedicated to lawmaking; the Collegio of twenty-six men in the upper half exercising executive power; and the doge at the top as head of state.[88] Harrington particularly liked the fact that the Great Council did not debate laws, but only voted on them when prompted. While letting the people both debate and decide had, according to him, ruined Athens and Rome, in Venice deliberation was reserved for a selected group of nobles. The Senate had the prerogative of proposing legislation, and even "sometimes resolving too."[89] Therefore, the Venetian "popular"

---

82. Judde de Larivière and Salzberg, "Le peuple est la cite," §21.

83. Venetian patrician Trifone Gabriele, quoted in Giannotti, "Della repubblica de' Viniziani," 46. Also cited in Judde de Larivière and Salzberg, "Le peuple est la cite," §14.

84. Venice had a population of about 170,000 in the mid-1500s. Ibid., §7.

85. Ibid., §29.

86. Harrington, *Oceana*, 160.

87. Ibid., 8.

88. Riklin, "Division of Power," 260.

89. Harrington, *Oceana*, 29.

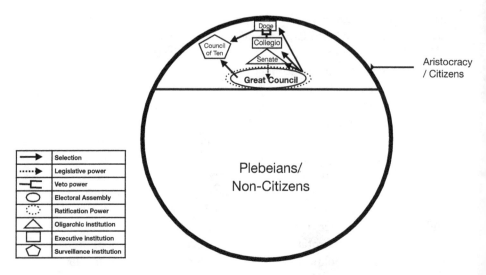

FIGURE 2.6. The aristocratic republic of Venice.

assembly not only was nondeliberative and limited to voting for candidates or motions but would sometimes yield its "resolving" function to the Senate, which had a monopoly over deliberating and proposing. Alongside ordinary institutions, like Rome, Venice also featured a dictatorial office: the Council of Ten. Even if the members of this council were elected by the Great Council, the office was not under the control of the people but tended to operate autonomously given that its main tasks were to guarantee security and fight corruption.[90]

Following the Venetian experience, Harrington proposes for Oceana a model based on three institutions fulfilling different functions—the Senate debating and proposing, the people resolving, and the magistracy executing. The law is debated and proposed by the Senate, sanctioned by the popular assembly, and adjudicated by the magistrates and the courts, which are considered a separate order, replacing the monarchical element of previous versions of the mixed constitution:

> The two first orders, that is to say the senate and the people, are legislative, whereunto answers that part of this science which by politicians is entitled *de legibus*, or of the laws; and the third order is executive, to which answers

90. The Council of Ten played the role of censors. See King, *Venetian Humanism*, 110–11.

that part of the same science which is styled *de judiciis*, or of the frame and course of courts or judicatories.[91]

For Harrington the best way to promote equality is to separate those who debate from those who resolve. He uses the example of two girls who want to eat a piece of cake. Only if one of them divides the cake and the other chooses, will the shares be equal. In the lawmaking process, dividing and choosing would translate as debating/proposing and resolving:

> If a council capable of debate has also the result, it is oligarchy. If an assembly capable of the result has debate also, it is anarchy. Debate in a council not capable of result, and in an assembly not capable of debate, is democracy.[92]

Despite his peculiar interpretation of democracy as a mixed constitution in which the senate proposes and the popular assembly decides, Harrington follows the ancients in arguing that liberty is the principle of the democratic regime. Democracy for him is "nothing but entire liberty."[93] Even if Harrington does not provide a definition of what he means by liberty, he states he is indebted to Thomas Hobbes's works *Human Nature* (1650) and *Of Liberty and Necessity* (1654), which are "the greatest of new lights, and those which I have follow'd, an shall follow."[94] According to Hobbes, liberty is not collective political action, but the "absence of external impediments" to individual action.[95] While in the state of nature liberty is absolute, lacking a supreme authority to impose limits, liberty under the state is for Hobbes necessarily nonpolitical since tolerating opposition to the will of the absolute, arbitrary sovereign could become an existential threat to the state. In the civil state liberty is limited by law and therefore ceases to be conceived in binary terms (either you ruled yourself and are free from domination, or you are a slave) and becomes a relative concept depending on the degree of power being curtailed by impediments. Since the law is an obstacle for action, in the civil state freedom is possible when the law is silent, and the more intrusive the legal system, the less liberty subjects have to engage in free action. In contrast to the republican interpretation of liberty, for Hobbes "freedom is undermined not

91. Harrington, *Oceana*, 38.

92. Harrington, *Oceana*, "A System of Politics," 280.

93. Ibid., 282.

94. Harrington, *First Book*, ch. 7. For an analysis of Hobbes's influence on Harrington, see Cotton, "James Harrington and Thomas Hobbes"; Rahe, *Republics Ancient and Modern*, 180.

95. Hobbes, *Leviathan*, ch. 14, 72. For further analysis of Hobbes on liberty, see Skinner, *Hobbes and Republican Liberty*, ch. 5.

by conditions of domination and dependence but only by overt acts of interference."[96] While Harrington criticized Hobbes's endorsement of absolute monarchy and his dismantling of the ancient taxonomy of regime forms, there is no indication that he does not agree with Hobbes about the meaning of liberty, which makes Harrington a "deeply idiosyncratic member of the English flock."[97]

Harrington's constitutional model, which he claims is democratic, is highly institutionalized, with thirty foundational "orders" determining groups, institutions, procedures, and functions:[98]

> The materials of the commonwealth are the people; and the people of Oceana were distributed by casting them into certain divisions, regarding their quality, their ages, their wealth, and the places of their residence or habitation.[99]

According to Jonathan Scott, Harrington embraced the mixed constitution only because it allowed him to divide society into groups and in this way control the passions. Against Machiavelli's agonism and closer to Platonic harmony, "Harrington's purpose was to do away with tumults, by rendering the passions impotent"[100] through division and rotation. This mechanistic interpretation of the mixed constitution as the separation of functions and as checks and balances would be reformulated procedurally a century later by Montesquieu, who argued Harrington had "examined the furthest point of liberty to which the constitution of a state can be carried" but that he had misunderstood what liberty actually meant.[101]

Even if Montesquieu argued against Hobbes's understanding of human nature as defined by the "desire to subjugate others"[102] and of the possibility of having liberty under a state based on fear, Montesquieu's definition of liberty seems in a paradoxical way very similar to Hobbes's. In *The Spirit of the Laws* (1748) Montesquieu defined liberty in a negative and procedural sense. Liberty is for him both an individual "tranquility of spirit" based on the absence of fear and a sense of security,[103] and "the power of doing what we ought to

96. Skinner, *Hobbes and Republican Liberty*, 212.

97. Jonathan Scott, "Classical Republicanism," 64. Rahe argues Harrington uses republican language to "camouflage" a new form of commonwealth. *Republics Ancient and Modern*, 181.

98. Harrington, *Oceana*, 75–217.

99. Ibid., 75.

100. Jonathan Scott, "Classical Republicanism," 74.

101. Montesquieu, *Spirit of the Laws*, II.11, 6.

102. Ibid., I.1, 2.

103. Ibid., II.11, 6.

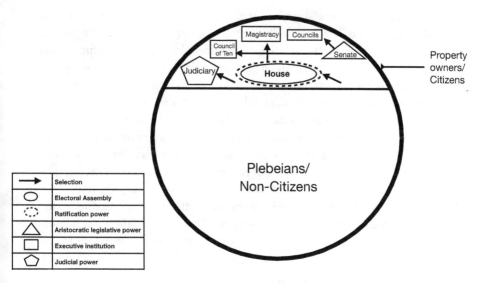

FIGURE 2.7. Simplified sketch of James Harrington's institutions
for the commonwealth of Oceana.

will, and in not being constrained to do what we ought not to will."[104] According to Annelien de Dijn, for Montesquieu security was more important in attaining human happiness than self-government, and thus monarchical subjects
could be as free as their republican counterparts owing to high levels of security of life and possessions under some monarchs.[105] While Hobbes argued
liberty is absolute in the state of nature and that the sovereign restricts liberty,
allowing for its secure enjoyment, Montesquieu reduces liberty to a feeling of
security that appears intrinsically related to the limited behavior allowed by
laws, mores, and customs. Because to be free is not only to act within the
bounds of the law, but also to will within these bounds, there is tranquility and
security. While Hobbes justified the absolute state on the need to provide
security from violence, Montesquieu, redefining liberty as security, argued for
embracing a mixed constitution as a way to guarantee liberty through
moderation.

For Montesquieu, constitution and law are bound to the *nature* and *principles* of government, the essential logic of the political form of rule.[106] While
the nature of a government is determined by who holds power (one, few, or

104. Ibid., II.11.3.
105. De Dijn, "On Political Liberty," 186–87.
106. Montesquieu, *Spirit of the Laws*, I.1, 3.

many), the principle is a "spirit," a sort of Aristotelian effective cause, as it were, that interacts with the laws, ideally "tighten[ing] all the springs of the government" and allowing for the principle to be refueled through a dynamic process of action and reaction.[107] Going against the ancient categorization of regimes and their corrupt forms, Montesquieu conceived of three types of government: republican, monarchical, and despotic. Republican government could take the form either of democracy—a regime in which the people as a whole are the sovereign—or of aristocracy—a regime in which power is in the hands of a few. Premised on a Platonist philosophical framework, for Montesquieu democracy is not a desirable form of government because it is not free; it is by nature a regime without moderation, in which power is easily abused.

After briefly surveying the different meanings that had been ascribed to the word *liberty* in different historical contexts, Montesquieu denounces democracy as recasting liberty as popular power to justify the government by the masses:

> As in democracies the people seem very nearly to do what they want, liberty has been placed in this sort of government and the power of the people has been confused with the liberty of the people.[108]

So, unlike Plato, who thought the principle of democracy was *liberty*, Montesquieu argued the spirit of the classic republic was not liberty but *virtue* understood as the "love of equality and frugality," a "feeling" of "love of the republic,"[109] and a desire to have "only one's equals as masters."[110] Montesquieu sees the power given by democracy to its citizens as a liability because "it has eternally been observed that any man who has power is led to abuse it; he continues until he finds limits."[111] Extreme, unbound democracy is a threat to liberty because of the advent of arbitrariness. "The more the people appear to take advantage of their liberty, the nearer they approach the moment they are to lose it."[112]

According to Montesquieu, the principle of democracy gets corrupted both when equality is lost and when there is extreme equality and the excess of virtue takes hold of the republic. For him, authority in a democracy is achieved through inequalities established by law between citizen and man, and between the citizens who rule and the rest. These distinctions, which are fundamental

107. Ibid., I. 5, 1.
108. Ibid., II.11, 2.
109. Ibid., I. 5, 2.
110. Ibid., I. 8, 3.
111. Ibid., II.11, 4.
112. Ibid., I.8, 2.

for the good functioning of the political system, arise from the principle of equality—because even if "men cannot render [the republic] equal services, they should equally render it services"[113]—and are not arbitrary because they are introduced through law, which is an expression of human reason. Consequently, when these necessary, nonsubjective inequalities are blurred, the republic incurs what Montesquieu calls extreme equality, a vice that brings its demise. The parallel with Plato regarding this point is very interesting. While Plato saw democracy as an inherently unstable system, which produced a deficit of power because of extreme *freedom*—to do whatever one pleases—which permanently undermines hierarchies, tradition, and rules,[114] Montesquieu uses Plato's same arguments to evidence the corruption of the republic but blames excessive *equality* instead. In other words, while in Plato's conception of democracy it is excessive liberty as the lack of interference that ruins the system, for Montesquieu it is the excess of interference toward equality that corrupts it. According to Montesquieu, democracy's excess makes the people want to do everything themselves, which causes a loss of respect for authority:

> Then there can no longer be virtue in the republic. The people want to perform the magistrate's functions; therefore, the magistrates are no longer respected. The senate's deliberations no longer carry weight; therefore, there is no longer consideration for senators or, consequently, for elders. And if there is no respect for elders, neither will there be any of fathers; husbands no longer merit deference nor masters, submission. Everyone will come to love this license; the restraint of commanding will be as tiresome as that of obeying had been. Women, children, and slaves will submit to no one. There will no longer be mores or love of order, and finally, there will no longer be virtue.[115]

Even though for both Plato and Montesquieu the democratic excess leads to despotism, for Plato freedom is lost because "excess in one direction generally tends to produce a violent reaction in the opposite direction," and for Montesquieu virtue and liberty are lost because excessive equality leads to arbitrariness and corruption, which are intrinsically related to despotism.[116] However, equality itself is not lost, because men are all equal both in a democratic government and in a despotic one: "in the former, it is because they are

113. Ibid., I. 5, 3.
114. Plato, *Republic*, bk. 8, 558a–563a.
115. Montesquieu, *Spirit of the Laws*, I.8, 2.
116. Ibid., I. 8, 2 and 5.

everything; in the latter, it is because they are nothing."[117] Hence, for Montesquieu, what is lost with the excess of democracy is virtue, the love of democracy and equality, but not equality itself. In other words, what is lost with the excess of equality is the passion, the feeling the keeps democracy in motion, the willingness to sacrifice one's own interests for those of the community.

A democratic republic is not only potentially despotic but also unfeasible because of the inadequacy of the spirit of virtue for the modern times. Because virtue in a republic is the love of frugality, one could argue that with the excess of equality this self-containment regarding material possessions and the accumulation of wealth can no longer be maintained, and individual ambitions burst into the republic, corrupting it at its core. Democratic virtue as love of equality and frugality is for Montesquieu too weak to be self-sustaining without a strong legal and social enforcement. Because virtue requires a continuous preference for the public interest over one's own, and thus it demands the creation of a sort of second nature in human beings, one that represses innate individual ambitions, "if one is to love equality and frugality in a republic, these must have been established by the laws."[118] However, laws are not enough to prevent the undermining of virtue. When "political men" argue that to sustain the republic only "manufacturing, commerce, finance, wealth, and even luxury" are needed, then "virtue ceases, ambition enters," and freedom *under* the law is exchanged for freedom *against* it.[119]

Both the painful and precarious sublimation required by virtue as the love of equality and frugality in an open, commercial society, and the lack of moderation of the egalitarian spirit,[120] brought Montesquieu to embrace the spirit of commerce, as a moderate, foundational force for the modern republic.[121] The principle of moderation, which he argues is what virtue means in an aristocratic republic, is for him the most perfect one, the closest to human nature and to freedom because it promotes the balance between inequalities of wealth and power.[122]

Like many of his contemporaries, Montesquieu conceived of commerce mostly as a benign, gentle force. Commerce would not only moderate mores and foster peace, but also produce exact justice—as opposed to a justice based

---

117. Ibid., I. 6.

118. Ibid., I. 5, 4.

119. Ibid., I. 3, 3.

120. Ibid., I. 5.

121. For the centrality of the principle of moderation in Montesquieu and its influence on the American Founders, see Cohler, *Montesquieu's Comparative Politics*.

122. Montesquieu. *Spirit of the Laws*. I.5, 8.

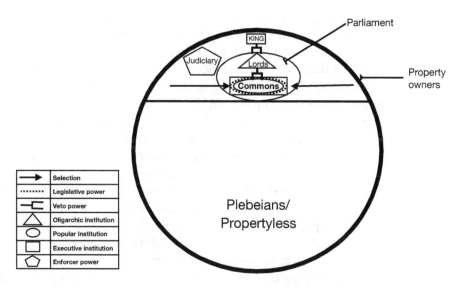

FIGURE 2.8. England in the time of Montesquieu.

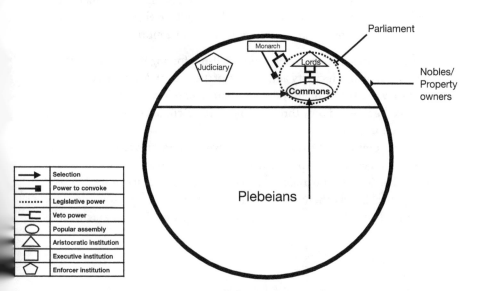

FIGURE 2.9. Montesquieu's aristocratic commercial republic.

solely on the public good or private interests.[123] This conception of "commerce as bring[ing] with it the spirit of frugality, economy, moderation, work, wisdom, tranquility, order, and rule"[124] appears at best naive and detached, on the one hand from the speculation bubbles and the extreme luxury of the upper classes fueled by Great Britain's trading boom of the mid-1700s, and on the other from the poverty and oppression of the popular sectors in the early years of the industrial revolution. Given this conception of commerce as a moderating factor—blind to the powerful, *immoderate* forces of finance— Montesquieu argued the spirit of commerce would provide a natural balance between collective well-being and individual ambitions.

Not only would his commercial republic be superior to ancient republics, but also becoming commercial would be the inevitable end of any republican government fostering peace and liberty.[125] The liberty generated in the republic would allow for each citizen to "have his own will and . . . value his independence according to his taste," and for all the passions to "appear to their full extent,"[126] including the ardor for enriching and distinguishing oneself. The security for investment and risk taking given by the political and legal structure of a stable republic would allow for economic development to be accelerated:

> one's belief that one's prosperity is more certain in these states makes one undertake everything, and because one believes that what one has acquired is secure, one dares to expose it in order to acquire more.[127]

Moreover, anticipating Adam Smith's self-reinforcing theory of economic growth based on productivity and the size of the market, Montesquieu argues the industry created through the security to acquire would foster new needs that would be satisfied only through commerce. Republics are thus bound to become commercial.

Because commerce thrives in republics where there are reliable public enterprises in which to participate, and where there is certainty about the laws— security that "makes one undertake everything" to "acquire more"[128]—the more political liberty there is in a state—understood as legal security—the more individuals will be inclined to pursue their own ambitions by taking risks

---

123. Ibid., III.20, 1.

124. Ibid., I.5, 6.

125. Ibid., III.19, 27. See also on the inevitability of the commercial republic. Rahe, *Soft Despotism, Democracy's Drift*.

126. Montesquieu, *Spirit of the Laws*, III.19, 27.

127. Ibid., IV.1, 4.

128. Ibid., IV.20, 4.

to acquire rather than being frugal to preserve. In other words, the more liberty there is in a state, the more commerce will be fostered, and the more accentuated risk taking will become. The evident implications of increased economic risk taking in society are inequality and abrupt socioeconomic change. The more possessions one has in a secure environment, the more inclined one is to risk part of them to acquire more. If the risk yields more wealth, inequality will abruptly grow between those who preserved and those who dared, a gap that is likely to become exponentially wider the more wealth is accumulated. The same happens when the risk taker makes a bad bet and losses his patrimony, falling into poverty.

Smith would argue a decade after Montesquieu that economic inequality inevitably comes together with commerce, and despite some benefits in productivity driven by luxury, a high degree of inequality is pernicious. Even if for Smith inequality was not intrinsically unjust, nor produced bad effects such as dependence, lack of social mobility, or corruption, as Dennis Rasmussen has convincingly shown, extreme inequality produces for Smith an even greater evil: a "distortion in our sympathies" that makes us favor the rich and neglect the poor, which "in turn undermines both morality and happiness."[129]

The same way that Cicero brought in normative considerations to justify the Senate's factual dominant position in Rome, Montesquieu theorizes a constitution that is based on a Whig interpretation of the English political system, proposing a hybrid commercial republic that incorporates the commercial spirit as a moderating force alongside the democratic virtue generated by popular sovereignty. The result is an elitist, proceduralist model in which the common people's only power is the right to elect representatives, while the few preserve their dominant position in the power structure through a formal institutional balance.

Following Cicero's elitist republicanism, Montesquieu argues that while man has a natural ability to perceive merit and elect, the people in general are not competent enough to be elected.[130] Thus, even if Montesquieu argued for extending the suffrage, giving the right to vote to all male citizens, excluding only those "whose estate is so humble that they are deemed to have no will of their own," for him the right of the people to legislate is exercised only indirectly, through representatives who are selected from the elites. Even though in a free state the legislative power is the prerogative of "the people as a body," Montesquieu argues "the people should not enter the government except to

---

129. Rasmussen, "Adam Smith on What Is Wrong with Economic Inequality."
130. Montesquieu, *Spirit of the Laws*, I.2, 2.

choose their representatives; this is quite within their reach."[131] Representation appears not as a device to bridge the gap between the people and power, but as a mechanism to keep the people *away* from power through the formal expansion of the aristocratic procedure of election[132] to the common people.[133] Montesquieu's commercial republic is a modified version of a mixed constitution in which the common people's sovereignty was limited to selecting representatives to "do all that they themselves cannot do,"[134] and the aristocratic element was predominant de facto within the organization of power.

Inspired by ancient republican experiences, he proposed a bicameral legislative institution composed of two separate bodies: one for the nobles—"people who are distinguished by birth, wealth, or honors"—and the other for the representatives of the people. Legislation entailed the faculty of both *enacting* and *vetoing*, and thus the ambitions of the nobles and the commons would be kept mutually in check through initiating, modifying, and stopping legal motions. In addition to the legislative power, he conceives of the executive power as one that should be in the hands of a monarch, owing to its requirement of immediate action, and of the judicial power as null and autonomous, limited to adjudicating the law.[135] The mechanical separation of these powers would keep these unequal bodies in a dynamic equilibrium, promoting stability and liberty.

It is not surprising that Montesquieu, who was part of the French aristocracy, would make a strong defense for preserving the political privileges of the nobility in the lawmaking process.[136] However, his defense of the necessity for an aristocratic institution was not based on the superior virtue of elites as in Cicero, but on the realist assessment that elites will aim at subverting liberty if they share an institution with the common people:

> If they [the nobles] were mixed among the people and if they had only one voice like the others, the common liberty would be their enslavement and they would have no interest in defending it, because most of the resolutions would be against them.[137]

131. Ibid., 11, 6.

132. See Manin, *Principles of Representative Government*.

133. Montesquieu, *Spirit of the Laws*, I.2, 2.

134. Ibid., II.11, 6.

135. For an analysis of judicial independence in Montesquieu, see Carrese, *Cloaking of Power*, chs. 1 and 2.

136. He also advocated for nobles to be judged by a special aristocratic tribunal to avoid the envy of the common people.

137. Montesquieu, *Spirit of the Laws*, II.11, 6.

Elite subversion of the constitution through negligence and passivity in an unmixed regime could then be interpreted as being justified as an act of self-defense stemming from the fear of domination by the common people. The only way to avoid this inevitable vulnerability, argues Montesquieu, is to institutionalize inequality by giving to the few their own institution with a role proportional to "the other advantages they have in the state," and veto power over the attempts by the representatives of the common people to "enslave" them. Even if he also gives the same powers of enacting and vetoing to the commons, and thus *formally* allows the people to resist further oppression from the few, Montesquieu's model of power allocation de facto entrenches power relations by giving the nobles political power commensurate with their socioeconomic power, and the faculty to stop any attempts at reform coming from below. While the formal equality of legislative prerogatives in Montesquieu's model obscures a status quo bias that gives political dominance to the elite, the introduction of representation through the extension of the suffrage to the common people as an alternative to class-specific institutions radically changed the interpretation of the mixed constitution.

Normatively, Montesquieu's procedural model is justified because it produces liberty. By defining liberty as "the right to do everything the law permits"[138] and then arguing that good laws are those resulting from the correct procedures and institutional checks and balances he endorses, Montesquieu pegs liberty to the rule of law, closing the possibility of legitimately questioning the law outside from formal political institutions that are effectively controlled by the few—hopefully the virtuous, moderate few. Under this constitutional framework, in which law is produced, executed, and adjudicated through a mechanistic division of functions aimed at preventing abuse, all individuals would be considered free simply because they "live under civil laws."[139]

If virtue conceived as love of equality needs to be established by law, and virtue as moderation lacks the mistaken beneficial force of commerce and therefore would also need to be established by law, then the making of the law is the most vulnerable point in Montesquieu's liberty-producing structure. Laws promoting equality and moderation would be aimed at limiting the few, which means that selected elites would be in charge of both making and executing rules aimed at limiting themselves. This problem of self-binding and self-policing is aggravated because Montesquieu gives equal formal power to the many, even if the few have *factual* dominance. The few are in an advantageous

138. Ibid., II.11, 3.
139. Ibid., III.26, 20.

position and need to protect what they have; the many need to protect themselves from new attempts at domination and push back against pervasive oppression by advancing their position. The preservation of the status quo works for the advantage of the few. Therefore, giving to the "senatorial" power a veto over demands for change coming from the popular sectors allows elites to legally, and peacefully, keep their dominant position. And even if in England the House of Commons ended up becoming the government, absorbing executive and legislative functions—something that was already happening under Walpole while Montesquieu was living in London—the supremacy of Parliament was not the result of an increase of popular power vis-à-vis the power of the few, but the result of the displacement of the old aristocracy from the real seat of power by the new commercial elite.

Even though Montesquieu praises England for always subordinating political interests to that of commerce,[140] he does not openly advocate for liberty as noninterference in relation to trade but still follows the republican conception of liberty in which law is the condition of possibility for public life:

> Liberty of commerce is not a faculty granted to traders to do what they want; this would instead be the servitude of commerce. . . . In agreements that derive from commerce, the law should make more of public convenience than of the liberty of a citizen.[141]

This tendency to decide in favor of the public interest instead of private ambition regarding lawmaking cannot be motivated by the spirit of commerce, but by virtue. But can virtue be maintained when the equality of fortunes that sustains frugality is relentlessly being undermined by the risk-taking spirit of commerce, when mores are being heavily influenced by new needs and ambitions? How can the law be kept independent from the servitude of commerce; how can freedom be sustained, if inequality, individual ambitions, and risk taking permeate mores and lawmaking itself, permanently pushing for laissez-faire? On the one hand, to follow one's ambitions is easy, natural, and encouraged by a legal context that secures individuals from arbitrary seizing of property by the state or other citizens. On the other hand, the cultivation of virtue, the suppression of individual interests for the common good, is difficult and demands of citizens a second nature born out of sublimation. Consequently, without strong legal restraints and a fierce republican ethos, it seems the spirit

---

140. Ibid., IV.20, 7. For an analysis of Montesquieu's critique of the English constitution, see Krause, "Spirit of Separate Powers."

141. Montesquieu, *Spirit of the Laws*, IV.20, 12 and 15.

of commerce does not merely come to moderate virtue, but to push for its extinction.

In the next section I will analyze how Montesquieu's model was adapted to establish the first modern representative government in the United States. I will begin by engaging with the conception of liberty that became functional to the justification for the new organization of power under the United States constitution, and then delve into a materialist analysis of the founding and of James Madison's constitutional thought.

From Mixed Constitution to Liberal Representative Government

The problematization of concepts has been at the core of political philosophy since ancient times. Because concepts and categories set up the theoretical framework through which we think about the political, the redefinition of a term as central as *liberty* fundamentally changes our understanding of what a free government is. Every form of free political rule is aimed at instituting freedom. The principle of ancient democracy was freedom understood as self-rule through the equal sharing of political power. Thus, citizens had equal rights to deliberate, legislate, and judge in turns.[142] The principle of the ancient Roman republic, which was based on the legal division between the elites and the common people,[143] was also to establish freedom, understood as non-domination, by giving each group its own political representative institution— the Senate and the Council of the Plebs led by the tribunes—with powers to check their mutual ambitions. While in ancient democratic theory, sharing in government was seen as constitutive of political liberty, and free political action—which presupposed the civil liberty of "living as one likes"[144]—was the highest *end* all citizens could aspire to, in the republican tradition, political participation, which recognized the right to legislate, judge, and veto laws and decrees, is only a *means* to assure security from domination. These two ancient conceptions of political freedom, which presupposed individual freedom to act, were put into question by the birth of liberalism and individualism.

Against Hobbes's conception of liberty as the lack of external impediments to action, and combining natural law and republican thought, John Locke also

142. Thucydides, "Pericles' Funeral Oration," in *History of the Peloponnesian War*, bk. 2, 37–50; Plato, *Republic*, VIII 556b; Aristotle, *Politics*, 1317b, 1–4.

143. Cicero, *On the Commonwealth*, in *"On the Commonwealth" and "On the Laws,"* I; Polybius, *Histories*, VI. 1, 2 and 5.

144. Aristotle, *Politics*, VI. 2, 1317b.

argued that liberty is limited, not by the will of the sovereign but by natural right. Natural, individual rights become the normative foundation of Locke's ideal political order in which the people are at the same time sovereign—limited only by natural and civil law—and ruled over based on their tacit consent. Locke attached liberty to the law, arguing that liberty is to dispose of "person, actions, possessions, and his whole property, within the allowance of those laws under which he is; and therein not to be subject to the arbitrary will of another."[145] Individual rights are in Locke's theory of government the fundamental limit on government—prepolitical entitlements that the government must never violate.

Although a protoliberal conception of freedom would predominate in the constitutional convention in Philadelphia, the first attempts at codifying rights and duties in state constitutions recognized strong political rights that went beyond election and mere protection from abuse. The preamble of the 1780 Massachusetts Constitution, for example, stated a twofold end for government: (1) to secure the existence of the body politic and (2) to give individuals the power to enjoy their natural rights. While the latter goal is based on a liberal understanding of the state, the objective of securing the political community is based on a republican understanding of politics in which the body politic is the source of freedom as nondomination, and the active role of citizens in checking the power of government is crucial for its maintenance.

Even though the newly constituted American states would institute indirect, representative government, the role of individuals in politics went well beyond the selection of magistrates. Moreover, the threat of oligarchy was explicitly recognized alongside the description of good government and the *political* rights of the people. Article VII of the 1780 Massachusetts Constitution, similar to a clause later proposed by James Madison[146] as a part of the First Amendment to the Constitution but ultimately discarded, recognized that

> government is instituted for the common good, for the protection, safety, prosperity, and happiness of the people, and not for the profit, honor, or private interest of any one man, family, or class of men; therefore the people alone have an incontestable, unalienable, and indefeasible right to institute government, and to reform, alter, or totally change the same when their protection, safety, prosperity, and happiness require it.

The recognition of the common good understood as the safety *and* prosperity of the people as the aim of government is a central feature in republican

145. Locke, *Second Treatise*, in *Political Writings*, ch. 5.57, 289.
146. Madison, "Speech Proposing the Bill of Rights."

thought, since relative socioeconomic equality was crucial for the preservation of the republic. The end of government is not the liberal protection of rights only to assure individuals the "enjoyment of their property in peace and safety,"[147] but to *guarantee* security, prosperity, and happiness. While the liberal state is conceived by Locke as a minimal state that comes only to fix what does not work properly in the natural state, as an impartial third party enforcing contracts and securing property, the aim of the republican state is more demanding because it first and foremost has the duty to assure the prosperity of the population as a whole, which may entail the limiting of individual rights for the benefit of the majority. Interference is necessary to preserve freedom as nondomination.

The republican constitution recognizes the power struggles within the community that may permeate the state, and that can be dealt with only through the active participation of the people in checking government action. Therefore, in a republican constitution, common citizens can legitimately constitute, direct, change, or overthrow a government, not only if there is evident usurpation and tyranny, but also if representatives are not advancing prosperity and happiness[148] properly because of their favoring of a specific class or group of citizens. The crucial role of the people in keeping government honest was therefore guaranteed in political rights that went beyond election.

Under article XIX the citizens of Massachusetts enjoyed the right to assemble with the specific aim to "consult upon the common good" and control elected officials,

> [to] give instructions to their representatives, and to request of the legislative body, by the way of addresses, petitions, or remonstrances, redress of the wrongs done them, and of the grievances they suffer.

What articles VII and XIX make evident is that, in the first state constitutions, private citizens were conceived not merely as authorizing through their consent a legitimate representative government, but as having an active role in political power as a counterbalance to the inefficiency of the state apparatus to guarantee prosperity for all, the usurpation of power by government officials, or the manipulation of government "for the profit, honor, or private interest of any one man, family, or class of men"[149] to exclude the majority from collective benefits. According to progressive historian Merrill Jensen, this

---

147. Locke, *Second Treatise*, ch. 11.134, 328.

148. Even if these are not properly republican goals, they work as democratic justifications for popular checking power.

149. Art. VII of the 1780 Massachusetts Constitution.

active role of the common citizens in securing popular sovereignty was part of the democratic legacy of the independence movements, which "shocked many American leaders who feared revolution within America" and prompted them to actively oppose any "fundamental changes in the political structure of American society."[150]

Despite the crucial legal role of ordinary citizens in keeping corruption at bay, their political power was kept only in the realm of individual rights, while the powers of representative government were codified and given institutional expression. In other words, while the constitution gave the different branches of government detailed institutional powers, the political rights of the people to contest the actions of government were not given institutional recognition. Assembly was seen as spontaneous—as had happened in the Committees of Correspondence formed to organize against the unjust actions of the British Empire—and collective demands and instructions lacked the necessary institutional command to coerce representatives into compliance. The active political rights of citizens, the rights to action and decision in political affairs, were as imperative as commands based on moral duty, relying only on the virtuous character of government officials. The constitution did not recognize the representative government's legal obligation to obey the organized multitude's complaints. Consequently, when the personal interests of government officials and the commercial elite that supported them came in direct conflict with those of a large group of private citizens, as it did during the 1780s debt crisis, formal rights were not respected, and the de facto rulers at that moment were revealed. As in the late Roman republic, the power of the "advisory" Senate came to the fore when agrarian reform led to a direct violation of institutional plebeian authority, and government officials disrespected citizen's political rights in order to protect the American oligarchy's right to profit.

At the early stage of the constituent moment, both the national government and the common citizens who were organized in councils and committees lacked institutional power vis-à-vis states governments. Referring to the fundamental defect of the Articles of Confederation, Thomas Jefferson stated that the power of Congress "was only requisitory, and these requisitions were addressed to the several legislatures, to be by them carried into execution, without other coercion than the moral principle of duty."[151] The same way that the national government lacked the tools to implement laws and statutes at the state level, individual citizens were institutionally powerless to counteract the machinery of state governments. While in the case of the national

---

150. Jensen, *Making of the American Constitution*, 19.
151. Jefferson, *Autobiography*, in *Political Writings*, 354.

government the lack of resources hinged on the unwillingness of states to cede sovereign power and autonomy, which was remedied by the 1789 Constitution, citizens' lack of institutional power to control their representatives endured because of an elitist interpretation of the mixed constitution.

According to John Mercer, delegate from Maryland to the Constitutional Convention and the leading voice against the Constitution, representative government was already a de facto aristocracy that could not be reined in by the citizenry:

> It is a first principle in political science, that wherever the rights of property are secured, an aristocracy will grow out of it. Elective Governments also necessarily become aristocratic, because the rulers being few can & will draw emoluments for themselves from the many. The Governments of America will become aristocracies. They are so already. The public measures are calculated for the benefit of the Governors, not of the people. The people are dissatisfied & complain. They change their rulers, and the public measures are changed, but it is only a change of one scheme of emolument to the rulers, for another. The people gain nothing by it, but an addition of instability & uncertainty to their other evils.[152]

According to Jensen, the main result of the American Revolution was the "enormous increase in the democratic potential" in politics and law.[153] The principle of universal suffrage, the regulation of commerce, state intervention in industry, and the alteration of taxation patterns according to the will of the sovereign people, who effectively controlled state legislatures through annual elections, were part of the legacy of the revolution. The new powers to regulate commerce were put in practice immediately after the war, when seven out of the thirteen states in the confederation took measures to alleviate the scarcity of money and the private debts of farmers, who petitioned the government to reprint paper money, abandoned during the war. Because of the fear of devaluation and loss of investment, paper money was bitterly opposed by merchants, planters, and creditors, but the pressure from yeomen farmers, who accounted for the majority of the population, could not be contained.[154] In the 1780s, the United States was for the most part composed of rural communities. Even though there was a powerful commercial elite settled in the costal urban

---

152. *Records of the Federal Convention*, 769.

153. Jensen, *Making of the American Constitution*, 28.

154. Ibid., 29. For another critical account of the American founding, see Rana, *Faces of American Freedom*.

centers, the bulk of the population still lived off the land and used barter instead of cash in most of their transactions.

The American Revolution brought about not only liberation from the British yoke and a desire for democratic rule, but also an economic recession.
While by severing ties with England the Unites States lost its most important
trading partner, the devastation left by the war meant a material contraction
of the economy. Personal income remained stagnant from 1774 to 1790,[155] and
especially for farmers, who endured the constant looting of their lands and
resources during the war, debt became a ubiquitous and constant threat to
property, liberty, and full citizenship.

Because of the recession, independent farmers—many of them war
veterans—became tenants on their own land, were often jailed, and lost
their political rights together with their property. Even though the idea of
universal male suffrage was starting a trend in several states, and at the time
of the Federal Convention the majority of states in the union had extended
the right of suffrage beyond freeholders, some states still required property
ownership to vote, and all of them except for Pennsylvania[156] required a
considerable amount of property to become an elected official, which effectively separated the common people from the elites who represented
them in government.

The 1780 Massachusetts Constitution granted the right to vote to male
owners of local property valued at least at sixty pounds or combined with
an annual income of three pounds.[157] Even though the provision requiring
pecuniary qualifications in order to vote was criticized by some of the towns
as an "infringement on the natural rights" and "a degree of slavery,"[158] the
rule opened the path to citizenship to the majority of war veterans, who
received a minimum of sixty pounds for three years of service.[159] However,
the political right of direct lawmaking and ruling was reserved for the
wealthiest individuals. To become a senator a citizen had to own five times
the minimum amount of property to be eligible to vote, and to become
governor, sixteen times.[160] Thus, although the property requirements to vote

155. See Global Price and Income History Group, http://gpih.ucdavis.edu/tables.htm.

156. 1776 Pennsylvania Constitution, art. VII. "That all elections ought to be free; and that
all free men having a sufficient evident, common interest with, and attachment to the community, have a right to elect officers, or to be elected into one."

157. 1780 Massachusetts Constitution, ch. 1, art. IV.

158. Extracts from a town-hall debate on voting rights in Massachusetts in 1780. Quoted in
West, *Vindicating the Founders*, 118.

159. Carpenter and Morehouse, *History of the Town of Amherst*, vol. 1, ch. 22, 96, 1896.

160. 1780 Massachusetts Constitution, ch. 1, §2, art. V; ch. 2, §1, art. II.

were not too stringent, which made the Massachusetts political process fairly inclusive at that time, the reins of government were still reserved for affluent citizens.

This inequality of wealth between the majority of private citizens and their representatives would prove pernicious when the debt crisis brought the interests of these two groups into direct conflict. As early as 1784, citizens affected by debt, taxes, and lack of currency began to spontaneously organize in committees or councils, from which emanated petitions for redress.[161] However, representative government remained deaf to the common people's demands and continued to enforce contracts and agreements, which threw many farmers out of their lands and into jail.

In addition to a damaged economy and debt collection, farmers were overwhelmed with new taxes being levied to fund the nascent republic. As an anonymous "Plough Jogger" argued in the press days before the debt rebellion started in 1786:

> I've labored hard all my days and fared hard. I have been greatly abused, have been obliged to do more than my part in the war; been loaded with class rates, town rates, province rates, Continental rates and all rates . . . been pulled and hauled by sheriffs, constables and collectors, and had my cattle sold for less than they were worth. I have been obliged to pay and nobody will pay me. I have lost a great deal by this man and that man and t'other man, and the great men are going to get all we have and I think it is time for us to rise and put a stop to it, and have no more courts, nor sheriffs, nor collectors nor lawyers, and I know that we are the biggest party, let them say what they will. We've come to relieve the distresses of the people. There will be no court until they have redress of their grievances.[162]

When the institutional path for rectification was exhausted, and the representative government remained unaccountable, the organized multitude engaged in direct action by closing and burning courthouses where debt records were kept.

According to the more conservative sections of the elite, the rebels were no more than criminals because they wanted to abolish private property and debts, and achieve land redistribution with the help of paper money. In a letter to John Adams, George Washington quotes General Knox's description of the radical group as accounting for a fifth of the population, "a body of twelve or

161. Main, *Antifederalists.*
162. Zinn, *People Speak,* 5–6.

fifteen thousand desperate and unprincipled men,"[163] positioning the rebels as a threat to the moral virtue of the republic. An echo of these arguments is present in Abigail Adams's concerned letter to Jefferson in the midst of the rebellion:

> Ignorant, wrestles desperadoes, without conscience or principals, have led a deluded multitude to follow their standard, under pretense of grievances which have no existence but in their imaginations. Some of them were crying out for a paper currency, some for an equal distribution of property, some were for annihilating all debts.[164]

However, the debt rebellion was not the work of a bunch of corrupt men or a deceived multitude, but a plebeian movement based on local committees organized for exercising their constitutional rights. Even though this rebellion was later known as "Shays's Rebellion," war hero Daniel Shays did not initiate the movement but only led its final armed struggles.[165] The power of the rebellion was not on its leader, but on the collective force of organized common people.

Jefferson was perhaps the only prominent official to recognize the beneficial element of the rebellion. For him freedom in the republic hinged on public education and local self-government,[166] and since the debt rebellion was based on local committees, it was the closest expression of his theory of elementary republics. Jefferson's idea of separation of powers and checks and balances referred not only to functions of government, but to the relation between ward, county, state, and national governments. For Jefferson, the ward was the ultimate bulwark of freedom, and the small landholders, the most valuable part of the state:

> The elementary republics of the wards, the county republics, the State republics, and the republic of the Union, would form a gradation of authorities, standing each on the basis of law, holding everyone its delegated share of powers, and constituting truly a system of fundamental balances and checks for the government. Where every man is a sharer in the direction of

163. Letter from George Washington to John Adams, November 5, 1786, https://founders .archives.gov/documents/Madison/01-09-02-0070.

164. Letter from Abigail Adams to Thomas Jefferson, January 29, 1787, https://founders .archives.gov/documents/Jefferson/01-11-02-0087. Irregular spellings are in the original.

165. See Gregory Nobles, "'Satan, Smith, Shattuck, and Shays': The People's Leaders in the Massachusetts Regulation of 1780," in Young, Nash, and Raphael, *Revolutionary Founders*, 218.

166. Letter from Thomas Jefferson to the Marquis de Lafayette, February 14, 1815, in Jefferson, *Political Writings*, 197–202.

his ward-republic, or some of the higher ones, and feels he is a participator in the government of affairs, not merely at an election one day in a year, but every day; when there shall not be a man in the State who will not be a member of some one of its councils, great or small, he will let the heart be torn out of his body sooner than his power be wrested from him by a Caesar or a Bonaparte.[167]

Following a plebeian interpretation of republican thought, Jefferson saw this kind of popular rebellions as constitutive to a good republic, because freedom is attained only through periodic resistance against oppression. For freedom to be preserved, rulers must be regularly warned of the power of the common people—"the tree of liberty must be refreshed from time to time with the blood of patriots & tyrants. It is it's natural manure."[168] Representative government and civil society are in permanent need of reconciliation, in a relentless struggle for and against inequality, and when the gap between state and local government is too wide, rebellion is necessary to coerce representative government to achieve more equality through a show of force of the collective power of the multitude.

This unusual view about the productive nature of rebellion was certainly not shared by the rest of the political leaders. The rebellion caused an element of "visceral fear"[169] that was a driving force for the calling of the constituent assembly and influenced the deliberation of the Founders.[170] But the Federal Convention was a response not only to an emotional reaction based on the violent acts themselves, but also to a rational, "prudential fear," a fear rooted on the logical expectations brought about by the equalizing effects of emancipation. Political leaders feared that the democratic force born with the revolution and enshrined in the Declaration of Independence would give preeminence to the leveling spirit, to the redistribution of property and the control of commerce for the benefit of all citizens. The fear of the American upper classes was a *prudential fear*—a logical conclusion derived from the principles of democracy and the continuing political equalization in society—which was

---

167. Thomas Jefferson to Joseph C. Cabell, February 2, 1816, in Jefferson, *Political Writings*, 205.

168. Thomas Jefferson to William Stephens Smith, November 13, 1787, in Jefferson, *Political Writings*, 110.

169. Jon Elster uses Robert Gordon's distinction between visceral or emotional fear of violence and prudential or rational fear. "Whereas the former is a genuine emotion, caused by the belief in an imminent danger to the agent, the latter does not amount to more than a simple belief-desire complex." In Elster, "Constitution-Making and Violence," 8.

170. Elster, "Constitution-Making and Violence," 9.

channeled and made effective thanks to the *visceral fear* ignited in the rebellion that ultimately galvanized support for a counterrevolution and the drafting of the Constitution.

According to Jon Elster, America fits the revolutionary pattern of "two steps forward, one step backward," a democratic revolution undone by a counter-revolution against democratic ideals.[171] Revolution of the fundamental structure of political society was rooted in the War of Independence. As Plato argues, the close encounter between the rich and the poor in a condition of war is likely to brings about the collapse of oligarchy because the people are able to see their rulers "carrying a good deal of superfluous flesh . . . wheezing and struggling," unworthy of their wealth and high-ranking position.[172] In the American colonies, war had also an equalizing effect that inevitably led to the desire for democracy and the "equal share in the constitution and public office."[173]

According to Jensen, the specific expression of democracy that ignited fear in the elites, and ultimately brought about the convention, was economic legislation aimed at "suspending or delaying the collection of debt and taxes" and the issuing of paper money.[174] James Madison made this clear at the beginning of the convention by stating that the interests of the majority were a threat to the rights of the minority:

> Debtors have defrauded their creditors. The landed interest has borne hard on the mercantile interest. The Holders of one species of property have thrown a disproportion of taxes on the holders of another species. The lesson we are to draw from the whole is that where a majority are united by a common sentiment, and have an opportunity, the rights of the minor party become insecure.

Even though the intellectual aptitude of the framers as lawyers and experienced politicians is the most significant feature often highlighted in historical accounts of the American founding, if one analyzes the composition of the Federal Convention, individual biographies reveal that it was finance, more than lawyering, that was more predominant among the members. While 56 percent of the framers were lawyers and politicians, 74 percent of them were lenders of some sort,[175] which puts the issue of debt and currency speculation

171. Ibid.

172. Plato, *Republic*, 8, 556d.

173. Plato, *Republic*, 8, 556–57.

174. Jensen, *Making of the American Constitution*, 40.

175. Of the fifty-five members of the Federal Convention, forty-one were lenders, thirty-one were lawyers and politicians, twenty-one were planters, seventeen were engaged in commercial

at the top of the list of the interests that delegates aimed at protecting when negotiating constitutional provisions. Therefore, the overwhelming majority of members were not only rich property owners—which foreseeably put the protection of property as the principal object of the new state—but also creditors threatened by popular measures advocating debt relief against the enforcement of contracts. The threat of social change came to reinforce the role of *prudential fear* in the constituent process regarding the protection of a specific type of property: financial assets.

Departing from the principles established in the Declaration of Independence, a basic premise in the discussions of those present during the 1787 Federal Convention was that the safety of property rights—not the happiness and prosperity of the people—was the main purpose of the state.[176] Except for a couple of dissenting opinions, there was general agreement among the delegates that the protection of property must be the fundamental aim of the new federation. Within the discussions surrounding representation in Congress, Governor Morris argued for property to be taken into account when estimating the proportion of representatives to the lower branch: "Life & liberty were generally said to be of more value than property. An accurate view of the matter would nevertheless prove that property was the main object of Society."[177] He was seconded by John Rutledge, planter and lawyer from South Carolina, and Rufus King, lender, merchant, and lawyer from Massachusetts, who stated that property was certainly the "primary object of society."[178] It is striking that the defense of property as the principal aim of the state was not argued for on normative grounds, but just taken for granted, an obvious claim almost all delegates—rich property owners—shared. The only delegate providing an explanation of this principle was Madison, who did so through a realist argument grounded on interest:

> In all civilized Countries the people fall into different classes having a real or supposed difference of interests. There will be creditors & debtors, farmers, merchants & manufacturers. There will be particularly the distinction of rich & poor. . . An increase of population will of necessity increase the proportion of those who will labour under all the hardships of life, & secretly sigh for a more equal distribution of its blessings. These may in time

---

enterprises, and thirteen were in real estate speculation. http://teachingamericanhistory.org /convention/delegates/.

176. *Records of the Federal Convention*, 405, 407, and 411.

177. Ibid., 405.

178. Ibid., 407 and 411.

outnumber those who are placed above the feelings of indigence. According to the equal laws of suffrage, the power will slide into the hands of the former. No agrarian attempts have yet been made in this Country, but symptoms, of a leveling spirit, as we have understood, have sufficiently appeared in a certain quarter to give notice of the future danger. How is this danger to be guarded against on republican principles?[179]

In this way, Madison reveals the protection of property *against* the dispossessed, as the central aim of the constitutional design based on republican principles. He argued that pressures for wealth redistribution coming from below would be inevitable because "according to the equal laws of suffrage, the power will slide into the hands of the [poor]."[180] The challenge for him was then how to guard against this "danger" coming from the masses on republican principles. For achieving this task, he relied mainly on Montesquieu—who he calls the "oracle"—and his elitist procedural model of the democratic republic based on universal suffrage, representative government, and separation of powers.

Despite being in favor of the continued recognition of hereditary aristocracy as necessary for liberty, Montesquieu became the most influential thinker during the founding of the first modern republic in America.[181] Based on the tenet that "power checks power" and that adequate distribution of powers[182] (executive, legislative, and judicial) was enough to avoid corruption, as seen in the previous section, Montesquieu's interpretation of the mixed constitution is decisively elitist and proceduralist, a mechanistic system of checks and balances designed to produce liberty through correct procedures and institutional interactions, with the people exercising sovereignty only when voting for representatives.[183]

Even though Montesquieu's *The Spirit of the Laws* was one of the most influential texts informing the theoretical framework propping up the Constitution, and the framers heavily relied on his model to accomplish the Lockean state as protector of property, the model of representative government and

179. Ibid., 328.

180. Ibid.

181. Donald S. Lutz's analysis of citations in American revolutionary political thought from 1760 to 1805 shows Montesquieu was the most-cited author, accounting for 8.3 percent of all citations to specific thinkers, "almost without peer during the founding era for prominence." Lutz, "Relative Influence of European Thinkers," 193.

182. Montesquieu refers to "distributed powers" (*pouvoirs distribues*) not separation of powers. *Spirit of the Laws*, XI.7.

183. Ibid., II.11, 6.

separation of powers established in America was different from what the "oracle" had envisioned. Montesquieu's republican model was a mixed constitution—an elitist regime based on the unequal relation between the elite and the people expressed in two separate representative bodies, with different interests and equal faculties for enacting and vetoing legislation. The American republic, on the other hand, was based on the liberal principle of universal equality, which made Montesquieu's mixed constitution, based on the institutional recognition of the division between the aristocracy and the common people, impossible. The nascent republic demanded the elimination of privilege and the embrace of popular government, which undermined the checks and balances between the elite and the people, one of the cornerstones of liberty in Montesquieu's model.

This elitist view of the republic was pervasive in the discussions in the Federal Convention. Regarding the mode of election to the House of Representatives, there was a strong opposition to the election by the people, and there was general agreement that the common people "should have as little to do as may be about the Government" because they are in want of information and "are constantly liable to be misled."[184] To the few objections against the aristocratic character of the constitution that, given "the inequality of representation," puts the state "at the mercy of its rulers,"[185] the antidemocratic faction argued the problem was not elite corruption but the inevitable corruption that people enable when entering the government. The problem was not that an oligarchic class could grow out of the House of Representatives but that giving political power to the common people would lead to corruption because of the material subordination of the working classes:

> Give the votes to people who have no property, and they will sell them to the rich who will be able to buy them. We should not confine our attention to the present moment. The time is not distant when this Country will abound with mechanics & manufacturers who will receive their bread from their employers. Will such men be the secure & faithful Guardians of liberty? Will they be the impregnable barrier against aristocracy? . . . The ignorant and the dependent can be as little trusted with the public interest.[186]

Endorsing Montesquieu's elitist argument that the spirit of democracy was potentially despotic, and the common people should have the power only to

184. Roger Sherman, lawyer and merchant from Connecticut, *Records of the Federal Convention*, 65.

185. James Wilson, in ibid., 214.

186. Governor Morris, in ibid., 680–81.

elect representatives, the American framers extensively discussed ways in which to undermine the "evils" that flow from the "excess of democracy"[187] by restricting suffrage to property owners. Freeholders were considered the best guardians of liberty, and "the restriction of the right to them as a necessary defense against the dangerous influence of those multitudes without property & without principle with which our Country like all others, will in time abound."[188] There was such agreement among the delegates that it was at first thought that the restriction of suffrage to property owners would not be too unpopular, since "the great mass of our Citizens is composed at this time of freeholders, and will be pleased with it."[189] However, because numerous states had already extended the right to vote to white males, regardless of property, this option was deemed unfeasible. Because it was such a "tender point, and strongly guarded by most of the State Constitutions," the delegates thought the people would not ratify the Constitution "if it should subject them to be disfranchised."[190] Consequently, the right to vote—what for Montesquieu was the people's sovereign action—was *left out* of the Constitution, reserved for the individual states to decide on expanding or restricting the suffrage.

In the American implementation of Montesquieu's model, the framers wanted to accomplish the Lockean state as protector of property. Even if there was no legal nobility in America, the Senate was conceived as the embodiment of the aristocracy, as the guardian of property against the common people.[191] The Senate was seen not only as being able to "filter" the passions of the common people, as famously stated in *Federalist* number 10, but also as *representing* propertied interests because "one of its primary objects [is] the guardianship of property."[192] Given that at least two-thirds of citizens in America were at that time yeomen farmers, the framers saw as the interest of the current majority to conceive of the Senate as a body representing property owners, guarding against a future majority of unpropertied citizens. Based on a realist assessment of the majority's leveling spirit, like Montesquieu's constitutional model, Madison's system was designed against the tyranny of the majority as the greatest danger to the republic.

To prevent corruption and domination *within* government Madison's mechanistic model of representative government relied on the division of functions and conceived "mutual relations" of the several departments of

187. Elbridge Gerry, in ibid., 65.

188. John Dickinson from Delaware, in ibid., 679.

189. Ibid., 679–80.

190. Oliver Elseworth, representative of Connecticut, lawyer and lender, in ibid., 679.

191. Ibid., 69.

192. Ibid., 433.

government as the "means of keeping each other in their proper places."[193] The most effective way to counteract power is to give officials of different departments the necessary "constitutional means and personal motives to resist encroachment of the others."[194]

In the American implementation of Montesquieu's model, the Senate was conceived as the embodiment of aristocracy and therefore as the guardian of property *against* the common people. The general object of the constitutional framework was

> to provide a cure for the evils under which the U.S. laboured; that in tracing these evils to their origin every man had found it in the turbulence and follies of democracy: that some check therefore was to be sought for against this tendency of our Governments: and that a good Senate seemed most likely to answer the purpose.[195]

The Senate was seen not only as being able to "refine and enlarge the public views," blocking "intemperate and pernicious resolutions" resulting from the people being "seduced by factious leaders,"[196] but also as *representing* propertied interest. The Senate was conceived as having as "one of its primary objects the guardianship of property,"[197] and thus as checking the "excesses against personal liberty, private property & personal safety." Not only would the Senate have the institutional role of being the guardian of individual liberties, but also the members of the Senate must be wealthy so to "have a personal interest in checking the other branch. . . . It must have great personal property, it must have the aristocratic spirit."[198]

What in Montesquieu was implicit—that the upper chamber *resists* changes to the socioeconomic order—becomes the main argument in the United States to establish a strong Senate through which rich property owners could defend property rights against redistributive claims. While in the Roman republic plebeian institutions were equipped to *resist* abuse from the nobility, the framers inverted the relation of domination and armed the "aristocratic" Senate with the power to stop legal attempts to modify this relation in favor of "plebeian" citizens. While in Rome plebeian laws were binding without the

193. Ibid., 187.

194. Hamilton, Madison, and Jay, *Federalist Papers*, no. 10, 71–79.

195. Edmund Randolph, planter, lender and real state speculator from Virginia in *Records of the Federal Convention*, 69.

196. Hamilton, Madison, and Jay, *Federalist Papers*, no. 62, 377.

197. Madison, in *Records of the Federal Convention*, 433.

198. Morris, in ibid., 388–89.

Senate's authorization, in the United States laws aimed at redistribution could be passed only with the Senate's acquiescence.

In addition to the aristocratic ethos that the framers wished the Senate to embody, the spirit of commerce was also thought of as foundational to the new representative republic. The overly positive view of commerce as the cure of all evils that Montesquieu embraces was also predominant in the Federal Convention, except for the caveat posed by a group of planters who saw commerce as a source of inequality from which a commercial nobility, "a new order of men will arise."[199] Nevertheless, in the constituent discussions, the commercial spirit of free trade triumphed over that of virtue as the foundation of the new constitutional order and was let free to "reign alone and not be crossed by another."[200] Moreover, going beyond Montesquieu's idea that the spirit of commerce would be a moderating force for democratic (egalitarian) virtue, the framers thought of democracy and free enterprise almost as opposing principles; while the evils of government were rooted in the "turbulence and follies of democracy,"[201] free trade was the source of moderation and liberty, the cure for the excesses of democracy. "Take away commerce, and the democracy will triumph."[202]

What Madison and the rest of the founders were explicitly establishing was not a democracy but a republic, which Madison defines simply as a "government in which the scheme of representation takes place."[203] This was a new regime type, defined by its representative character, by "the delegation of the government ... to a small number of citizens elected by the rest."[204] For this "elected aristocracy" to be considered a free form of government it needed, as "sufficient" conditions, for the "persons administering it be appointed, either directly or indirectly, by the people," and for them to hold their office according to the law.[205] Consequently, the central institution of this new form of republic is for Madison the procedure of election, which is both the method of selecting a ruling elite and the source of normativity for the regime, the "essence of a free and responsible government."[206] If one follows Montesquieu's criteria for determining regime types, the nature of the representative republic is defined by who has political power. In the American republic's case,

199. General Pinkney of South Carolina, in ibid., 309.

200. Montesquieu, *Spirit of the Laws*, I.5.6, 48.

201. Randolph, in *Records of the Federal Convention*, 69.

202. Morris, in ibid., 389.

203. Hamilton, Madison, and Jay, *Federalist Papers*, no. 10, 76.

204. Ibid.

205. Hamilton, Madison, and Jay, *Federalist Papers*, no. 39, 237.

206. Madison, *Virginia Report*.

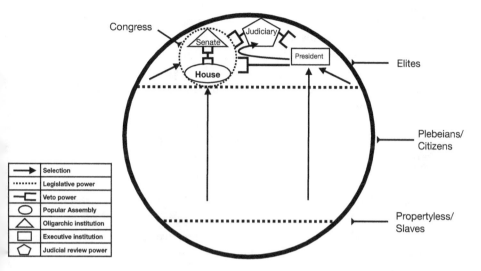

FIGURE 2.10. The American republic.

the holders of power are not the few or the many, or a mixture of both, but the representatives: a government by the few authorized and checked by all citizens.

Because procedurally the government is legitimate if elected by majority under set rules, the burden of producing legitimacy and good leaders is placed not on individual elites but on the "right to elect," a procedure that was for Montesquieu inherently aristocratic.[207] The whole complex federal structure of power put in place by the framers was built on the right to elect, procedure that was not thought of as faithfully representing the will of citizens, but as a better way to approximate the common good than direct democracy. "The public voice, pronounced by the representatives of the people, will be more consonant to the public good than if pronounced by the people themselves, convened for that purpose."

The supposed superiority of representation over the democratic method of popular assembly however did not blind Madison to the tyranny likely to occur in such a system in which "men of factious tempers, of local prejudices, or of sinister designs, may, by intrigue, by corruption, or by other means, first obtain the suffrages, and then betray the interests of the people."[208] Even if he feared the tyranny of the majority the most, Madison knew corruption could also come from the elites who are supposed to protect liberty:

207. See also Manin, *Principles of Representative Government.*
208. Hamilton, Madison, and Jay, *Federalist Papers,* no. 10, 77.

I wish, among other reasons why something should be done, that those who have been friendly to the adoption of this constitution, may have the opportunity of proving to those who were opposed to it, that they were as sincerely devoted to liberty and a republican government, as those who charged them with wishing the adoption of this constitution in order to lay the foundation of an aristocracy or despotism. It will be a desirable thing to extinguish from the bosom of every member of the community any apprehensions, that there are those among his countrymen who wish to deprive them of the liberty for which they valiantly fought and honorably bled.[209]

Madison responded to the challenge political corruption posed for representative government with an argument based on the beneficial effect of the size of the republic, and another based on the effectiveness of the surveillance exerted by the press and public opinion over public officials. The first argument, developed at length in *Federalist* number 10, is mostly probabilistic, premised on the idea that more and larger are better. Madison argues that because the probability of having good candidates standing for election and of selecting them increases proportionally with the pool of candidates and the electorate, a large republic is "most favorable to the election of proper guardians of the public weal." But having a larger electorate not only would be beneficial in terms of selecting good representatives; it also would decrease the probability of domination by the majority:

> Extend the sphere and you take in a greater variety of parties and interests; you make it less probable that a majority of the whole will have a common motive to invade the rights of other citizens; or if such a common motive exists, it will be more difficult for all who feel it to discover their own strength and to act in unison with each other.[210]

Given the factual pluralism in a large republic, majorities are difficult to attain and mobilize because of the collective action problems that make it harder to transform the will of citizens into actual political power.[211] Therefore, for Madison having a representative government in a large republic would constitute in itself a guard against the tyranny of the majority by effectively hindering the capacity of organization of the masses at a grand scale. The federal structure would further enhance this antimajoritarian—but mostly antiplebeian—feature of the large representative republic, by making it less

---

209. Madison, "Speech Proposing the Bill of Rights" (June 8, 1789).
210. Hamilton, Madison, and Jay, *Federalist Papers*, no. 10, 78.
211. Olson, *Logic of Collective Action*.

likely for "a rage for paper money, for an abolition of debts, for an equal division of property, or for any other improper or wicked project . . . to pervade the whole body of the Union."[212]

The structural protection against the domination of the majority, however, does not apply as well to the domination coming from the powerful few, who do not experience the collective action problems of the masses. While separation of functions and jurisdictions is meant to counteract ambition with ambition, mechanical checks deal only with the existence of factions within representative government, not with the quality of the representatives, which hinges on the electoral procedure. For Madison, to elect good representatives it is necessary to scrutinize them, and thus the right to free speech and to a free press is the most fundamental political right in the republic giving "value and efficacy" to the right of electing by enabling the censorial power of public opinion and allowing for government accountability.[213]

Even if the American Constitution contained a detailed organization of the powers of representative government, it had little recognition of individual rights[214] and did not recognize the rights to vote or to freedom of speech. Madison was initially opposed to a formal recognition of rights because a list of rights could never be exhaustive or properly enforced and thus would only account for "parchment barriers" against government oppression.[215] Nevertheless, the first ten amendments to the Constitution—the Bill of Rights—contain a list of individual rights as conceived, in a Lockean fashion, *against* the power of the federal government. It is this fundamental antagonism between government power and individual rights that establishes perhaps the original, most decisive rule of interpretation in American constitutional jurisprudence: a categorical approach to rights in which freedoms are understood as absolute vis-à-vis the government. At least in theory, the government must not infringe on individual rights, and thus liberty acquires a "negative" character: lack of state interference.

Madison puts forward an interpretation of the right to free speech as functional—because aimed at enabling the proper exercise of the right to elect—and absolute, not subject to abridgment. Freedom of the press and speech are not ends in themselves, but means to achieving accountability and virtuousness in politics, expected to expose the truth about public officials

212. Hamilton, Madison, and Jay, *Federalist Papers*, no. 10, 79.

213. Madison, *Virginia Report*, 227.

214. Habeas corpus (art. I, §9); bills of attainder and ex post facto laws (art. I, §10); treason procedure (art. III, §3).

215. Hamilton, Madison, and Jay, *Federalist Papers*, no. 48, 305.

and affairs, so citizens can adequately judge characters and measures, and elect good leaders. Absolute free speech, understood as the right to scrutinize public officials, was conceived by Madison both as a necessary premise for exercising the right to elect and as the ultimate guard of liberty, allowing for the formal structure of power based on separation of functions and veto powers to reproduce liberty through the normal functioning of political institutions.

According to Madison freedom of speech should be conceived as absolute because it is a natural right and therefore the federal government lacks the authority to control it "on the original ground of not being delegated by the Constitution, and consequently withheld from government."[216] In addition to the philosophical and jurisdictional justification for conceiving free speech as an absolute right, Madison claims that limiting speech is impossible without undermining the surveillance role of the press and the whole republican structure. Good and abusive speech are for Madison inseparable. Even if the press is "checkered . . . with abuse," it is impossible to cut the "noxious branches" without injuring the "proper fruits."[217] If free speech is curtailed (either by prior restraint or by posterior criminal actions), valuable information about political leaders and the policies they sponsor would be lost, and citizens would choose corrupt leaders, who would govern for their own interest or that of a faction. The burden of virtue in the Madisonean republic is thus placed on citizens' informed election of representatives, which depends on the surveillance role of the press and the unveiling of truth about candidates, laws, and policies.

Neorepublican Mixed Constitution: Popular Power as Discursive Control

Today perhaps the greatest exponent of the elitist proceduralist strand of republican constitutional thought is Philip Pettit, who interprets liberal democracies as mixed constitutions and seeks to develop the institutional checking power of the people to its highest degree. Searching for a "social philosophy that is at once anti-collectivist and anti-atomist," Pettit found in modern republican thought a conception of liberty that is "intermediate between the ideals of non-interference and self-mastery."[218] According to his reading of republican thought, republican freedom as nondomination would, on the one hand, justify *nonarbitrary* interference, and on the other, require the *absence*

---

216. Madison, *Virginia Report*, 229.
217. Ibid, 222.
218. Pettit, *Republicanism*, 27.

of mastery, providing an alternative between the liberal and democratic conceptions of liberty. To be free in a republic would be to have the status of being subject only to interference that "is not arbitrary and does not represent a form of domination: when it is controlled by the interests and opinions of those affected, being required to serve those interests in a way that conforms with those opinions."[219]

Even if Pettit's proposed conception of liberty is certainly thicker than a purely Hobbesian one, and he would never endorse the antidemocratic ideas that were pervasive at the moment of the American founding, his proposal is unable to escape the elitist framework of formal equality and the preservation of socioeconomic hierarchies. He not only takes the constitutional order as a given but also interprets it as a form of mixed constitution in which the checking power of the people is exercised individually through the courts and collectively through neutral, technocratic elite bodies. The popular element not only does not have an institution to assemble and exercise direct collective power but also has the *duty* to individually resist oppression through the resources provided by the system. Formally egalitarian, when seen through a plebeian lens, the status quo bias embedded in the connection between nonarbitrariness and individual interests comes to the fore.

Since in many political decisions there are winners and losers, under Pettit's normative framework any interference by the state to change the balance of socioeconomic power, depriving a minority to empower a majority, would be a form of domination because it would not track the interests of the few being forced to give up part of their property. According to Pettit, the goal of intensifying nondomination supports state provision of social services to fulfill what Amartya Sen describes as the basic capabilities for functioning in society, even if it is hostile to material egalitarianism:

> In order for the state to provide one person with extra resources, and thereby to extend their undominated choices, it must deprive another person of those resources, and must thereby reduce the extent of that person's undominated choices. There is no reason to think that the transfer will make for a gain. On the contrary, the costs of the state intervention will almost certainly mean that less is given to the second person than is taken from the first and that the transfer makes for a decrease in the extent of undominated choices overall.[220]

---

219. Ibid., 35.
220. Ibid., 161.

A strict application of Pettit's definition that demands the state to be "controlled by the interests and opinions of those affected" would not allow for redistributive policies beyond universal social services, such as the motion to allow the state to expropriate property without compensation, recently passed by the South African parliament.[221] The result is the preservation of the status quo and its current socioeconomic hierarchies based on patterns of accumulation and dispossession that cannot be modified without domination. This seems closer to a liberal conception of freedom in which individual rights are conceived as absolute against the state, rather than to a republican view of liberty in which rights are inherently political, and thus subject to legitimate abridgement and even outright violation, like in the case of expropriation of property, if it is necessary for preserving a free republic.

Following Montesquieu's positivist interpretation of the rule of law as the mark of liberty, Pettit argues that freedom as the lack of arbitrary interference is possible only in a regime with separation of powers in which the people elect representatives. However, for Pettit these are not sufficient conditions for freedom, and he therefore proposes to enhance the "contestatory" nature of liberal democracies. Even if the American republic was not conceived as a mixed constitution but as a representative government with separation of powers and checks and balances, Pettit argues our current system of government is a form of mixed constitution,

> insofar as it lets final decisions on law and policy be determined, whether simultaneously or sequentially, on the basis of interaction between different centres, civic and official, executive and legislative, constitutional and judicial.[222]

Through Pettit's framework, the mixed constitution is not an institutional structure giving political power to the few and the many, but a "contestatory constitution" based on an "acceptability game" that allows for the rise of "shared policy-making norms," and that guarantees multiple "sites of opposition" such as electoral debates, public justification of policy, and political exchanges in the media.[223] By abstracting the ancient checking role exerted by the people through class-specific institutions, and conceiving it as a system of "popular control" that influences and gives direction to government directly

---

221. Government estimates show that 72 percent of the nation's private farmland is owned by white people, who make up 9 percent of South Africa's population. In February 2018 a motion was made for land reform by South Africa's radical opposition party, the Economic Freedom Fighters (EFF), to allow the state to use eminent domain to seize white settler land.

222. Pettit, *On the People's Terms*, 283.

223. Ibid., 261.

and indirectly, Pettit attempts to reinterpret the representative republic as a mixed constitution in which the people are able to exert discursive control over the state.

Even if Pettit correctly diagnoses the shortcomings of liberal democracies, highlighting the current lack of effective control of the people over law and policy, his attempt to empower individuals within the current structure does not allow him to exit the elitist constitutional tradition. He rightly argues that the electoral system is deficient in guaranteeing "the people an unconditioned sort of influence" on certain aspects of government because of public officials' unwillingness to comply with popular authority.[224] The best way to force government to yield to popular influence would be, according to Pettit, to embrace a form of mixed constitution that would

> ensure the separating of the many powers of government, the sharing of each of those powers by different authorities, and the recognition of popular acquiescence as the ultimate guarantor of the constitution.[225]

While separation of powers and sharing of prerogatives are already institutional features of liberal representative governments, the third normative goal of having popular consent as ultimate guardian of the constitution has endemic problems in terms of the recognition of true consent and the enforcement of indirect popular influence on government.

To address the institutional weakness of popular influence, Pettit proposes a "dual-aspect model" of democracy aimed at enhancing popular control over government by providing citizens with an "individualized, unconditioned, and efficacious influence that pushes [government] in a direction that they find acceptable."[226] The duality of Pettit's model comes from the two temporal registers in which popular influence operates: while in the short term a plurality of citizens exert influence on law and policy, in the long term the people, conceived as a "group entity, taking the form of a singular agency," constitutes the state itself by ensuring the compliance of law and policy with the norms that frame the exercise of political power.[227]

Based on the ideal conceptions of "public interest"—understood as "those goods that anyone who accepts the necessity of living in equal terms with others is likely to have collectively guaranteed or promoted"—and the "invisible-hand mode"—through which electors, seeking their particular

---

224. Ibid., 304.
225. Ibid., 305.
226. Ibid., 239.
227. Ibid., 309.

interests, would promote a "utilitarian version of the public interest"—Pettit argues that the three requirements for achieving a more perfect mixed constitution (individualized, unconditioned, and efficacious popular influence) are already present in our political regimes. While the electoral system would provide for "individualized contestation," the unconditioned character of this contestation would be based on the "resistive character of the citizenry," and its efficacy would depend on the "insulation of the channels of popular influence against the distorting effects of electoral pressures and private lobbies."[228]

To force the state to be influenced by the people and track individual interests, Pettit argues that the constitution must establish democratic institutions with both a "positive search-and-identify dimension" equivalent to an "authorial" form of control, and a "negative scrutinize-and-disallow dimension," which he understands as an "editorial" form of control.[229] Accordingly, through democratic institutional channels ordinary people would be able to formulate as well as criticize law and policy, exercising the type of popular control proper to a mixed constitutional regime.

Despite Pettit's attempt to empower individual citizens by giving them negative and positive authority to author and edit law and policy, the powers he gives to ordinary citizens are far removed from the common account of authorial and editorial powers, and from the power mixed constitutions have historically afforded to the popular element. For Pettit the people are "indirect, electoral authors" because they "choose the personnel who will author the laws and decisions."[230] This is a highly controversial claim that he does not philosophically substantiate. Even if individual citizens would contribute with their selection of representatives to the collective legislative and policy-making process, they are certainly not authors. The same way that the selection of my favorite group of artists to make a sculpture under certain guidelines does not make me an indirect author of that piece of art, the selection of representatives to make law and policy does not make citizens authors of what is produced by representative government. Citizens indirectly *authorize* the law through their election of representatives,[231] but they do not *make* the law. And even if one

228. Ibid., 239.

229. Pettit, *Theory of Freedom*, 159.

230. Ibid., 161

231. Even if Hobbes makes the connection between author, actor, and authority, this does not apply to all representatives. "Of persons artificial, some have their words and actions *owned* by those whom they represent. And then the person is the *actor*; and he that owns his words and actions is the AUTHOR: in which case the actor acts by authority. For that which in speaking of goods and possessions is called an *owner*, and in Latin *dominus*, in Greek κύριος; speaking of

were to concede that electing lawmakers is akin to indirectly making the law, this tenuous connection between the right to elect and the right to author becomes even more dubious given the fact of what Pettit calls the discursive dilemma: "that even if all representatives endorse a consistent set of policy judgments, the effect of aggregating their votes may be to support an inconsistent package."[232]

In addition to conceiving citizens as indirect electoral authors, Pettit argues citizens have an editorial power capable of "rigorously scrutinizing and eliminating those candidate policies and those modes of policy-implementation that do not advance common avowable interests."[233] However, the popular editorial power he proposes is not strictly editorial—having the authority to modify law and policy, and even to veto them—but rather a "power of challenge" or "contestation" that is exercised through procedural resources, such as separation of powers and depoliticized decision-making bodies,[234] consultative opportunities for nonbinding citizen input, and the judicial system. More than *editors* able to direct and edit the content of law and policy, in Pettit's framework citizens are better understood as *subscribers* of the government who can challenge the direction and content of law and policy through petitions, public statements, and the courts, but certainly have little pull to make substantial changes to the "editorial line" of the government.

If we compare the powers Montesquieu gave to common citizens within an elitist mixed constitution to the power Pettit gives to the people in his ideal dual-aspect model of democracy, it becomes clear that common citizens in Pettit's framework would have even less power to resist the oppression coming from elites than in Montesquieu's commercial republic. In addition to giving citizens the right to elect representatives, Montesquieu gave to the representatives of the people the powers of introducing legislation and vetoing attempts at domination coming from the nobility. In Pettit's model, by contrast, citizens have the power only to elect representatives and contest laws and policies individually, mainly through the courts, even if in his latest work he also

---

actions, is called author. And as the right of possession is called dominion; so the right of doing any action is called AUTHORITY. So that by authority is always understood a right of doing any act: and *done by authority*, done by commission, or licence from him whose right it is." Hobbes, *Leviathan*, ch. 16, 111. Despite his authorization model, Hobbes would not argue that individuals *make* the law through their representatives.

232. Pettit, *On the People's Terms*, 246.

233. Pettit, *Theory of Freedom*, 160.

234. These institutions are equivalent to what Pierre Rosanvallon calls "counter-democratic" institutions. *Counter-democracy*.

endorses referenda as a desirable way of exercising popular control—not too different from what some state constitutions allow citizens today. According to Pettit, the existence in liberal democracies of "a multi-dimensional, multi-centred system of popular interaction and decision-making" would mean that "the people rule themselves" to the extent that their influence is present throughout the system of checks and balances,[235] which ultimately gives legitimacy to government and normativity to the law.

Pettit's interpretation of the mixed constitution as a "contestatory" framework in which individuals and groups have procedural, consultative, and appellate resources to challenge government decisions is, under a plebeian lens, decisively elitist, since it does not conceive of strictly popular institutions and gives to the people only weak channels to effectively control government. This neorepublican model is not only antimajoritarian but also proceduralist, and thus blind to systemic corruption.

Given Pettit's conception of liberty as the lack of arbitrary interference that equates liberty to the rule of law under contestatory conditions, structural forms of domination cannot be properly addressed without putting into question rules, procedures, and institutions. If liberty is achieved under a rule of law that presupposes contestatory institutions and procedures in the making of the law, then there would be no need for extralegal action such as political protest and social movements to exert radical social change. Civic virtue and contestatory institutions would be enough to keep systemic corruption in check, by constant, multidimensional, multicentered resistance to forms of oppression by individual citizens. The obvious problem is that while the majority of liberal democracies have all or a great number of Pettit's contestatory institutions and procedures, civic virtue—and the minimum conditions for civic virtue to exist—is lacking, which undermines effective and efficacious popular resistance against oligarchic domination and liberty itself. This endemic problem allows for structural forms of domination such as sexism[236] and racism[237] not only to exist alongside the rule of law, but also to be reproduced through institutions, laws, and procedures that effectively keep gender and racial oppression in place. How are these structural forms of domination going to be dismantled piecemeal if it is mainly up to the victims of domination to act, not only by resisting, but also by actively challenging domination?

235. Pettit, *On the People's Terms*, 286.
236. Gädeke, "Does a Mugger Dominate?"
237. Spitz, "Is Structural Domination a Coherent Concept?"

While the burden of virtue in the republic was for Cicero placed on elites, for Montesquieu on the system of checks and balances, and for Madison on the procedure of election premised on the right to free speech, Pettit places the burden of virtue on the "resistive" character of the citizens who need to scrutinize and resist potentially dominating decisions by the government. As I argued in the previous chapter, to place the virtue of the system on the "vigilance" of individual citizens, who perhaps already live in conditions of oppression, puts an unduly heavy burden on individuals without providing the infrastructure to really guarantee active civic resistance. This would be the equivalent to leaving representative institutions to their own devices.

3

On Material Constitutional Thought

THERE IS MUCH controversy within critical theory about the meaning of materialism and its centrality within the Marxist tradition.[1] I do not wish to contribute here to this philosophical debate but rather to use materialism as a method to study the constitutional structure and its legality, as a lens to analyze the organization of political and economic power, rights, and law as constructed in a specific conjuncture,[2] conditioned by existing power relations and their ideological justificatory structures.

A materialist interpretation of the constitution necessarily originates in the factual organization and exercise of power that is allowed and enabled by foundational institutions, rules, and procedures—or the lack thereof. Material constitutionalism is therefore premised on the idea that the organization of political power cannot be analyzed without taking into account the socioeconomic power structure, and how the state enables some kinds of actions while disabling others, targeting specific groups not only through the criminalization of certain behaviors (e.g., loitering) and the legalization of others (e.g., campaign finance), but also through the selective enforcement of rules and penalties that appear as neutral. The materialist constitutional lens, because it allows for the engagement in a dialectical analysis of the relation between

---

1. For an overview of this debate, see Timpanaro, *On Materialism*. Timpanaro makes an important contribution to the conception of materialism by reincorporating biological and ecological conditions into the materialist analysis, but I fundamentally disagree with his natural determinism.

2. I follow Louis Althusser's conception of the conjuncture as a historical singularity in which social power struggles are recognized, and the overdetermination of the contradictions of the system as well as the imprints this imbalance leaves behind on the structure are revealed. Althusser, *Machiavelli and Us*. See also Lahtinen, *Politics and Philosophy*.

power and law[3]—the material conditions of society and the legal, juridical, and formal provisions that (are supposed to) determine them—would enable a constitutional ideology that would stand opposed not only to legal positivism and formalism—which deny the political nature of constitutions and reduce their analysis to jurisprudence, excluding the application of law and its consequences in material terms—but also to proceduralism, which enables the masking of inequality and domination flourishing under democratic rules of political engagement.[4]

The material constitutionalism I present here is not the school of constitutional interpretation that developed in Germany after the 1958 Lüth case, which expanded the sphere of constitutional rights into the relation among individuals.[5] Even if it endorsed the application of constitutional norms to private law—which established the foundation for what has been called the "horizontal effect" of constitutional law, a strategy that has proven successful in accounting for rights violations coming from private agents as well as the state[6]—the "material" aspect of German constitutionalism refers not so much to the relation between power and law, but to an "expression of 'the substantive' in law,"[7] as a system of values centered on the principle of human dignity.[8] The materialist constitutionalism I develop here, on the contrary, does not have a preexisting ethical "substance" but rather is premised on the recognition that norms develop in relation to society and are the result of conflict. Law carries normativity not because it conforms to a predetermined substance or supreme principle, but because of the role it serves in the material conflict between domination and emancipation. In order to asses if a given institution, procedure, or law is "good" and thus part of the normative framework of a free society, material constitutionalism would take into account not only the degree of conformity of institutions, procedures, and laws to the basic democratic principle of equal liberty,[9] but also their effects in enabling emancipation and discouraging oppression on the ground.

---

3. Close to sociological constitutionalism. See Teubner, *Constitutional Fragments*; Thornhill, *Sociology of Constitutions*. For a critique of sociological constitutionalism, see Goldoni and Wilkinson, "Material Constitution."

4. I deal with proceduralism and elitism in chapter 2.

5. Lüth case, BverfGE 7, 198 (1958) B.II.1.

6. Gardbaum, "'Horizontal Effect' of Constitutional Rights"; Tushnet, "Issue of State Action."

7. Bomhoff, *Balancing Constitutional Rights*, 74.

8. 1949 German Constitution, art. 1.1 "Human dignity shall be inviolable. To respect and protect it shall be the duty of all state authority."

9. Identified as the principle of representative government for the first time by Condorcet. For an analysis of the principle, see Urbinati, *Representative Democracy*.

Material constitutionalism would also differ from Constantino Mortati's realist interpretation of the Italian constitutional order in its transition to fascism. Mortati, attempting to infuse positivism with a material point of reference to give stability to the state, finds in the material constitution a "supreme source of order"[10] and in the political party a constitutive element of the modern state, the "subject from which the fundamental constitution emanates."[11] For Mortati, the party is the "active element of the original institution" of the state, allowing for the state to assume its "political form."[12] In this way, the material constitution understood as the sociopolitical regime of political parties is the normative anchor of the formal constitution, enabling the integration of society into the constitutional order. Material social relations, articulated through the party, would constitute a normative basis for the stability of the state, which renders this constitutional theory as conservative of existing sociopolitical hierarchies.

In contrast to liberal constitutionalism—which sees the constitution as a set of "metaconstraints,"[13] laws as limits on governmental power, and the rule of law as neutral, even if its final interpretation is the monopoly of the judiciary[14]—under the materialist lens the constitution appears as a political document that is dynamic, constantly undergoing modifications, some of them radical enough to have been considered effectively equal to constitutional amendments, able to change the trajectory of society independently from procedural amendments to the original text.

According to Bruce Ackerman, the US Constitution is "an evolving language of politics"[15] and a "historical practice"[16] that is punctured by "constitutional politics"—extraordinary political moments such as the "successful struggle by the New Deal Democrats to place activist national government on solid constitutional footing."[17] Revolutionary reforms originating in popular mobilizations were "constitutionalized" by Supreme Court decisions,

10. Mortati, *Constitución en sentido material*, 16 and 23.

11. Ibid., 84.

12. Ibid., 83.

13. For an interpretation of the constitution as having both regulatory and constitutive rules, see Holmes, "Precommitment and the Paradox of Democracy."

14. Even if Montesquieu insisted that when judges effectively become lawmakers "the life and liberty of the subject [are] exposed to arbitrary control." *Spirit of the Laws*, 11.6.

15. Ackerman, *We the People*, 22.

16. Ibid., 34.

17. Ibid., 47. He also argued that the so-called Reagan revolution "was a failed constitutional moment" (56). Today it is evident that Reagan's neoliberal state (lean and mean) prevailed in the long run.

changing the substance of the Constitution and the trajectory of society without the need of a formal amendment. Ackerman's controversial idea, that there are distinct processes of higher lawmaking that do not align with the procedures established in article V, and that judges tend to adjudicate based on these unwritten, informal changes resulting from constituent politics, puts under the spotlight peak moments of the exercise of constituent power. However, it does not account for the progressive dismantling of the legal structure put in place by that constituent moment. I would argue that Ackerman's recognition of informal constituent changes based on limit cases involving strong popular mobilization is insufficient to unveil the cumulative effects of the steady ramification of smaller constituent changes coming out from every other judicial decision affirming and deepening sociopolitical conditions. The only way to account for these subtler changes is if we recognize the material constitution as dynamic. Through this lens the constitutional framework could be radically transformed not only through judicial interpretation, which opens and closes paths for adjudication and material possibilities for oppression and emancipation, but also through the power of the state to selectively realize these legal paths. Therefore, to track the progression of the material constitution, one needs not only to go beyond legal norms, procedures, and adjudication, but also to incorporate their enforcement and the effects of the constitutional framework on society. Thus, a relative consequentialism, in which the legitimacy of the norm would hinge on its material effects in preventing and containing oppression, would be an integral part of a materialist analysis of the constitution.

Seen through the materialist lens, I would argue the liberal rule of law should no longer be defended as a marker of equal liberty.[18] Because liberalism conceives of individual equal rights as immunities against the state (e.g., "Congress shall make no law . . . abridging the freedom of speech") and interprets them as a form of negative liberty, as noninterference from the state, the constitutionalization of equal rights not only is insufficient to guarantee their equal protection against the state but also does not offer any security against the violation of rights in social relations in cases were the law is silent, vague, or disregarded. Instead of a rational framework aimed at furthering the common good or realizing a specific principle, legality reveals itself as a means that could be used to liberate individuals from oppression as well as to enforce relations of domination.

18. For an analysis of how neoliberalism coopted the concept of rule of law, see Vatter, "Neoliberalism and Republicanism."

That having "rule" of law does not necessarily translate into equal liberty is perhaps best exemplified in the role played by the Supreme Court in defending segregationist legality in the American South. By nullifying the 1876 Civil Rights Act that aimed at enforcing the equal protection clause of the Fourteenth Amendment—which would have given African Americans a legal recourse to resist social oppression—the court enabled Jim Crow laws, forcing former slaves to suffer almost one hundred extra years of domination through legal segregation and discrimination. Congress, only after years of popular mobilizations, passed the Civil Rights Act of 1964, the enforcement of which has been mediocre at best. Despite their formal equal status, black Americans are discriminated against,[19] brutally oppressed by the police and the criminal justice system, and systematically stripped of voting rights. They are two times more likely to be stopped by police, six times more likely to serve jail time and be sentenced to mandatory minimums for nonviolent offenses, and four times more likely to lose their voting rights.[20] Therefore, even if they formally have equal rights on a par with white Americans, seen from a materialist perspective, their oppression, allowed and enabled by legal regulation or the lack thereof, denies this equality. The same could be said regarding the status of women, gender and ethnic minorities, and the working class, whose exclusion and exploitation has been systematically enabled by the law or its absence.[21]

Democratic constitutionalism tends to be formal and procedural in its analysis, and it is representative and liberal in its basic structure. While the study of the formal constitution requires analyzing the original constituent moment, the structure of power and body of norms derived from it, the interpretation of these norms, and legal changes to rules and procedures, the material constitution necessarily differs from the conception of the constitution exclusively as text and jurisprudence. I argue materialist constitutionalism demands a far more complex examination because it conceives of the constitution as an embedded set of norms that can be adequately grasped only if we integrate the political, economic, and social spheres into the analysis of forms of higher law. The proper study of the material constitution demands, in

19. See Taylor, *Race for Profit*.

20. One out of every thirteen African Americans has lost their right to vote because of felony disenfranchisement compared to only one in every fifty-six nonblack voters. Bill Quigley, "18 Examples of Racism in the Criminal Legal System," *Huffington Post*, October 3, 2016, https://www.huffpost.com/entry/18-examples-of-racism-in-criminal-legal-system_b_57f26bf0e4b095bd896a1476.

21. For the arbitrariness of rules, see Kennedy, "Form and Substance in Private Law Adjudication," 1685–89.

addition to the formal analysis of norms, an account of (1) the superstructure, basic political and social institutions,[22] and the power they factually exercise; (2) the rules and procedures enabling this exercise of power; (3) the institutionalization and exercise of constituent power; and (4) the social effects of the constitutional framework in terms of socioeconomic inequality and the racial, religious, and gender disparities in the application of the law.

Plebeian Constitutionalism

Even if a material interpretation of constitutions can be traced back to Plato, for whom socioeconomic inequalities were integral to the structure of political orders, his material assessment of the constitutional power structure did not have an emancipatory thrust nor was aimed at uncovering concealed forms of domination but rather helped enforce social hierarchies. Instead of correcting for material and social inequalities, *elitist material* constitutional thought recognized the impact of these inequalities on political power but nevertheless promoted the political dominance of the few and the exclusion and subordination of the many as desirable. Even if materialist in its acknowledgment that conflict between the few and the many is at the center of politics, elitist thought rejected democracy and its equal liberty. Moving away from materialism in its constitutional proposals, elitist thought often turned to idealism by proposing the suppression of conflict and the embrace of harmony, tranquility, security, and peace as foundational principles.[23]

In addition to the suppression of conflict being impossible to sustain—like a pressure cooker building up steam without periodic release—after the idea of equal natural rights became hegemonic in the West, elitist material constitutional thought could no longer be defended as a legitimate normative basis for a political order. Its proposed constitutional structures, based on cast systems, hereditary citizenship rights, and class-based institutions, are certainly not compatible with liberal democracy. Arguably Plato's ideal republic of guardians in which every individual had a rigid designated role, or Aristotle's preferred agrarian democracy in which the many were toiling away in the fields and did not actually exercise their voting rights, or Harrington's democratic aristocracy in which the many were excluded from citizenship, or

---

22. I follow here a broad understanding of the superstructure such as the one discussed by G. A. Cohen. "The superstructure consists of legal, political, religious, and other non-economic *institutions*," e.g., president, Congress, courts, political parties, churches, social organizations, media outlets, and social media networks. G. A. Cohen, *Karl Marx's Theory of History*, 45.

23. Plato, *Republic*; Hobbes, *Leviathan*; Montesquieu, *Spirit of the Laws*.

Guicciardini's electoral aristocracy in which elections meant de facto *ottimati* rule[24] would not be adequate models from which to draw lessons to reform modern democracies, since they do not promote equal liberty but the dominance of the few over the many. Building on such models is likely to further increase the systemic corruption of republics, accelerating their oligarchization instead of reverting it. Given that elitist material constitutional thought was effectively truncated after the modern revolutions, in a postliberal world elitist thought has embraced proceduralism as a way to justify the rule of the few on democratic grounds. Instead of active popular deliberative and decision-making power, freedom of expression and suffrage became the two normative pillars of representative government in the constitutional structure.[25]

The *plebeian material* constitutional thought I attempt to reconstruct here recognizes the influence socioeconomic inequalities have on political power, embraces conflict as the effective cause of free government, and seeks to channel its emancipatory, anti-oligarchic energy through the constitutional structure to produce and maintain liberty as nondomination. This strand of thought, commenced by Machiavelli,[26] sees conflict as productive of liberty and seeks to justify on republican grounds the active participation of the many to control those in power: as necessary for keeping the republic free from oligarchic domination. In addition to supporting institutional means for common people to engage in political decision making at the level of ordinary politics, plebeian thought also has proposed ways to institutionalize the constituent power—the power to intervene in the basic structure—which has been conceived in radical democratic theory as a form of extraordinary politics opposed to the constituted order,[27] and in republican thought as the revolutionary spirit that allows for the republic to renew its foundational principles.[28] Given the pivotal role afforded to conflict in the constitutional structure, in plebeian thought the constituent power is conceived not as a threat to

24. "The fruit of liberty and the object of establishing free republics was not to enable everyone to rule, since only those who are qualified and deserve it should do so." Guicciardini, *Dialogue on the Government of Florence*, 173; McCormick, *Machiavellian Democracy*, 107–10.

25. Urbinati, *Representative Democracy*.

26. There is also the utopian materialist strand of thought of which Thomas More is the most prominent thinker.

27. Andreas Kalyvas analyzes Weber, Schmitt, and Arendt as theorizing a politics of the extraordinary that prompts a change of paradigm. *Democracy and the Politics of the Extraordinary*.

28. Condorcet, "A Survey of the Principles Underlying the Draft Constitution," in *Condorcet: Foundations of Social Choice and Political Theory*, 190; Arendt, *On Revolution*, 26–27.

the constituted structure, but as a source of periodic renewal of the constituted order to update its anti-oligarchic capabilities, as a necessary means to preserve the original thrust of the constitution of a free government built on popular actions against domination.

Plebeian constitutionalism would aim (1) at establishing a normative framework designed to achieve equal liberty as nondomination—which is currently foreclosed for the majority of wage workers, women, and racial, religious, and gender minorities, who suffer oppression from bosses, men, and social majorities through the rules and penalties enforced by the state—and (2) at maintaining this equal liberty by actively dismantling emergent patterns of domination through the institutional exercise of plebeian constituent power. The political thinkers I identify as contributing to this plebeian constitutional thought could be grouped into two major camps depending on their conception of conflict and the rule of law: the *revolutionary reformers*, who proposed institutional solutions to the problem of oligarchy and the negation of agonistic politics, and *critical theorists*, who do not propose solutions but reveal law as an enabler of domination, which seems crucial for an adequate development of anti-oligarchic thought. While the two strands begin with Machiavelli's political philosophy, the institutionalist strand developed by Condorcet, Jefferson, and Arendt, and more recently by John McCormick and Lawrence Hamilton, is strictly political and propositive of new sites of popular self-rule (democratic) and forms of control over oligarchic power (republican). The critical strand commenced by Karl Marx, followed by Evgeny Pashukanis, and Antonio Negri, and more recently by Marco Goldoni and Michael Wilkinson, has remained anti-institutional and averse to proposing solutions to oligarchy, given the tight connection between the capitalist mode of production and the rule of law. Nevertheless, its contribution to the theorizing of the connection between law and domination, and the difficulty of achieving emancipation through the law within a superstructure controlled by the few, is crucial for the radical questioning of the legitimacy of law that is possible through plebeian constitutional thought. This distinction between the institutionalist and critical approaches to the republic is bridged by Rosa Luxemburg's proposal to establish a system of workers, soldiers, and peasant councils alongside representative government as the condition of possibility for proletarian law.

Revolutionary Reformist Legal Theory

Machiavelli was the first constitutional thinker to have a materialist interpretation of the republic and an institutional proposition aimed at correcting socioeconomic and political inequality to prevent the inevitable drift of republics into oligarchy.[29] He not only celebrated conflict as the foundation of "good laws" but also gave to the many the role of "guardians of liberty" and armed them to fulfill their function not only with legislative and military power but also with constituent power.[30] This meant not only that Machiavelli's ideal constitutional structure would have plebeian institutions exercising decision-making power during normal politics, but also that the many would have the extraordinary power to intervene in the basic structure, able to create new institutions and rules to periodically renew the republic and liberate it from oligarchic domination. As I discuss in detail in chapter 4, in Machiavelli this form of plebeian constituent power is not only creative, but also avenging, aimed at punishing those who actively undermine liberty. According to Machiavelli, to have a republic free from corruption the people must renew its foundations by periodically modifying its basic structure *and* inflicting extraordinary punishment on corrupt elites to remind the ruling few of the mighty force of plebeian foundational power. Without this material enforcement of liberty through plebeian authority, the republic would be doomed, corrupted through its own structures and procedures.

The contribution of Machiavelli to materialist constitutional thought was systematically revisited only in the eighteenth century. The renewed interest in Machiavelli, the mixed constitution, and plebeian constituent power sprang from a critical approach to the American constitution coming from the revolutionary experience in France. Perhaps the strongest critic in the Girondin camp was the Marquis of Condorcet, who argued the system of separation of powers put in place in America was a complicated machine that could not replace the mixed constitution, and only served to conceal a parallel ruling system based on "intrigue, corruption and indifference."[31] Condorcet was the last of the philosophes and the only one to provide a constitutional proposal to institutionalize the revolution in France. As a rationalist who embraced knowledge as a necessary condition for liberty, he included general education and the exercise of public judgment at the center of his ideal constitutional framework. But as a republican thinker, Condorcet was principally concerned not with how to advance human intellectual flourishing but with how to prevent corruption, the inevitable degradation of the system of restraints and incentives aimed at limiting representative government, "the vices which will

29. For further analysis of the relation between inequality and constitutions, see McCormick, "'Keep the Public Rich, but the Citizens Poor.'"

30. For an account of the relation between plebeian liberty and the citizen army in Machiavelli, see Barthas, *L'argent n'est pas le nerf de la guerre.*

31. Condorcet, "Survey of the Principles," 199.

corrupt even the best organized constitution if it remains unaltered."[32] His constitutional plan for France, which I analyze in detail in chapter 5, offers a three-pronged cure for corruption: frequent renewal of the representative assembly, an institutional popular "protest power" exercised through primary assemblies to check on representative government, and the periodic popular revision of the constitution.

Public education and local government were also embraced by Thomas Jefferson, who considered these elements crucial for the "continuance of republican government."[33] Jefferson, who was a diplomatic envoy in Paris after the American Revolution, argued in a series of letters to his friends in the United States that liberty for the many is impossible without tumults, and that conflict was a necessary evil to prevent the otherwise inevitable "degeneracy of government."[34] Even if Jefferson's constitutional proposals followed closely Machiavelli's, endorsing the periodic reactivation of the constituent power and the renewal of the constitutional order "every 19 years,"[35] his main argument is not strictly republican (functional) but rather democratic (end in itself). He supports periodic constitutional renewals not because of their anti-oligarchic benefits but as necessary for self-determination, as giving every generation the chance to be bound by laws of their own making.[36]

Jefferson's approach to extraordinary foundational violence was also different from Machiavelli's. Plebeian desire for redress and revenge does not relate to the institutionalized collective power of extraordinary public juries to ruthlessly punish corrupt elites, as Machiavelli would propose, but is rooted in rebellion, which according to Jefferson should always be allowed to spontaneously arise. To prevent "degeneration," rulers must be periodically warned that the revolutionary spirit is still present in the people; government needs to allow for spontaneous revolts and be prepared to "pardon and pacify" the rebels:

> A little rebellion now and then is a good thing, & necessary in the political world as storms in the physical. . . . The tree of liberty must be refreshed from time to time with the blood of patriots and tyrants. It is its natural manure.[37]

---

32. Ibid., 221.

33. Thomas Jefferson, "Letter to the Marquis de Lafayette," February 14, 1815, in Jefferson, *Political Writings.*

34. Jefferson, "Letter to James Madison," January 30, 1787, in ibid., 108.

35. Jefferson, "Letter to James Madison," September 6, 1787, in ibid., 596.

36. Jefferson, "Letter to Major John Cartwright," June 5, 1824, in ibid., 384.

37. Jefferson, "Letter to James Madison," January 30, 1987, in ibid., 108; "Letter to William Stephens Smith," November 13, 1787, in ibid., 110.

Jefferson also endorsed a republic of wards, a local form of government in which every man would be an "acting member of the common government, transacting in person, a great portion of its rights and duties."[38] Similar not only to the *Committees of Correspondence* that self-organized against the actions of the British Empire before and during the War of Independence, but also to the local meetings from which Shays's debt rebellion sprang, citizens in Jefferson's small republics would be organized and active to plan and demand certain courses of action from their representative government. But even if he agreed with Machiavelli and Condorcet that local popular governments as well as periodic conflict and creation are necessary to keep a republic free, as with his arguments for the renewal of the constitution, for him the establishment of a republic of wards was aimed not at eliminating corruption, but at promoting self-government—the positive liberty of men and the need for individuals to choose collectively their own fundamental rules.

While Jefferson justifies popular uprisings using republican anticorruption arguments—to keep representative government in check—his support for local government was based on democratic rather than republican principles. This democratic variation of republican thought was then advanced in the mid-twentieth century by Hannah Arendt, who proposed a republican conception of liberty in combination with a democratic form of self-government in the council system alongside representative government. In chapter 6 I analyze Arendt's thought, which combines the democratic and republican traditions, and allows for interpretation of the mixed republic from the point of view of revolution: as a juridical and spatial structure built to house and preserve the revolutionary spirit by enabling political action. For her, political liberty is achieved in action, and therefore the constitution of liberty needs to create spaces for political action to take place. It is in the councils, spaces in which individuals disclose their opinions and engage in political judgment, where liberty is exercised, and new beginnings may arise to found the republic anew.

Pushing back against Arendt's conception of freedom as political action, Lawrence Hamilton, based on the South African experience, has argued to conceive political freedom as a "power through representation" that requires the involvement of citizens "to the extent that is possible and necessary."[39] For him Arendt's conception of freedom is unrealistic because "under modern conditions we cannot all be involved actively in *virtuosi* political acts."[40] Hamilton proposes instead to understand political freedom as the power of citizens

---

38. Jefferson, "Letter to Major John Cartwright," Monticello, June 5, 1824, in ibid., 385.

39. Hamilton, *Freedom Is Power*, 193.

40. Ibid., 38.

to exert control over the "general trajectory of the state's macroeconomic path"[41] through representation. To achieve this, he proposes a combination of popular institutions with advisory power, a plebeian electoral procedure, and an "updated tribune of the plebs," which builds on the class-based institution aimed at curbing oligarchic power that was proposed by John McCormick in *Machiavellian Democracy*.[42] Loyal to Machiavelli's anti-oligarchic political philosophy, McCormick proposes to institutionalize plebeian power by establishing a People's Tribunate with the power not only to curb the excesses of the ruling elite, but also to legislate, opening the possibility for establishing plebeian law. I critically engage with both proposals in chapter 8.

Critical Legal Thought

In addition to this "positive," institutionalist strand of materialist constitutionalism, Machiavelli's thought—predicated on the conflict between the few and the many—also influenced a critical theory of law that was predominantly "negative," constructed *against* the legal system under capitalism and grounded on the conflict between capital and labor.[43] While revolutionary reformers have proposed institutional solutions to the problems of oligarchy and the negation of agonistic politics, critical theorists have focused mainly on revealing representative government and the liberal rule of law as enablers of domination. While the reformist strand advocates for the institutional participation of common people in politics, the critical materialist line, developed through Marx *against* the superstructure of capitalism, has tended to follow a path closer to anarchism in its distrust of institutions and laws to bring about real liberty for the proletariat.

Marx's radical critique of capitalism, the liberal republic, and its juridical system proposed, instead of institutional reforms, an alternative system, communism, conceived as a "*real* movement which abolishes the present state of things,"[44] eliminating the structure of production based on private property, overcoming class, and therefore also what for Machiavelli is the socio-ontological divide between the few and the many.[45] Consequently, the overlap

---

41. Ibid., 194.

42. McCormick, *Machiavellian Democracy*.

43. Even if Marx does not cite Machiavelli, he carefully studied his thought in mid-1843, as has been found in his *Kreuznach Notebooks*. Hudis, *Marx's Concept of the Alternative to Capitalism*, 47n53.

44. Marx, "German Ideology," 162.

45. For a radical interpretation of this divide from the point of Althusser's "aleatory materialism," see Lahtinen, *Politics and Philosophy*. For an analysis of the postcapitalist society in Marx, see Hudis, *Marx's Concept of the Alternative to Capitalism*.

between republicanism and Marxism can be only partial. While plebeian republican thought aims at institutionalizing plebeian power as supreme authority within a mixed constitutional structure, Marxism aims at transforming the foundations of society to abolish class and in this way enable society, as a divided whole, to become a species-being.

As a theorist of emancipation concerned with the material and juridical foundations of society, Marx should be situated within plebeian constitutional thought.[46] One of his greatest contributions to this strand is his critical analysis of individual rights and legal emancipation. In *On the Jewish Question* Marx leveled a critique against the formal interpretation of individual rights because it allows for the endurance of alienation and social forms of domination. Emancipation through formal individual rights is for Marx only a partial form of liberty that is not conducive to actualizing our species-being. While "free conscious activity" rests on the recognition that individual power is inextricably social, individual rights codify the barriers protecting individuals against the state as well as separating individuals from each other, which negates the social character of individual power:

> Political emancipation is a reduction of man, on the one hand to a member of civil society, an *independent* and *egoistic* individual, and on the other hand, to a *citizen*, to a moral [juridical][47] person. Human emancipation will only be complete when the real, individual man has absorbed into himself the abstract citizen; when as an individual man, in his everyday life, in his work, and his relationships, he has become a *species-being*; and when he has recognized and organized his own powers (*forces propres*) as *social* powers so that he no longer separates this social power from himself as *political* power.[48]

For Marx liberty through equal individual rights not only is inherently partial but also contributes to the reproduction of relations of domination that are presupposed even if legally abolished.[49] He developed further his critique of the legal system in *The Grundrisse* where he argues the juridical structure is a "stabilizing" force that influences and reproduces specific forms of distribution and production,[50] legalizing the domination of the few over the many:

46. For a republican interpretation of Marx, see Leipold, "Marx's Social Republic."

47. Translation in the Marxist archive, https://www.marxists.org/archive/marx/works/1844/jewish-question/.

48. Marx, *On the Jewish Question*, in *Marx-Engels Reader*, 46.

49. Ibid., 33. For a discussion on relations of production as effective power and legal ownership, see G. A. Cohen, *Karl Marx's Theory of History*, 63.

50. Marx, *The Grundrisse*, in *Marx-Engels Reader*, 235.

Every form of production creates its own legal relations, form of government, etc. . . . This principle [of might makes right] is also a legal relation,
and that the right of the stronger prevails in their "constitutional republics"
as well, only in another form.[51]

The principle of the strongest prevails not *despite* the law, but *through* the
law, complacent with it.[52] Making a parallel between laws and the structure
of distribution, Marx seems to suggest that laws determine the distribution of
rights and burdens at the same time that they are being produced as commodi-
ties, determined by the structure of production:

> The structure of distribution is completely determined by the structure of
> production. Distribution is itself a product of production, not only in its
> object, in that only the results of production can be distributed, but also in
> its form, in that the specific kind of participation in production determines
> the specific forms of distribution, i.e. the pattern of participation in
> distribution.[53]

The legal superstructure, which stabilizes relations of distribution, is conceived as being determined by the structure of production. Because socioeconomic inequalities based on relations of production determine the patterns of
distribution, which are preserved or modified through the law, the trajectories
of the economic and legal spheres should be seen as developing dialectically.
From this initial insight, Evgeny Pashukanis developed in 1924, in *The General
Theory of Law and Marxism*, a materialist theory of legal forms that takes as its
object of analysis the legal relation, "the cell-form of the legal fabric."[54] For
him legal relations are premised on social relations, with the law coming to
give legal form to what is already happening on the ground:

> The economic relation of exchange must be present for the legal relation of
> contracts of purchase and sale to arise. Political power can, with the aid of
> laws, regulate, alter, condition, and concretise the form and content of this

51. Ibid., 226.

52. An insight Corey Robin has recently brought back to the political discussion: "The worst
things that the US has done have always happened through American institutions and
practices—not despite them." "American institutions won't keep us safe from Donald Trump's
excesses," *The Guardian*, February 2, 2017, https://www.theguardian.com/commentisfree/2017
/feb/02/american-institutions-wont-keep-you-safe-trumps-excesses.

53. Marx, *The Grundrisse*, in *Marx-Engels Reader*, 233.

54. Pashukanis, *General Theory*, 85. For an extended analysis of Pashukanis, see
Head, *Pashukanis*.

legal transaction in the most diverse manner. The law can determine in great detail what may be bought and sold, how, under what conditions, and by whom.[55]

Against Hans Kelsen's "formal-juridical method,"[56] which saw law as the aggregation of norms, "merely a lifeless abstraction," Pashukanis argues the law should be analyzed as a legal relation that is rooted in material conditions, which always have "primacy over the norm":[57]

> Nevertheless, to assert the objective existence of law, it is not enough to know its normative content, rather one must know too whether this normative content materializes in life, that is in social relations. The usual source of errors in this case is the legal dogmatist's way of thinking—for him, the specific significance of the concept of the valid norm does not coincide with that which the sociologist or the historian understands by the objective existence of law.[58]

Pashukanis rejects the equation of law and norm because of the relation of law with the capitalist mode of production. He argues that the final cause of the legal system in a capitalist society is "commodity circulation,"[59] and thus the power of law to influence the patterns of distribution and production would not be able to produce real emancipation. According to his commodity exchange theory of law, "the logic of juridical concepts corresponds to the logic of the social relations of a commodity producing society,"[60] a relation between subjects who are individual bearers of property rights; law therefore would not be a proper tool for emancipatory structural change. Because his aim was to question private law and the system of private property, Pashukanis argues it is not a norm but the relation among subjects, and thus the power struggle inherent in that relation, that produces law. The legal superstructure is rooted on material relations of domination and is thus unable to upend these relations. As China Miéville has argued, Pashukanis appears to be

> hostile to law, inasmuch as he understood it to be a reflection of capitalist property relations, an integral part of a class society where the market has

---

55. Pashukanis, *General Theory*, 93.

56. Ibid., 87, also 52; Kelsen, *Das Problem der Souveränität*.

57. Pashukanis, *General Theory*, 87.

58. Ibid., 87.

59. Ibid., 100.

60. Ibid., 96.

a commanding role, and he did not believe that it would last as communism flowered.[61]

Pashukanis's materialist constitutional thought thus did not transcend his critique of capitalism and the Marxist dogma that the state and its rule of law are mere tools at the service of the capitalist class and thus no longer necessary when property and class are abolished.[62] This reductionism made him dismiss the possibility of "proletarian law," which was for him an oxymoron given the intrinsic connection between law and capitalist relations of exploitation:[63]

> The withering away of certain categories of bourgeois law (the categories as such, not this or that precept) in no way implies their replacement by new categories of proletarian law. . . . The withering away of the categories of bourgeois law will, under these conditions, mean the withering away of law altogether, that is to say the disappearance of the juridical factor from social relations.[64]

Pashukanis's refusal to conceive of the possibility of having emancipatory laws working to dismantle socioeconomic hierarchies, instead of only reifying them, is connected not only to his reduction of legal forms to private property, but also to his reduction of material conditions to social relations of exchange under the capitalist mode of production. For him the legal subject "is the abstract commodity owner elevated to the heavens," and his legal desires are "to alienate in acquisition and to acquire in alienation,"[65] and therefore the agency of legal subjects would also be determined by capitalist relations of exchange. These reductions not only obscure other relations of domination that precede and transcend capitalism[66] but also made him dismiss the possibility of radical constitutional change through legal means.

Seen from a republican perspective, Pashukanis's denial of the possibility of proletarian law hinges on his conception of conflict. While Machiavelli attributed to conflict a normative force, as being productive of good laws, Pashukanis argues there is always conflict at the base of every legal relation, which

61. Miéville, *Between Equal Rights*, 98.

62. Engels, *Socialism: Utopian and Scientific*, in *Marx-Engels Reader*, 713; Lenin, *The State and Revolution*, ch. 5, "The Economic Basis of the Withering Away of the State," in *Collected Works* 25; Evgeny Pashukanis, "Economics and Legal Regulation" (1929), in *Evgeny Pashukanis: Selected Writings*, 268–69.

63. Miéville, *Between Equal Rights*, 99.

64. Pashukanis, *General Theory*, 61.

65. Ibid., 121.

66. Shoikhedbrod, "Estranged Bedfellows." See also Fine, *Democracy and the Rule of Law*, 157.

"comes into being only at the moment of dispute. It is dispute, conflict of interest, which creates the legal form, the legal superstructure."[67] Going against Hegel and Kelsen, Pashukanis argues material conditions are at the origin of the legal structure, and even if the relation between matter and form is dialectical after that original point, the premises of law are always "rooted in the material relations of production."[68] Therefore, for Pashukanis conflict is not seen from the side of popular resistance to oligarchic power—as productive of liberty—but as a permanent feature of *all* legal relations, which are not derived from basic principles or acts of resistance but are "directly generated by the existing social relations of production."[69] Conflict is not productive because it is reduced to the subjacent conflict implied in all relations of domination, denying the possibility that conflict coming from popular pushback against domination could generate emancipatory law.

A reengagement with a critical analysis of law was enabled in the late 1970s by the critical legal studies (CLS) movement, which aimed at engaging critically with the law while moving away from Marxist determinism. The two overriding concerns of CLS were, on the one hand, the critique of legal formalism and objectivism, and on the other, the "purely instrumental use of legal practice and legal doctrine to advance leftists aims."[70] While CLS was successful in demystifying the law by pointing to its indeterminacy, internal "disharmonies,"[71] and political character,[72] the few institutional proposals that came out of this critical analysis were merely reformist. For instance, in the late 1990s Roberto Unger proposed a "democratizing alternative to neoliberalism"[73] that would expand equal access to capital and democratize "the partnership between government and business," in tune with a liberal-left political project.[74]

Marxist thought also yielded a radical democratic interpretation of law, the constitution, and the constituent power, mostly anti-institutional and anarchic. Writing soon after the fall of the Berlin Wall, the defeat of communism, and the triumph of capitalism and constitutional democracy as the dominant economic and political systems, Antonio Negri analyzed the emancipatory nature of the constituent power as "crisis" and "living labor," and its relation

---

67. Pashukanis, *General Theory*, 93.

68. Ibid., 94.

69. Ibid., 96.

70. Unger, *Critical Legal Studies Movement*, 567.

71. Ibid.

72. Ibid., 578. See also Collins. "Roberto Unger."

73. Unger, *Democracy Realized*, 235.

74. Ibid., 273.

to the constituted order. Through a radical democratic interpretation of Machiavelli, in which the republic is equivalent to an absolute democracy, Negri not only generates an interpretation of constituent power as "the passion of the multitude,"[75] "absolute and untamable,"[76] but also posits the need for a constitutional model in permanent becoming, "capable of keeping the formative capacity of constituent power itself in motion."[77]

For Negri the constituent power is in constant movement and is at the same time creative and destructive, subject and strength, "a radical subjective foundation of being,"[78] the basis of the political: an absolute, unfinalized process that "comes from the void and constitutes everything,"[79] that is always referring to the future and implies a multidirectional plurality of time and spaces. He also recognizes in the constituent power "the negative power par excellence,"[80] due to the destructive force inherent in the process of permanent becoming. The double nature of the constituent power, as positive/creative and negative/destructive, is realized in relation to its opposition to the constituted order, which, instead of being the basis of the political, is its summit, an accomplished finality, a rigidified and formal framework always referring to the past, which implies a limited time and space:

> Sovereignty presents itself as a fixing of constituent power, and therefore as its termination, as the exhaustion of the freedom that constituent power carries.[81]

Against this ossified structure and the death of the political, "the only possible concept of constitution" is for Negri "that of revolution: precisely, constituent power as absolute and unlimited procedure."[82] A working proposition for this kind of constitutional framework, able to accommodate permanent constituent revolution as constant becoming, is yet to be elaborated, and thus Negri's contribution to plebeian constitutional thought remains at the level of pure critique.[83]

More recent Marxist legal analyses have also preferred to remain in the critical description rather than engage in the normative and prescriptive.

---

75. Negri, *Insurgencies*, 304.
76. Del Lucchese, "Machiavelli and Constituent Power," 6.
77. Negri, *Insurgencies*, 25.
78. Ibid., 319.
79. Ibid., 16.
80. Ibid., 21.
81. Ibid., 22.
82. Ibid., 24.
83. See also Abensour, *Democracy against the State*.

Despite acknowledging that the strength of the material constitution rests on the social "support for the political aims (or even finality) of a regime,"[84] Marco Goldoni and Michael Wilkinson explicitly embrace the explanatory over the normative analysis of the material constitution. From a postliberal perspective,[85] bringing pluralism into critical legal analysis, they argue that the study of the material constitution cannot be "reduced to the study of the underlying economic base" because economic and politics are interrelated.[86] As a way to escape the reduction of politics to economics, they negate Pashukanis's insight of the factual dominance of material conditions over the norm by arguing that in this interrelation "the economic base must not be presented as over-determining the material constitution."[87] In their account conflict is not primarily between the few and the many, capital and labor, but is "conducted by a plurality of subjects whose positions are conditioned but not determined by already established relations."[88]

The replacement of class struggle with agonistic pluralism,[89] and the negation of the factual dominance of material conditions over politics by putting economic and political power in equal standing, is not to my mind a materialist analysis of the constitution, since the dominance of the few over politics has been a constant feature since the origins of representative government.[90] The political influence of lenders, real estate speculators, and slave owners produced in the United States a constitution constructed explicitly against democracy and the power of the popular sectors.[91] All members of the constituent convention agreed that the constitution they were writing was not a democracy but a representative government, which had as its principal objective the protection of private property.[92] To put the power of politics as equal to material power both obscures factual oligarchy and overestimates the

84. Goldoni and Wilkinson "Material Constitution," 591.

85. I understand a postliberal perspective as embracing the basic tenants of political liberalism such as the respect of individual rights and pluralism. A postliberal Marxist interpretation is by necessity a hybrid.

86. Goldoni and Wilkinson, "Material Constitution," 587.

87. Ibid. They limit their analysis to "four ordering forces of the material constitution: political unity; a set of institutions; social relations, and fundamental political objectives" (567).

88. Ibid., 589.

89. For the political philosophy of agonistic pluralism, see Mouffe, "Deliberative Democracy."

90. See Manin, *Principles of Representative Government.*

91. Of the fifty-five members of the Federal Convention, forty-one were lenders. For the antidemocratic sentiment, see *Records of the Federal Convention,* 65.

92. Ibid., 69 and 433.

political power of individuals to exert changes to the superstructure. As a result, similar to *elitist* republicans, Goldoni and Wilkinson place on individuals the burden of achieving and protecting liberty:

> Political subjects are thus essential in the formation and then preservation of a particular political economy, as well as in fomenting change through putting pressure on reforming the political-economic structure.[93]

This postliberal contribution to critical legal studies is liable therefore to the same problems as proceduralism, in which the burden of the maintenance of liberty is placed on individuals, which is, as I have argued before when discussing Philip Pettit's neorepublican model, practically equivalent to leaving the system to its own devices. Structural oppression makes individuals powerless to resist domination and exert changes to the legal structure if collective power is not institutionalized in the constitution.

Despite the lack of a model for a plebeian materialist constitution, critical constitutional thought has provided a strong critique of legal formalism, strengthening the cause for establishing a mixed constitution. In addition, its push for connecting the power of the many in Machiavelli with the theory of constituent power has greatly contributed to plebeian constitutionalism by allowing for a partisan conception of the power to renew the republic. Finally, even if the anti-oligarchic side of plebeian thought precedes Marx, the current radical republican interpretation of Machiavelli put forth by McCormick owes much to Marx's analysis of capitalism and class struggle, even if indirectly via an interpretation of Machiavelli through the lens of critical political economy. Through a post-Marxist[94] (but not postliberal)[95] application of Machiavellian thought, McCormick has placed class struggle, the threat of plutocracy, and the need for class-based institutions to control the rich at the center of material constitutionalism.

93. Goldoni and Wilkinson, "Material Constitution," 588.

94. I understand a post-Marxist perspective as embracing basic tenants of Marxism such as class struggle. Even if I agree with Pedullà that McCormick "does not place Machiavelli in Marx's shadow," his interpretative lens appears to have been influenced by critical theory and the current conjuncture determined by oligarchic power. Pedullà, *Machiavelli in Tumult*, 5.

95. Class-based institutions and penalties are not postliberal in the sense that they do not embrace formal equal rights and political equality.

PART II

Plebeian Constitutional Thought

4

Machiavelli on the Plebeian
Power to Create and Punish

THE TRADITION of elitist-procedural republican thought, which took inspiration from the English mixed government of the 1700s and crystalized in the establishment of an antimajoritarian, electoral constitutional framework in the United States, stands in stark contrast to the materialist plebeian strand that developed from Machiavelli's assessment of the Roman republic, from the viewpoint of the democratic experience of the Florentine republic (1494–1512). While under the Medici Florence had a *governo stretto* (narrow government) directed by the *ottimati* (nobility), after taking power Girolamo Savonarola embraced *governo largo* (broad government) by establishing in 1494 the Great Council as a popular legislative and electoral assembly. The new constitutional structure of the Florentine republic, which acquired its definite form in 1499, was a new mixed *ordini* that lasted until 1512. The introduction of a democratic assembly with about one thousand citizens who participated in turns,[1] alongside other councils and magistracies, meant that for the first time the plebeian sociopolitical element was institutionalized in Florence.

As a public official in the Florentine republic, Machiavelli had a firsthand experience of the inner workings of institutions and the struggle between social groups to exert influence on government. I argue that his support for a mixed constitution in which the few would govern within limits and the many would be active guardians of liberty, both in the *Discourses on Livy* and in his *Discourse on Remodeling the Government of Florence*, is rooted in his direct

---

1. Citizenship was restrictive since it demanded membership in one of the seven great guilds. The Council had between 1,150 and 2,400 members who could effectively participate. Citizens were divided into three sections to deliberate and decide. Rubinstein and Raillard, "Early Years of Florence's Grand Council," 103–6. Najemy, *History of Florence*, 388–89.

assessment of the limitations of democratic rule to contain the informal power of the great in Florence.

The Republic as a Mixed Constitution

From radically different methodologies, both Leo Strauss and the Cambridge school[2] interpret Machiavelli's work as advocating for a republic ruled by elites. However, Machiavelli's conception of mixed constitution departs from the predominant, elitist strand of republicanism initiated by Cicero and picked up later by Montesquieu, which gives to the aristocratic element (the selected few) the reins of government, while reserving for the many only the power to choose representatives.[3] For Machiavelli, to live in liberty plebeians must not only approve or reject policies, but also dictate them, not only obey laws and institutions, but also establish them. As John McCormick has shown, these elitist interpretations of Machiavelli distort his theory of the plebeian republic because they "underemphasize class conflict," disregard the necessary role of active, popular participation in political rule, and conceive of liberty in a formal, narrow manner, which "rather meekly addresses forms of social domination aside from slavery."[4] For *elitist* republicans, only the best citizens should control the government because they contribute much-needed moderation to the republic; the many should be limited to elect the best citizens to rule.[5] On the contrary, for Machiavelli a regime of liberty demands a dynamic balance of power between the few and the many that is achieved only through institutionalized political conflict, allowing for the few to satisfy their ruling ambition and for the many to defend liberty through their active participation in political power.[6]

Machiavelli's materialist constitutional analysis begins with his interpretation of the Roman plebeian experience recorded in detail in the *Discourses*, work that according to Gabriele Pedullà aims at recovering "the actual political prudence of the Romans through a hermeneutics of the ancient historical

2. Pocock, *Machiavellian Moment*; Skinner, "Machiavelli on the Maintenance of Liberty"; Viroli "Machiavelli and the Republican Idea of Politics."

3. For an extensive critique of the aristocratic strand, see McCormick, *Machiavellian Democracy*.

4. McCormick, *Machiavellian Democracy*, 9–10; McCormick, "Machiavelli against Republicanism."

5. Cicero, *On the Commonwealth*, 1.52, 23; Montesquieu, *Spirit of the Laws*, I.3.4 and II.1.6; A. Hamilton, Madison, and Jay, *Federalist Papers*, no. 62, 374–80.

6. Pedullà, *Machiavelli in Tumult*; Brudney, "Machiavelli on Social Classes and Class Conflict"; Bonadeo, *Corruption, Conflict and Power*, 37–71.

narratives," achieving with his republic of tumults an alternative to "the classical and humanistic tradition of concord."[7] In Rome's *ordini*, while the authority of the Senate and the consuls rested in tradition, the authority of the tribunes was not based on the sacred, original foundation of Rome, but on the force exerted by the plebeians owing to their crucial role in defending the republic. The authority of the people was rooted in their actual power to extract political concessions from the elite by deserting and, thus, paralyzing the city.[8] Machiavelli's critical engagement with the Roman republic evidences the need to account for different forms of power and authority in the mixed constitution springing from the fundamental split of society between the great and the people.

In the Roman republic, while authority based on tradition, seniority, knowledge, and wealth rested with the Senate, which legitimately directed government action, the authority to protect liberty, through the right to legislate and veto government action, lay with the organized multitude. The authority of the consuls, who were co-administrators of government with the Senate, was based on the recognition of leadership through election. As commanders of the army, the consuls wielded legal power—the right to execute policies within the boundaries of the law and the counsel of the Senate. The other source of power was the people, who could command only the power of presence, the sheer power of numbers, which is exerted through extralegal means (e.g., mobilization, occupation of public space, violence). Different from the power of the army—a hierarchical command structure susceptible to cooptation and instrumentalization—the power of the people, being inseparable from their physical presence, cannot be commanded. It can certainly be invoked and demanded, but the response of the people is always uncertain. Soldiers have proper weapons and training to risk their lives; common citizens have neither, which means that while the influence of the Senate over the consuls gives the elite the power of the army, the assembled people of Rome as guardians of liberty armed their representatives, the tribunes, only with a "sacrosanct" authority and an uncertain threat of collective violence.[9]

---

7. Pedullà, *Machiavelli in Tumult*, introduction, 8.

8. In 494 BC, while Rome was at war with two neighboring tribes, plebeian soldiers refused to march against the enemy and instead seceded to the Aventine Hill, leaving the city to its fate. Tenney, *Economic History of Rome*.

9. Sacrosanctity "implies that the plebeians had formed a separate body in the state and had compelled the government to take an oath to respect the persons of their representatives under penalty of divine vengeance." Tenney, *Economic History of Rome*, 47. See also Lintott, *Constitution of the Roman Republic*, 33, 121–24.

Despite their institutional and material weakness, plebeians were successful in extracting concessions from the few. Plebeians gained access to lawmaking and magistracies through open conflict, but these gains were lost because institutional means were not enough to back up plebeian legal authority after corruption had taken root. Rome is for Machiavelli both a model of a tumultuous republic and a warning, the tragic example of a free republic apparently ruined by its own effective cause: conflict. While the institutionalized conflict between the elite and the people constituted for him the republic's normative energy, yielding "all the laws made in favor of liberty,"[10] it was also the cause of its ruin[11] because the authority of the tribunes was never entirely severed from the popular force through which it had originated, and thus never entirely respected by the ruling elite. Therefore, the evolutionary way in which the Roman republic was constituted created a precarious dynamic balance of power between the few and the many that was finally upended with the complete disregard of plebeian institutional power by the Senate. The ruin of the Roman republic was brought about by conflict, by the refusal of the Senate to sanction the reforms to the Agrarian Law[12] passed by the people in 133 and 122 BC, and the violent upheavals that ensued, in which the tribunes Tiberius and Gaius Gracchus were murdered. I argue Machiavelli wants to correct the institutional imbalance created in a constitution made through class struggle—on popular authority conceded through active resistance—by constitutionalizing what in Rome was grounded on the physical power of the people. In other words, Machiavelli seeks to perfect the Roman republican experience by formally constitutionalizing the power of the many to resist the domination coming from the few.

According to Althusser, Machiavelli is a materialist philosopher who inaugurates a conjunctural approach to politics and the law in which liberty is attained only through conflict.[13] Machiavelli's "aleatory materialism"[14] begins for him from the foundational theoretical premise of the ontological split of society between the few and the many, the grandi and the popolo, animated by two unequal battling humors: to oppress and resist oppression:

---

10. Machiavelli, *Discourses*, 1.4.

11. Ibid., 1.37.

12. Ibid. For a politico-historical analysis of the period, see Millar, *Crowd in Rome*.

13. Althusser, *Machiavelli and Us*. For an analysis of Althusser on Machiavelli, see Bargu, "Machiavelli after Althusser"; Vatter, "Machiavelli after Marx"; Gaille, "What Does a 'Conjuncture-Embedded' Reflection Mean?"

14. Althusser theorizes an aleatory materialism he derives from Machiavelli. *Écrit Philosophiques et Politiques I*, 543–48. See Lahtinen, *Politics and Philosophy*.

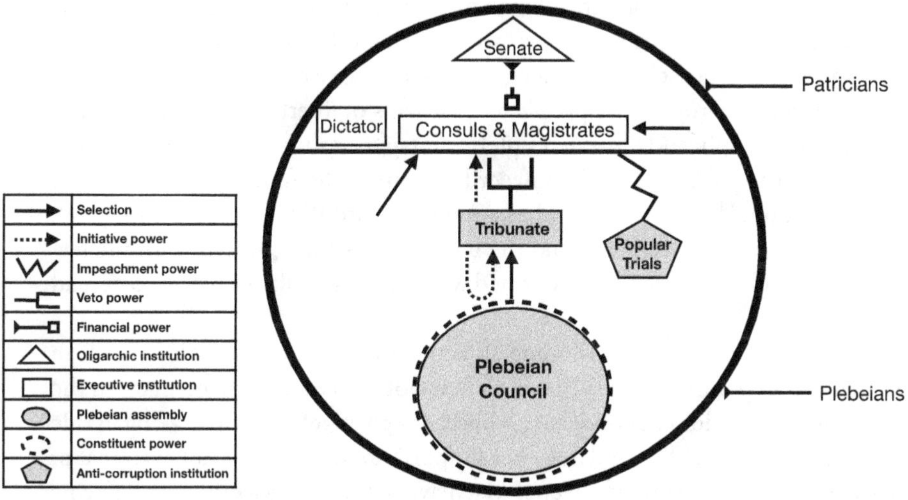

FIGURE 4.1. Simplified interpretation of Machiavelli's description of the Roman republic.

A small part of them wishes to be free in order to rule; but all the others, who are countless, wish freedom in order to live in security.[15]

The rich desire to dominate the people, the people desire not to be oppressed by the rich, and the perpetual struggle in a republic between these opposing desires, argues Machiavelli, generates liberty. The power of the organized few to direct government is checked by the power of the organized multitude to initiate legislation and stop governmental action. Liberty is the result of this institutional conflict between the few and the many; desires and conflict are expressed through institutions and procedures, and in this way tamed and oriented for the good of the republic. However, liberty is not caused by the institutional *balance* of two unequal forces like in Polybius, but by the periodical pushback of the many against the inevitable, constant overreach of the powerful few.

While theoretically a precarious balance could be achieved between the few and the many, the crucial guardianship of liberty—the right to make the last decision—must always rely on one side. Machiavelli chooses the people over the elites as stewards of liberty because the former merely long not to be ruled, "and as a consequence [have] greater eagerness to live in freedom, since they can have less hope of taking possession of it than the great can."[16]

15. Machiavelli, *Discourses*, I.16, 237.
16. Machiavelli, *Discourses*, I.5.

Even though it is a difficult task to completely separate Machiavelli's description of the Romans from his own ideal model in the *Discourses*, his general statements suggest the Roman republic would have benefited from a formalization of the role of the people as guardians of liberty. This interpretation not only implies Machiavelli's plebeian partisanship—which was already evident to John Adams who described him as the founder of a "plebeian philosophy"[17]—but also implies a mixed constitutional structure in which the power of both the few and the many are institutionalized, with the few ruling and the many properly armed with legal and military power to defend liberty.

Despite certainly envisioning an active role for the common republican citizen in politics, I argue Machiavelli is not a theorist of democracy, in the sense that he does not understand liberty as positive[18]—the partaking in rule as an end in itself[19]—and does not support monocratic rule, not even that of a democratic assembly.[20] Even if Machiavelli is certainly a critic of oligarchic republics, and explicitly advocates for direct participation of the people through lawmaking, voting for magistrates,[21] judging in political trials,[22] and choosing their own, *exclusive* representatives—the Tribunes of the Plebs— this does not mean he is sponsoring unmixed popular or democratic government. Even though he praises the specific characteristic of the people and their form of government, he advocates for an increase of popular power *within* a republican framework grounded on his theory of humors in permanent conflict. In other words, Machiavelli does not envision the popolo ruling on its own, but for the popolo to have enough power to curb the power of the grandi and protect liberty. Liberty is for him nondomination and, therefore, different from the democratic ethos, in which active engagement in politics is an *end* in itself—the most virtuous activity the common man could ever perform[23]— for Machiavelli citizen participation in everyday politics is functional, a necessary *means* for maintaining a republican structure conducive to liberty. Moreover, while liberty is enjoyed by all, he reserves glory for the few able to perform extraordinary actions aimed at benefiting the republic. In Machiavelli

17. "Defence of the Constitutions and Government of the United States of America," in *John Adams, Works*, 396. See Barthas, "Machiavelli in Political Thought."

18. Berlin, "Two Concepts of Liberty."

19. Democracy is to rule and be ruled in turns, and the exercise of politics is a virtuous action, which is an end in itself. Aristotle, *Nichomachean Ethics*, I.8.

20. Against this interpretation, see Barthas "Il pensiero costituzionale di Machiavelli."

21. Machiavelli, *Discourses*, I.18; III.34.

22. Machiavelli, *Discourses*, I.7–8.

23. Aristotle, *Nicomachean Ethics*, I.2.1094b, 5.

the many participate in government primarily to defend their liberty—not to be virtuous or attain glory.

Remaking Florence as a Mixed Constitution

Machiavelli's preoccupation with oligarchy, corruption, and the active resistance of the people was embedded in the extraordinary democratic experiment of the republic of Florence, which began in 1494 with the establishment of the Great Council, a form of direct democracy that allowed for extensive citizen participation in legislative, electoral, and judicial authority. During the brief democratic experiment in Florence, of which Machiavelli was a leading figure, the elites lost the monopoly over government and were constantly trying to regain their dominance. As Jérémie Barthas has showed, despite the extensive powers of the Council, the republic remained effectively dependent on the financial oligarchy owing to its reliance on mercenary armies, and Machiavelli's most important task as secretary and second chancellor of the republic was to liberate the republic from oligarchic control by introducing a project of mass conscription.[24]

After the return of the Medici and the end of the Florentine democratic experience, Machiavelli argues to remodel Florence so at to give the city a lasting republican structure that satisfies all "those elements that must be contented"[25] and creates a mechanism to "establish fear in great men."[26] He criticizes the institutional framework of the Florentine republic of 1494 because it neither adopted a form that would endure, based on the satisfaction of the fundamental elements of society, nor established the punishment of elites who set up factions to satisfy their own interests. Machiavelli argues there are three different kinds of individuals, "the most important, those in the middle, and the lowest."[27] Because some citizens are ambitious and desire to outrank others, this desire needs to be satisfied in the republican organization of power if the regime does not want to end up having the same fate as Florence's democratic experiment, which "fell for no other cause than that such group was not satisfied."[28] Because the grandi seek glory, the best constitution is the one able to satisfy the interest of the elite in a manner conducive to

24. Barthas, "Machiavelli, the Republic, and the Financial Crisis," 273; Barthas, L'argent n'est pas le nerf de la guerre.

25. Machiavelli, A Discourse on Remodeling the Government of Florence (1520), in Machiavelli Chief Works, vol. 1, 101.

26. Ibid., 102.

27. Ibid., 107.

28. Ibid., 108.

liberty.[29] Instead of satisfying their desire for social distinction through riches or power, the few should have an institutional space to attain glory and distinguish themselves in the service of the republic. Machiavelli also uses this same argument of satisfaction of desires through institutional means to push for the reopening of the Great Council in Florence.

In his *A Discourse on Remodeling the Government of Florence* Machiavelli argues that a constitution that does not satisfy the people after they have already experienced the exercise of political power would be certainly short-lived.[30] "Without satisfying the generality of the citizens, to set up a stable government is always impossible."[31] But even if Machiavelli is certainly sponsoring republican institutions and the reopening of the Great Council, his main argument is not that the council of the people should be the *only* institution, but that it should be restored because the common citizens also needed to be satisfied as well as the elites. Machiavelli's proposal for Florence envisioned, on the one hand, a consolidation of the executive councils into the Council of Sixty-Five[32] from which the gonfalonier of justice would be selected, and the legislative councils into the Council of Two Hundred (of the Selected), and on the other, a reempowerment of the popolo with the reestablishment of the Great Council and the creation of a surveillance office: the Council of Provosts.

In terms of its membership, the Great Council should be considered a plebeian institution. While only guild members were eligible for the executive and legislative councils, and 80 percent of the members selected to serve were taken from the major guilds, which represented the richest merchants and artisans,[33] the membership of the Grand Council was broader, given the establishment of the *beneficio dei tre maggiori*, which allowed officeholders of the three major offices and their descendants to serve. This meant that about a quarter of its members were drawn from either the Council of the People or the Council of the Commune,[34] and thus from plebeian ranks.

29. Ibid., 102–3.

30. Ibid., 101–2 and 106.

31. Ibid., 110.

32. The Council was divided in two groups, each governing in alternate years. The Council would be divided into groups that would carry on all executive functions, finance and trade, foreign and military affairs.

33. Guilded members eligible for these offices accounted for only one-third of the male adult population of Florence. See Najemy, "Guild Republicanism in Trecento Florence."

34. Rubinstein and Raillard, "Early Years of Florence's Grand Council," 102. See also Najemy, *A History of Florence*, 387–90.

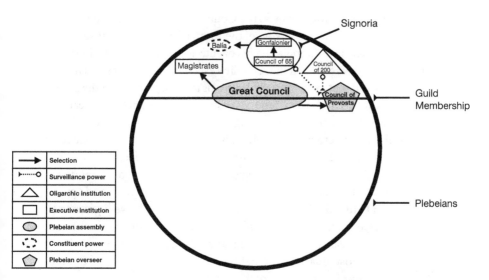

FIGURE 4.2. Simplified interpretation of Machiavelli's proposal to reform Florence.

It is clear from this constitutional proposal that Machiavelli, as a theorist of the republic as mixed constitution, aimed at giving an appropriate place in the constitution both to the elite, so to channel their desire to rule (analogous to the ancient Roman Senate or the English Parliament), and to plebeians by creating stronger popular institutions to effectively censure and control those who rule. Reaffirming this republican line of interpretation, in addition to reopening the council open to the many, Machiavelli proposes to add a Council of Provosts: a popular surveillance office aimed at providing a tiebreak vote in matters of discord within political institutions and, more importantly, to oversee government officials, taking away their power and appealing their decisions, in case they do things opposed to the common good.[35] The Council of Provosts, composed of sixteen gonfaloniers of the Company of the People, would take turns in supervising government action. This anti-oligarchic institution, whose members could not be part of the Council of Sixty-Five, was dedicated to controlling government officials and "mak[ing] them abstain from actions that are not good."[36] The provosts would take turns residing in the palace with the *signores* to be witnesses of their proceedings.

35. Machiavelli, *Discourse on Remodeling*, 112.
36. Ibid., 111–12.

According to John McCormick, the Council of Provosts should be understood as being an improved version of the Roman Tribunate because the provosts would function as "popular agents of elite accountability," serving as "the people's eyes and ears in both the republic's executive committee and its senatorial council and that explicitly wields veto or referral power over the policies proposed within them."[37] Even if the provosts' surveillance power is clear, their power to actually obstruct dominating motions coming from the few is far removed from the veto power wielded by the tribunes in Rome, since the provosts "would not have other authority than to delay a decision" by the executive council by appealing to the legislative council, and "could not do anything other than take a case away from the Council [of Selected] and appeal it to the Grand Council."[38] Despite the weak powers Machiavelli gives to the provosts, McCormick argues this office is radically democratic in the sense that it provides "invaluable political education" by allowing common citizens to "observe in close quarters the deliberations and decisions of the most powerful and prominent citizens of the republic."[39]

The recognition of the need for popular institutions strong enough to control the ruling elite also makes evident in Machiavelli the relativity of law and the need for popular constituent power as a necessary condition for attributing an emancipatory character to the rule of law. Because corruption, which is linked to oppression, begins both in individuals—when "a citizen is allowed to get more power than is safe"—and in laws—"the nerve and life of free institutions"[40]—liberty cannot be equated with the rule of law, because laws can be manipulated and used as tools for oppression. The rule of law is not necessarily conducive to liberty, and, because of unavoidable corruption, even an originally emancipatory rule of law would tend to uphold and sustain domination instead of combating it, thus legalizing domination, allowing for only the mere illusion of liberty. Neither should freedom be reduced to the lack of arbitrary rule[41] because, as Machiavelli argues, the reestablishment of freedom demands moments of arbitrariness—of suspension of the law—to reorganize power and regain liberty by bringing greater equality and introducing new methods, institutions, and laws into the constitution.[42] Consequently, the principle of liberty must not be reduced to law, which is just a *means* to keep individuals free from subjection. Without the people being effective guardians

37. McCormick, *Machiavellian Democracy*, 106.
38. Machiavelli, *Discourse on Remodeling*, 112.
39. McCormick, *Machiavellian Democracy*, 106.
40. Machiavelli, *Discourses*, I.33.
41. Skinner, *Liberty before Liberalism*.
42. Machiavelli, *Discourses*, I.18.

of liberty, a constitutional framework would inevitably become corrupt, "a naked oligarchy."[43]

As I showed in chapter 1, Machiavelli argues that the procedure of election and the individual right to speak in the assembly ended up allowing for the people to be manipulated into decreeing their own ruin. But despite the perverse outcome of these corruption-enabling methods, Machiavelli does not want to eliminate them but to create new ones so as to counteract their negative, unintended results. Consequently, as opposed to Rousseau, who entirely forsakes representation and deliberation in the sovereign assembly,[44] Machiavelli wants to keep equal access to election and *isegoria*, and complement it with new methods aimed at "enforcing" the foundation. He argues ordinary exercise of popular legal power is not enough, and that periodical extraordinary measures are needed to keep the oligarchic tendencies of the ruling class in check. In the next section I analyze the two extraordinary methods he proposes in the *Discourses* for the containment of corruption: (1) periodic revision and creation of fundamental laws and institutions, and (2) extraordinary popular punishment to remind elites of the founding fear in which plebeian liberty was gained through force.

Plebeian Constituent Power

Even if Machiavelli is a theorist of extraordinary politics, concerned primarily with the mutation of the constitutional order,[45] his work has not been seen as contributing to the theory of constituent power that developed within democratic thought.[46] The five-hundred-year anniversary of *The Prince* in the aftermath of the 2008 financial and political crisis, however, allowed for a renewed engagement with Machiavelli's work, from which emerged a radical democratic interpretation concerned with extraordinary politics.[47] Filippo Del Lucchese recently proposed to trace back to Machiavelli the genealogy of

43. McCormick, *Machiavellian Democracy*, 107.

44. Rousseau, *Social Contract*, II.1 and 3.

45. See Pedullà, *Machiavelli in Tumult*; Torres, "Tempo e politica."

46. Modern democratic theories of constituent power have been traced back to Marsilius of Padua in the early fourteenth century. For an analysis of the concept in the history of ideas, see Kalyvas, "Constituent Power."

47. Even if Negri was the first to propose reading Machiavelli through the theory of constituent power, his interpretation, heavily influenced by Spinoza, was not systematic but merely instrumental to his theory of insurgent democracy. For the latest radical democratic interpretations of Machiavelli, see the edited volume *The Radical Machiavelli*.

the concept of constituent power as a "living force within the social order,"[48] highlighting Machiavelli's theory of sociopolitical humors and the dialectic relation between laws and orders derived from it, as major contributions to the understanding of the conflictual nature of constituent power.[49] Even if Antonio Negri and Miguel Vatter had already analyzed Machiavelli's conception of constituent power,[50] Del Lucchese offers the first systematic reading of Machiavelli's thought on extraordinary politics. In what follows I argue that the attempt to read Machiavelli through a democratic theory lens, which begins from the premise of a community constituting itself, inevitably obscures the originality of Machiavelli's *republican* conception of constituent power, which is predicated on the socio-ontological split between the few and the many, which Vatter briefly analyzes from the perspective of a "modified, 'no-rule' republicanism."[51]

Through a critical analysis of Del Lucchese's interpretation of Machiavelli, in what follows I argue that the constituent power in Machiavelli is not a bridge between basic principles and politics, but rather the power to resist oppression by restraining oligarchic power. While in democratic theory the constituent power has been conceived as the *autopoietic* power of the community, a republican theory of constituent power would be defined functionally, determined by the goal of achieving liberty as nondomination. Republican thought conceives of constituent moments happening within an already constituted reality in which the community is never whole or in a vacuum, but existing in the perpetual struggle between the few and the many, and the legal reality attempting to stabilize it. The constituent power is the power to establish liberty, and thus, as Machiavelli argues, only the civil prince, allied with the people, is able to constitute a republic:[52]

48. Del Lucchese, "Machiavelli and Constituent Power," 9.

49. Ibid., 7. He also analyzes Machiavelli's theory of dictatorship, even if he recognizes the dictator was indeed a "commissarial" one within Carl Schmitt's categorization, and thus as Marco Geuna has convincingly argued, it should be conceived as an ordinary mode to deal with extraordinary circumstances, and not an office called on to impose social change. Geuna, "Extraordinary Accidents." Also, Del Lucchese argues that Machiavelli's theory of dictatorship and theory of humors and the relationship he establishes between laws and orders correspond to "three classic pillars of a theory of constituent power, namely its subject, its temporality and its will." I cannot refute this correspondence here, but I do not see any relation, to which Del Lucchese refers only loosely.

50. Negri, *Insurgencies*; Vatter, "Quarrel between Populism and Republicanism."

51. Vatter, "Quarrel between Populism and Republicanism," 244. For a discussion of the plebeian desire not to be dominated, see Vatter, *Between Form and Matter*.

52. Machiavelli, *The Prince*, ch. 9.

Though one alone is suited for organizing, the government organized is not going to last long if resting on the shoulders of only one; but it is indeed lasting when it is left to the care of many, and when its maintenance rests upon many.[53]

While in extraordinary moments the founder would exercise constituent power by establishing lasting foundations for liberty that can be maintained after the founder's death,[54] the many should be the bearers of the power to resist oppression during ordinary politics, able to add anti-oligarchic institutions to the constitutional structure in order to address inequality and the corruption of older institutions. The constituent power is the power used both to establish a constitutional framework that liberates plebeians from the domination of the nobles, and to maintain this emancipation. While democratic constituent power presupposes the community as the subject of constituent power, republican constituent power would not be defined by the political subject and its sovereign will, but by its final cause (i.e., establishing liberty as nondomination) and the fundamental premise of a society that is irremediably split between the few and the many. While the *one* exercises constituent power by establishing a republic with lasting foundations for liberty, the *many* need to exercise constituent power to preserve this liberty, by recreating the founding through amendments to the institutional structure and extraordinary public trials.[55]

Even though Del Lucchese recognizes the centrality of the division between "the people and the great" in Machiavelli, and duly criticizes the democratic theory of constituent power because of its focus on the "attribute of the will and the homogeneity of the constituent subject,"[56] his analysis of Machiavelli does not escape the democratic tradition and the unitary conception of the constituent power connected to the original founding moment of the community. This lens leads him to miss the role of constituent power in counteracting corruption. According to Del Lucchese, laws would be "ineffective and incapable of resisting corruption" because of the inadequacy of their enforcement, which is "anchored to the originary constituent situation."[57] Abstracting Machiavelli's ideas from the material conflict between the few and the many, he argues that corruption derives from a disconnect between the

53. Machiavelli, *Discourses*, I.9.

54. Ibid., I.11.

55. For a comparison between Machiavelli and Guicciardini on public trails, see McCormick, *Machiavellian Democracy*, ch. 5.

56. Del Lucchese, "Machiavelli and Constituent Power," 10.

57. Ibid., 19.

founding principles and political contingency—rather than corruption arising from the ambition of the great.

Even if he recognizes that for Machiavelli corruption is a systemic phenomenon, an "unavoidable mutation that all republics must endure," Del Lucchese argues corruption in Machiavelli expresses not the overreaching of oligarchic power but "a tension between laws and orders, or rather between constituent principles embodied in orders, and the juridical and political life of the republic, embodied in laws."[58] Therefore, the constituent power in Machiavelli would be a "bridge between the juridical and the political."[59] This abstraction from material conditions, and the projection of the dualism between constituent and constituted power onto Machiavelli's political philosophy seems misguided since in Machiavelli the fundamental "tension" is not between constituent principles embodied in orders and laws that arise conjuncturally, but between the desires and actions of the orders, which are legalized through political processes, and the effectiveness of basic institutions to counteract the natural tendency of the republic to drift into oligarchy.

The lack of engagement with the threat of oligarchy and the specific function of constituent power in a republic also leads Del Lucchese to inject into Machiavelli a pluralism that is not reflected in his political philosophy, which is predicated on the split between the few and the many. Despite acknowledging Machiavelli's plebeian partisanship, "in favour of the many, and against the few,"[60] Del Lucchese does not take this into account when analyzing Machiavelli's conception of constituent power. For him the "people" in Machiavelli is "irreducibly partial and partisan," but only a part "among many, a humour among other humours."[61] Even if this is accurate and the popolo is only one of the *umori*[62] in a republic, that the popolo is a partiality does not mean it is equal to other partialities, only one among many. Machiavelli is a plebeian thinker because for him plebeians—owing to their *exclusion* from political rule, "the condition that makes it possible for the plebs to act as a constituent power to make equal law"[63]—are the only legitimate guardians of liberty, and thus not simply a part among many.

Giving constituent power to the people is what radically defines Machiavelli's partisanship. It is clear that for him most of the "very great disturbances"

58. Ibid.

59. Ibid.

60. Ibid., 14.

61. Ibid., 12.

62. Machiavelli also recognizes the soldiers as being a third *humour. The Prince*, ch. 19. For an analysis, see Rahe, "Machiavelli and the Modern Tyrant."

63. Vatter, "Quarrel between Populism and Republicanism," 244.

in a republic are caused by the few, who fear to lose their position, not by the many, who hope to gain what they do not have; the rich need to secure their possessions by acquiring more in order to have greater resources to ignite rebellion and instill in the many the wish to possess and dominate.[64] Consequently, the few must not have the final say on the liberty of plebeians, because they will try to undermine it and effectively enslave them. The few, given the position of power they hold in society, could never be the bearers of constituent power. The regime the few would impose would not be a republic but an oligarchy.

Because for Machiavelli liberty is to not be dominated—a state that is gained through conflict and tumults—the preservative power of free government would be the power of the people to replicate this gaining of liberty, to redraw the boundaries of what is considered permissible and what is deemed oppressive. Only the many—who desire not to be oppressed and do not partake in ruling—should be the guardians of liberty. The constituent power belongs to plebeians "in so far as it maintains itself as that part which does not participate in rule" and thus is not something plebeians possess owing to their class per se; to resist oppression the many must not be in a position to dominate.[65] The case of the Ciompi revolt in 1378 and the betrayal of plebeian leadership should then be seen as a warning. The wool workers overthrew the government and installed a plebeian revolutionary regime under the leadership of Michele di Lando, a comber from humble origin, who Machiavelli depicts as "barefoot and wearing little clothing."[66] After becoming the standard-bearer of justice and *podestà*, di Lando "became a Thermidorian figure, clashing with the radical wing of the workers and thwarting their more egalitarian demands,"[67] and ultimately unleashing the slaughter of the Ciompi by reformist forces.[68] The plebeian origins of di Lando did not make him a plebeian partisan; it was his ruling position, in which he had the ability to dominate, that ended up determining his antiplebeian behavior.

According to Machiavelli, plebeians, given the position of no-rule they occupy in the political structure, should be not merely the guardians of the constitution or the founding principles, as it is today the judicial branch, but the defenders of liberty itself, which could even run against established law. Consequently, we should consider the many as the bearers of constituent power,

---

64. Machiavelli, *Discourses*, I.5.

65. Vatter, "Quarrel between Populism and Republicanism," 259.

66. Machiavelli, *Florentine Histories*, III.16. Winter, *Machiavelli and the Orders of Violence*, 170–78.

67. Winter, "Plebeian Politics," 742.

68. Najemy, *History of Florence*, 124–76.

the power to amend the basic institutional and juridical structure of society. During the normal functioning of free government only the many are the bearers of the self-emancipatory force wielded by the plebeians against oligarchic domination in Rome; only the common people are the rightful bearers of this "conflictual power that precedes, drives and exceeds constituted power, not moving beyond law, but rather occupying its centre and transforming its nature."[69]

The constitutionalization of plebeian ordinary and extraordinary powers would be for Machiavelli a necessary condition for keeping a republic free from domination. In a republic the common people need not only to actively participate in deciding on motions, initiating and vetoing laws in plebeian assemblies, and selecting their tribunes, but also to collectively offer fundamental changes to the constitutional structure and inflict punishment on those who have become too powerful, so to bring the republic back to its beginnings and keep plebeians free from the domination of the great. Machiavelli argues citizens must periodically "examine themselves" (*si riconoschino*) and go back to the beginning, to their mighty republican founding. This self-examination of the people vis-à-vis the legal and institutional order, which allows for the renewal of the republic, would happen either by an external "accident" or by an internal change triggered either by law or by the "striking words" and "vigorous actions" of a virtuous leader.

At the beginning of book 3 of the *Discourses*, Machiavelli identifies these two means—law and virtue—as the appropriate ones for a republic to periodically be brought back to its beginnings and remain free. There is nothing more necessary for a republic than to regain

> the reputation as it had in the beginning, and to strive that either good regulations or good men may produce this effect and that it will not need to be done by an external force.[70]

Since the birth of republics is marked by creation and punishment—institutionalization of popular power and foundational violence[71]—Machiavelli proposes a periodic renewal of the republic through law, triggering a periodic constituent moment, and an extraordinary public impeachment of those who have transgressed the egalitarian foundations of the republic.

Basing his observations in Rome, Machiavelli argues in favor of the reconciliation of law and liberty through the creation of new institutions such

69. Del Lucchese, "Machiavelli and Constituent Power," 7.

70. Machiavelli, *Discourses*, III.1.

71. Ibid.

as the "Tribunes of the People, the Censors, and all the other laws that opposed the ambition and pride of the citizens."[72] Machiavelli's response to corruption and oppression is thus not to get rid of institutions and procedures that have become corrupted but to add new institutions and legal means of popular censure to restrain the ambition of the few. However, he cautions that the mere establishment of anti-oligarchic institutions does not guarantee liberty since they would be ineffective if they were not "brought to life by the wisdom of a citizen who courageously strives to enforce them against the power of those who violate them."[73] Consequently, even if laws and institutions against corruption are established, the courage of extraordinary popular leaders to enforce them appears in Machiavelli as inescapable. Legal means without *virtù* would amount only to "parchment barriers" against oppression, as James Madison referred to the Bill of Rights of the US Constitution.[74]

In addition to institutional innovation to create new means of controlling the few backed by adequate enforcement, Machiavelli adamantly argues for extraordinary instances of punishment as necessary violence exerted against those who have violated liberty. The republic needs to deal harshly with those who have machinated against liberty such as the sons of Brutus, who conspired against the republic to "profit unlawfully,"[75] the Decimviri, who usurped political power and became tyrannical, and Melius the grain dealer, who sought to buy the favor of the masses by feeding the people at his own expense.[76] From his experience in the Florence of the Medici, Machiavelli identifies fear[77] as a crucial emotion that must be present both in the founding of liberty and in renewal moments. Therefore, going "back to the beginnings" is not only about reconciling law and liberty through the creation of new institutions, but also about instilling the same fear of punishment to those who "had done wrong" as it was experienced during the founding. Thus, Machiavelli conceives of this foundational power as essentially creative *and* avenging, as a constituent power able to create institutions and laws in favor of equality, and ruthlessly punish individuals profiting from the corrupted constituted order. This

72. Ibid.

73. Ibid.

74. Hamilton, Madison, and Jay, *Federalist Papers*, no. 48, 305.

75. "There is no more powerful remedy [against the troubles of a new republic], none more effective nor more certain nor more necessary, than to kill the sons of Brutus." *Discourses*, I.16.

76. Machiavelli, *Discourses*, III.1.

77. This constitutive fear is different from the fear of God that Numa, the second founder of Rome, had to establish in order for the citizens to obey the law. Civil religion and fear of the divine are part of the constituted order.

constituent power as extraordinary enforcement of liberty should be, according to Machiavelli, legally convoked with

> a lapse of not more than ten years, because, when that time has gone by, men change their habits and break the laws; and if something does not happen to bring the penalty back to their memories and renew fear in their minds, so many offenders quickly join together that they cannot be punished without danger.[78]

Because Machiavelli, as I have argued, wants to constitutionalize the evolutionary political institutions of Rome, he argues for normalizing these instances of constituent creation and punishment, so to avoid the overgrowth of inequality and the extreme violence necessary to check it. He proposes to imitate the Romans, who periodically established new institutions and laws in favor of liberty, and were "accustomed to punish large numbers of those who did wrong."[79] Therefore, a good republican constitution should codify these instances of constituent power to periodically examine and reconcile the legal framework with social reality through the creation of new methods of *adaptation* and *deterrence* to periodically curb corruption and the overgrowth of oligarchy. Only through the constitutionalization of periodic instances of constituent creative and avenging power can the republic remain free from domination.

In addition to this periodic reactivation of constituent power as creation and punishment through law, Machiavelli argues a periodic refounding is also possible through "the mere excellence of one man."[80] Citizens are able to recognize good leaders by their reputation, and nothing gets individuals greatest reputation than extraordinary political action. Machiavelli's new methods thus would work in synergy with elections and free speech, rules and procedures that are crucial for allowing extraordinary, virtuous leadership to arise:

> Men born in a republic should, then, follow this formula, and early in life strive to become prominent through some unusual action . . . either by proposing a law for the common benefit, or by bringing a charge against some powerful citizen as a transgressor of the laws.[81]

Excellent men are able to accomplish a renewal of the republic based only on their virtue, "without reliance on any law," by their extraordinary reputation and example that lead other good men "to imitate them."[82] For Machiavelli,

78. Machiavelli, *Discourses*, III.1.
79. Ibid., III.49.
80. Ibid., III.1.
81. Ibid., III.34.
82. Ibid., III.1.

elections—which imply the possibility of attaining glory through virtuous action, allowing for the moralizing authority of kingly power[83] to emerge in defense of liberty—and the equal access to political speech—the equal right to propose a law and speak in favor or against it in the assembly—are *necessary*, but not *sufficient* methods to maintain liberty over time. Adding new methods for adaptation and deterrence through periodic popular creation and punishment would make the republic incorruptible:

> If such instances of enforcement as I mentioned above, together with such individual examples, had appeared at least every ten years in that city, their necessary result would have been that Rome would never have become corrupt.[84]

83. From the obedience to the first good chief came "understanding of things honorable and good, as different from what is pernicious and evil." *Discourses*, I.2.

84. Ibid., III.1.

5

Condorcet on Primary Assemblies

NICOLAS DE CONDORCET was one of the most progressive and creative thinkers of the eighteenth century. He was a radical egalitarian who vigorously advocated for the abolition of slavery, citizenship rights for women, equal protection for homosexuals and sex workers, equal and free public education, and active political participation of the masses.[1] As a materialist political philosopher,[2] Condorcet was particularly adept at seeing the gap between formal rules and procedures, and the actual exercise of rights and their consequences in society.

Living in a moment of intense revolutionary activity, in which the old corporate structures of the ancien régime, already hollowed out by incipient capitalist markets and secularism, were crumbling, Condorcet sought to play an active role in the making of new "enlightened" institutions. Based on his own experience as a legislator as well as the radical change coming out of the Paris Commune and the storming of the Tuileries, he came to comprehend that equal liberty needed strong popular institutions to properly channel protest coming from the masses and to limit the domination coming from representative government. His constitutional project was therefore designed to protect the republic against what he identified as a new form of domination: "indirect despotism," a regime in which there is a procedurally sound representative government, but in which representation is "neither equal nor real,"[3] a de

---

1. Popkin, "Condorcet, Abolitionist."

2. Condorcet followed Claude Adrien Helvétius's material philosophy, which proclaimed the radical equality of human beings and the development of their faculties through physical sensation and experience. He rejected however the principle of self-interest that seemed to underlie Helvétius's utilitarianism. For a discussion between Condorcet and Turgot on Helvétius, see Baker, *Condorcet*, 215–18. For an analysis on Helvétius's influence on Condorcet, see Carson, *Measure of Merit*, 32–36.

3. Condorcet, "On Despotism," in *Condorcet: Political Writings*, 164. Urbinati interprets indirect despotism as a "degenerated form of representative government." *Representative Democracy*, 189.

facto oligarchy within the bounds of the rule of law. Given our own ongoing "crisis of democracy," in which there is a general sensation that "the game is rigged" even if the rules are generally being followed, revisiting Condorcet's constitutional theory, which he constructed against the threat of de facto oligarchy concealed through proceduralism, appears as timely as ever.

Even if his contributions to the application of probability theory to voting have been sufficiently acknowledged,[4] his insights as a political philosopher have "been judged from the point of view of defeat"[5] and therefore have mostly gone unappreciated and understudied.[6] Raised as part of the nobility but advocating for equality, the Marquis de Condorcet was a class traitor, an aristocrat who betrayed his class interest and embraced democracy. Because he was a nobleman of letters, and thus part of the intellectual structure of the monarchical regime,[7] the Jacobins saw him with suspicion, as a "timid conspirator," despite his radical egalitarian agenda.[8] And even the most liberal part of the bourgeoisie, the Girondins, did not trust him, seeing him "as a weak reed at best, and as a tool of the Jacobins at worst."[9] As a result, Condorcet's

---

4. Condorcet's voting scheme was tried out in Geneva. Even if it was not successful, his theory of voting was influential. See, for example, the influence of Condorcet's jury theorem on James Madison in Schofield, *Architects of Political Change*, ch. 4. I do not engage with Condorcet's jury theorem because it applies only to approximations to truth: if the number of people deciding is large enough, their "guessing" of what is true is more likely to be true. This works in a jury trial, where individuals have to decide if a crime was committed or not based on the evidence provided. There is a truth to be "discovered." As Arendt argues, politics is about not truth but opinion. Political judgment does not lead to truth, but primarily to our collective assessment of what is just or unjust. The jury theorem, even if it claims that more people deciding makes it more likely for truth to be reached (or for "better" decisions based on some truth), does not adequately apply to political judgement. This is why Condorcet does not even mention it in his constitutional writings since he reserves it for truth-seeking (not political) decisions.

5. For example, Condorcet is analyzed in *The Critical Dictionary of the French Revolution* edited by François Furet and Mona Ozouf from the point of view of his failure to set the agenda for the revolution. This is also highlighted by Urbinati in *Representative Democracy*, 179.

6. There are only a handful of books and articles in English and French that touch on the constitutional question, but none dedicated exclusively to it.

7. Member of the Académie Française and permanent *secrétaire* of the Académie Royale des Sciences.

8. Robespierre, *Moniteur*, May 8, 1794. Cited in Schapiro, *Condorcet and the Rise of Liberalism*, 97. The Jacobins were a left-wing group that had its stronghold of support in the Paris Commune, and took over government in 1793, initiating the Terror.

9. Schapiro, *Condorcet and the Rise of Liberalism*, 96.

1793 constitutional proposal was first discarded by the Jacobins and then disavowed by the Girondins and has remained largely dormant since then.[10]

As the only philosophe who was an active participant in the French Revolution, Condorcet's ideas on how to harness the revolutionary spirit against systemic corruption from the point of view of praxis are of special interest. As a journalist and political pamphleteer, Condorcet followed closely the proceedings of the newly elected French constituent assembly (1789–91). In 1790 he became a member of the municipal council in Paris while keeping up "a deluge of criticism and advice to the Assembly."[11] After the 1791 constitution was unveiled, he strongly criticized it for establishing property qualifications for suffrage and holding public office.[12] In October 1791 he was elected to the Legislative Assembly, of which he served as president. His most important achievement (even if tabled) was to introduce a report on public education that recommended the establishment of equal, secular, and free public education from elementary school to college.[13] Given his legislative track record and his furious defense of equality in the press, Condorcet gained the reputation of being "a champion of the people, without being tainted by violent demagoguery," which made him become elected in 1792 to the National Convention, and then appointed to preside over the commission that would draft the new republican constitution.[14]

The constitutional proposal that came out of that commission established a "popular branch" composed of local primary assemblies with the power to elect, censor, and reconstitute the republic. The project was endorsed by the Girondins, which were the majority in the commission, presented by Condorcet to the convention in February, but only discussed for about a month in mid-April 1793. Le Girondine, as the constitutional project is commonly known, was bitterly opposed by the Jacobins, who saw in Condorcet's proposal for establishing a system of primary assemblies a scheme devised to bolster conservative strongholds in the provinces and dilute the power of the Paris Commune.

Seeing their material power under threat by this radically democratic, decentralizing proposal coming out of a Girondin-dominated commission, in June the Jacobins expelled the Girondins by force, took over the convention,

10. Analyses of Condorcet's constitutional proposal remain partial and scarce. An exception is Rosenkranz, "Condorcet and the Constitution."

11. Schapiro, *Condorcet and the Rise of Liberalism*, 85.

12. Condorcet, *Adresse à l'Assemblée Nationale, sur les conditions d'éligibilité.*

13. Condorcet, *Cinco memorias sobre la instrucción pública y otros escritos.* His report is considered part of the canon in the history of education.

14. Robespierre lost the election. Schapiro, *Condorcet and the Rise of Liberalism*, 95.

and approved (but never implemented) a mutilated version of *Le Girondine* that, although it instituted primary assemblies, limited their capacity for opposition and binding decision-making power and did not include procedures or ways to enforce the popular will.[15] It also did not include the right to education, which was for Condorcet a necessary condition for the proper exercise of sovereign power in these assemblies. If implemented by the Jacobins, the primary assemblies would likely end up having a toothless "advisory" role with no incentive for commoners to participate, and no procedural or material educational support for them to exercise political judgment. During the referendum on the new constitution Condorcet published a pamphlet condemning the project and urging citizens to vote against it.[16] The Jacobins denounced this as a seditious act, and the convention decided to arrest him on treason charges in early July. After escaping arrest for eight months, Condorcet was finally apprehended and died in a prison cell while awaiting to be guillotined.[17] The revolutionary experience, unable to produce a stabilizing constitutional framework, would end five years later in the coup d'état of 18 Brumaire and the return of kingly power to France.

In what follows I seek to recuperate Condorcet's neglected wisdom during this revolutionary period in which old structures were being destroyed and there was no suitable blueprint for a postrevolutionary future. I engage first with Condorcet's critique of separation of powers and the American Constitution and then analyze his constitutional plan, focusing on his proposal to institutionalize the popular protest power that arose with the revolution. I argue we should understand Condorcet's proposal as a mixed constitution that institutionalizes the power of the many within the framework of the modern state. His proposed popular institution does not share in government—as a branch alongside the executive, legislative, and judiciary branches—but is conceived as censorial, as exerting control over government through political judgment. Because "nothing could be easier than to devise forms which would

15. Primary assemblies had only a forty-day window to protest a law. Within this period, at least one-tenth of all primary assemblies in the country would have to protest for the law to be vetoed (art. 59). If there is protest, the legislative body calls together all primary assemblies to decide on the matter (art. 60). However, there is no article dedicated to procedures or enforcing decisions made by primary assemblies, so the power could be interpreted as nonbinding.

16. Condorcet, *Aux citoyens français: Sur la nouvelle constitution*, https://archive.org/details /auxcitoyensfrancoocond/mode/2up.

17. When he was arrested, Condorcet was in a precarious health condition. He was found "half-starved, footsore, with a copy of Horace in his pocket." Schapiro, *Condorcet and the Rise of Liberalism*, 106.

create and then preserve bad laws,"[18] representative constitutions need a non-ruling power able to periodically judge—from outside of government—law and policy. The constitutionalization of this no-rule, protest power appears for Condorcet as the only reasonable guarantee against systemic corruption and slow-moving, relentless oligarchic domination.

The Modern Mixed Constitution

While the first to write on a mixed constitution in which the people had the final say on law, policy, and punishment was Machiavelli, who sketched a plebeian republic in which good laws are the result of the conflict between the few and the many, Condorcet was the first one to write a full-fledged plebeian framework constitutionalizing the power of the many and giving them constituent power. Building on old participatory structures, his 1793 constitutional plan for the French republic seeks to reform and entrench the village assemblies that were convened for the elections of the Estates-General,[19] and the self-governing experience of the communes to establish a "popular branch": a decentralized network of radically inclusive local assemblies with the power not only to elect officials but also to initiate and veto legislation, and exercise periodic constituent power.

As a republican thinker, Condorcet's main concern was to prevent systemic corruption, the process in which "slow and secret abuses" take hold of institutions, allowing for the few to control representative government.[20] Even if for him "the true perfection of man" was certainly a central duty of society,[21] his constitutional project was not so much aimed at the "enactment of political autonomy" but, rather, based on a "negative" conception of political liberty, at enabling *resistance* against tyranny.[22] Following Machiavelli, for whom

18. Condorcet, *Letters from a Freeman of New Haven to a Citizen of Virginia on the Futility of Dividing the Legislative Power among Several Bodies (1787)*, letter 3, in *Condorcet: Foundations of Social Choice and Political Theory*, 316.

19. Communal gatherings for putting together *cahiers de doléances*. After the electoral statute was promulgated, local assemblies were convoked to elect delegates and put together a list of grievances. See Jones, *Peasantry in the French Revolution*, 62–64; Crook, "Persistence of the Ancien Régime." For the importance of popular reunions and committees at this time, see Dalotel, Faure, and Freiermuth, *Aux origins de la Commune*; Dautry and Scheler, *Le Comité Central Républicain*; Johnson, *Paradise of Association*; Ross, *Emergence of Social Space*.

20. Condorcet, "A Survey of the Principles Underlying the Draft Constitution," in *Condorcet: Foundations of Social Choice and Political Theory*, 221.

21. Condorcet, "Sketch for a Historical Picture of the Progress of the Human Mind," in *Condorcet: Political Writings*, 126.

22. Urbinati, *Representative Democracy*, 188.

corruption is enabled by the methods of selection and decision making,[23] Condorcet criticizes Montesquieu's doctrine of separation of powers and its proceduralism[24] and rejects the constitutional framework put in place in America, based on this doctrine, as not sufficient for controlling corruption and guaranteeing liberty.[25]

In Montesquieu's constitutional model, liberty is an individual "tranquility of spirit" based on the absence of fear and the sense of security that result from good procedures that presuppose a division of functions and a balance of power.[26] For Condorcet, this separation of powers does not provide an adequate mechanism for maintaining liberty because it "only tend[s] to separate and complicate individual interests."[27] Condorcet argues that seeing the executive, legislative, and judicial powers as independent forces that, by seeking their own interest, balance and regulate one another against the encroachment of liberty denies the possibility of domination happening despite this formal division of government functions:[28]

What becomes of public freedom if, instead of counterbalancing one another, these powers unite to attack it?[29]

James Madison, too zealous against the tyranny of the majority and too confident on public opinion and electoral procedures, did not provide the constitutional structure with any recourse against oligarchy and the corruption of foundational institutions, except for a constituent process requiring supermajorities and excluding the direct participation of the people.[30] He saw separation of powers as an "auxiliary precaution" to prevent corruption and the negative effects of factions,[31] which together with a free press would protect the republic from vicious political leaders.

---

23. Machiavelli, *Discourses*, I.18.

24. Condorcet, *A Commentary and Review of Montesquieu's "Spirit of Laws,"* https://oll .libertyfund.org/titles/tracy-a-commentary-and-review-of-montesquieus-spirit-of-laws.

25. Shortly after the draft of the Federal Constitution, Condorcet published his *supplément*, in which he criticized it. John Adams responded to this criticism in "Defence of the Constitutions of America."

26. Montesquieu, *Spirit of the Laws*, II.11, 6.

27. Condorcet, *Commentary and Review of Montesquieu's "Spirit of Laws,"* "Letter I: Letter of Helvetius to President Montesquieu."

28. For a discussion on the difference between separation of powers and functions, see Pasquino, "Machiavelli and Aristotle."

29. Condorcet, "Survey of the Principles," 199.

30. US Constitution, art. V.

31. Hamilton, Madison, and Jay, *Federalist Papers*, no. 10.

According to Condorcet's account of the principles that should undergird republican institutions—"equality, economy, and simplicity"[32]—the new American constitution, which chose "identity of interests rather than equality of rights" as organizing principle,[33] and which enshrined the separation of powers as the best design to keep the republic uncorrupted, would stray too far from the republican tradition and thus was unlikely to serve as a real bulwark for liberty. While embracing interest over equality of rights would increase rather than ameliorate "artificial" inequalities and the forms of domination they reproduce,[34] Condorcet criticized the system of separation of powers because it "disfigured" the simplicity of constitutions. Not only would separation of functions be unsuccessful in keeping corruption at bay, but it also would allow for its concealment and reproduction:

> Experience everywhere has proved that these complicated machines destroyed themselves, or that another system emerges alongside the legal one, based on intrigue, corruption and indifference; that, in a sense, there are two constitutions, one legal and public but existing only in the law books, and the other secret but real, resulting from a tacit agreement between the established powers.[35]

Separation of powers thus not only is an inadequate framework to keep corruption in check but also would serve to obscure the actual domination being exerted "off the books" through the actual collusion of representative institutions against equal liberty. Without a popular censorial power making sure elites are not self-serving, the American Constitution put "the fate of the State dependent on the degree of stubbornness or corruption in each branch":[36]

> When the people of a nation are reduced to fearing the errors, passions or corruption of their own representatives, they have to entrust other men, chosen just as much by chance, with the authority to prevent these representatives from abusing their power. The nation's fate is not therefore in the

---

32. Condorcet, "The Theory of Voting," in *Condorcet: Foundations of Social Choice and Political Theory*, 210.

33. Condorcet, "Lettre d'un Théologien," cited in Constance Rowe, "The Present-Day Relevance of Condorcet," in *Condorcet Studies*, 21.

34. Rowe, "Present-Day Relevance of Condorcet," 30.

35. Condorcet, "Survey of the Principles," 199.

36. Condorcet, "Letters from a Freeman of New Haven," letter 3, in *Condorcet: Foundations of Social Choice and Political Theory*, 322. For further analysis of Condorcet's critique of the American Constitution, see Mintz, "Condorcet's Reconsideration of America."

hands of the reason, virtue and identity of interest of its citizens and their representatives. On the contrary, it is prey to the balance of opposing passions, of conflicting interests and clashing prejudices. In both administration and legislation, we must try to find a way of binding men to their duties when it is only chance, masquerading as free choice, which has endowed them with power in the first place.[37]

For Condorcet representative government without a proper surveillance power censoring it is equivalent to trading one form of despotism for another, "suffering under several types of oppression rather than fearing just one."[38] And even if not all those in power have oligarchic tendencies or are inept at protecting the interest of the people against them, having a few good leaders does not guarantee the dismantling of structures of domination. Condorcet learned through his experience in politics that reasonable arguments and truth are unlikely to carry the day, and thus the fate of the system cannot be placed on representative institutions:

> Indeed, the major defect of all known assemblies is not that they lack talented men and virtuous citizens, but that they are full of stupid and corrupt men.[39]

From a critical engagement with the American constitutional model, especially the Constitution of Pennsylvania, which instituted a checking power in the Council of Censors in its article 47, and Turgot's plan of local assemblies,[40] Condorcet proposed a republican organization of political power aimed at addressing the inevitable erosion of law and its democratic foundations. As an alternative to the liberal constitution established in the United States, Condorcet proposed a mixed constitutional framework in which the ruling power of making laws and decisions about administration and foreign affairs would

---

37. Condorcet, "On the Form of Election," in *Condorcet: Foundations of Social Choice and Political Theory*, 169.

38. Ibid., 169.

39. Ibid., 178. He had so little faith on the virtue of candidates that he designed his electoral system to "ensure that the plurality of the votes will always be obtained by men who have a perhaps mediocre, but sufficient, amount of the qualities necessary to fulfill the functions entrusted to them" (169).

40. Anne-Robert-Jacques Turgot, *Mémoire sur les Municipalités* (1775), https://www .institutcoppet.org/oeuvres-de-turgot-188-memoire-sur-les-municipalites/. Among the many departures Condorcet took from Turgot's plan was the latter's endorsement of property as a requirement for active citizenship.

be concentrated in a government that would be constitutionally bound to obey decisions reached in local assemblies. By giving the administration of the states to representatives, he made "the sovereign [the people in assemblies] unencumbered and thus the best candidate to be the judge of government and its agents."[41] As opposed to Madison's theory of factions, in which ambition counters ambition and the most effective way to counter the pernicious effects of factions is to multiply them,[42] Condorcet proposes a government composed of different bodies (administrative, executive, legislative) that are not designed to check each other but to fulfill a particular role at different levels of government, and an external popular power to check corruption and push back against oligarchic domination.[43] While the American constitutional structure gave citizens the *individual* right "to petition the Government for a redress of grievances"[44] without providing any enforcement mechanism to see that petitions are taken into proper account in governmental action, Condorcet's popular branch would constitute an *institutionalized* popular power aimed both at electing the members of government and at censoring their decisions. Rather than embracing the idealist position of trusting elite self-policing, Condorcet follows a material approach to the constitution and gives the censoring power to popular primary assemblies, which are conceived as the institutionalized form of collective protest power.

Spontaneous assemblies appear as constitutive to a free society born out of revolution, and they are the central pivot of Condorcet's constitutional plan to stabilize the thrust of the French Revolution and preserve its recently gained but fragile liberty.[45] Given that he recognized that such a decentralized institution of decision making would not be able to enforce its own decisions against the centralized power of government, Condorcet saw the need for another institution dedicated to oversee that the law was properly applied and enforced: a council of national overseers selected by the people. In the following sections I first analyze the system of primary assemblies, then focus on the procedures to initiate a constituent process, and finally examine the Council of Overseers from a plebeian point of view.

41. Urbinati, *Representative Democracy*, 217.

42. Hamilton, Madison, and Jay, *Federalist Papers*, no. 10, 78.

43. Condorcet also proposed an independent public treasury able to contain "the greed or ambition of the leaders of the government." "Survey of the Principles," 207.

44. US Constitution, First Amendment.

45. Counterrevolution was at its highest. See Mayer, *Furies*.

Constitutionalizing the Revolutionary Spirit:
Primary Assemblies

Condorcet was ahead of his time and was very aware that unveiling truth would make him a target of "ridicule."[46] He was one of the first to call out the absurdity of excluding women from active citizenship and of the legality of slavery. His materialist approach to law allowed him to understand the mechanism behind these exclusions and the justifications that are constructed based on the material conditions of dependency of women and slaves. For him the same way that men have negatively determined women's education and aptitudes by making "oppressive laws against them," establishing a "huge inequality among the sexes,"[47] and then sanction their incapacity for active citizenship, "we deprived the Negro of all his moral faculties and then declare him inferior to us, and consequently destined to carry our chains."[48] For Condorcet the causes of inequality are not individual faculties, but the social structures that condition human development. His project is therefore aimed at eliminating the man-made distortions of the natural equality of "being capable of reason and moral ideas," by establishing an egalitarian legal and institutional infrastructure in tune with the principle of equal rights coming out of the French Revolution:

> Our hopes for the future condition of the human race can be subsumed under three important heads: the abolition of inequality between nations; the progress of equality within a single people; and true perfection of man.[49]

Given Condorcet's radical egalitarian worldview and his material constitutional lens, the framework he proposes is aimed not at suppressing the revolutionary spirit and demobilizing the people by reserving political action for the enlightened few, but at creating the institutional structure necessary to harness the emancipatory nature of popular politics for the benefit of the republic. According to him, "grouping the citizens into primary assemblies is more a means of reconciling peace with freedom than a threat to public tranquility."[50] Because this foundational framework would need to accommodate his egalitarian position, Condorcet's model is a radically inclusive one

---

46. Condorcet, "Letters from a Freeman of New Haven," letter 2, 299.

47. Ibid., 297.

48. Condorcet, "Rules for the Society of the Friends of Negroes," in *Condorcet: Foundations of Social Choice and Political Theory*, 342.

49. Condorcet, "Sketch," 126.

50. Condorcet, "Survey of the Principles," 196.

in which the state has the duty to provide for basic welfare and education, and all adult residents participate in politics at the local level. These social, educational, and political guarantees would establish the minimal conditions for adequate human development.

In his constitutional proposal all males who were twenty-one years old and residents for more than a year could become active citizens,[51] even if to his mind there was no reason beyond social dependence to exclude women from education and active citizenship. Despite *Le Girondine* not giving the franchise to women, in terms of the degree of inclusiveness and participation, its proposal is quite radical since it argued not only for equal civil rights, but also for equal political rights, which were previously restricted to property-owning citizens in the 1791 constitution. Even if Condorcet considered legitimate the exclusion from the franchise based on a state of dependence in which an individual "no longer obeys his own will," he denied the legitimacy of social relations perpetuating dependence in society and denounced the 1791 legal framework not only as incapable of "destroying all vestiges of this dependence" but also as "helping to consecrate it in our new laws."[52] He found wealth requirements for voting and holding public office a baseless malice:

> We could be neither stupid nor contemptible enough to believe that rich men are less prone to vice and corruption than poor ones. The only justification for a condition of this kind would be the advantage of choosing men who had received a better education and who could therefore be assumed to be more enlightened. We would consequently have to require a fortune of some considerable size. Clearly, all conditions of this kind are either illusory or lead to oligarchy.[53]

The only requirement Condorcet endorses for the exercise of political rights, in addition to local residency, is a proper "theoretical education" enabling individuals to enjoy their rights, the very exercise of which forms part of a second, "political education."[54] Because without knowledge and the skills

51. *Le Girondine*, title II., art. 1.

52. Condorcet, "Survey of the Principles," 213. He also criticized youth discrimination and opposed the high age requirement to serve in office in the United States Constitution, which was set at thirty-five years for the president. For him this was not legitimate and would prevent great leaders—such as Scipio Africanus, who defeated Hannibal at age twenty-two—from coming to power. Billias, *American Constitutionalism Heard Round the World.*

53. Condorcet, "Survey of the Principles," 216.

54. Ibid., 215. This idea of political rights as inherently active, of the exercising of political judgment as a learning-by-doing process, would be later invoked by J. S. Mill as part of an ideal constitution in *Considerations on Representative Government* (1861).

to judge critically we do not have the capacity to recognize truth from false-ness, ignorance undermines the "genuine improvement of the human person," and therefore proper education must be a constitutional right, guaranteed by the state to every citizen:[55]

> Society thus has another duty—to provide all individuals with the means of acquiring the knowledge of their intelligence and the time they are able to spend on educating themselves put within their reach. The probable re-sult is that the scales will be weighted in favor of those who have more natural talent and those with private means, giving them freedom to spend longer on their studies; but if this kind of inequality does not subject any individual to another, and if it affords support for the weak without impos-ing a master on them, it is neither an evil nor an injustice; indeed, a love of equality that is afraid of swelling the ranks of the enlightened and adding to their knowledge would be a most sorry thing.[56]

The expansion of general instruction to all citizens was so crucial for Con-dorcet that a year before his constitutional proposal he presented to the French National Assembly a project to make education compulsory to men and women—a necessary condition for his participatory constitutional project. Because for Condorcet true political liberty entails being free from ignorance, having the necessary knowledge to enjoy our rights and be truly independent, compulsory instruction would be the "price for liberty."[57] This necessary learn-ing process takes place not only in classrooms but also in political assemblies where political knowledge is created and shared, and political judgment is exercised and perfected through decision making.

The radical inclusion of *Le Girondine* in terms of citizenship was coupled with a participatory institutional framework aimed at forming the general will of all assembled citizens to elect and check representative government. Pri-mary assemblies of between 450 and 900 citizens would be established by law in every district *alongside* representative government,[58] which means that the nascent French republic could have had about seven million active citizens organized in as many as sixteen thousand local assemblies[59] had *Le Girondine*

---

55. *Le Girondine*, "Déclaration des droits naturels, civils et politiques des hommes," art. 23, guarantees elementary education to all members of society.

56. Condorcet, *Cinco memorias sobre la instrucción pública y otros escritos*, "Primera memoria: Naturaleza y objeto de la instrucción pública," 85.

57. Ibid.

58. *Le Girondine*, title III, art 1.

59. Even though there is no accurate record of the percentage of the population of voting age, for a population of twenty million, roughly seven million are likely to have been males older

been established. This bottom-up process of will formation based on a multiplicity of times and spaces of sovereignty and deliberation[60] not only would be superior in terms of determining the general will, rather than having only district or national representatives,[61] but also would provide the opportunity for the political education of the people, which is necessary for the full enjoyment of their rights. Condorcet's material approach to the constitution directed him to build on already existing popular organizations as a springboard for radical change. His intention was to formalize the "partial, spontaneous protests and private voluntary gatherings" that arose with the revolution into primary popular assemblies, which "following legally established procedures, [would] carry out precisely determined functions."[62]

Condorcet is against allowing for private forms of protest to drive government action because it would be a source of inequality:

> Sporadic protests and the rebellions or movements which may result from them will have more influence if they occur in or near the town where the national powers are based.[63]

Because his constitutional framework was designed to "suit a people in the final stages of a revolution" by bringing order "without weakening the public spirit,"[64] he acknowledges these extralegal popular councils born out of the revolutionary experience as existing *outside* of the constituted order and in need of institutionalization.

Even if as a rationalist Condorcet was primarily concerned with good deliberation and decision making, I argue his primary assembly system is not democratic in the sense that his constitutional scheme does not give primary assemblies ruling power (*kratos*), but only the power to check government, as a reactive power responding to the (in)actions of the representative body. His constitutional proposal conceived of the power of lawmaking and passing administrative measures as a monopoly of the national representative assembly;[65]

than twenty-one.

60. Urbinati "Condorcet's Democratic Theory of Representative Government."

61. Condorcet, "On the Constitution and the Functions of Provincial Assemblies," in *Condorcet: Foundations of Social Choice and Political Theory*, 168.

62. Condorcet, "Survey of the Principles," 190.

63. Ibid., 197.

64. Ibid., 190.

65. Members to a unicameral representative assembly would be elected by primary assemblies in each department through a two-tiered system. I will not focus on this electoral function of the assemblies, but just briefly refer to it. To avoid corruption in the selection process, Condorcet proposed a voting system in which the citizens gathered in primary assemblies would

"all other authorities will be required simply to execute the laws and resolutions which this assembly produces."[66]

Besides giving primary assemblies the power of electing candidates for the national assembly, and thus the power to constitute government, Condorcet conceived of local assemblies as the site for the people's institutionalized form of appeal, a "legal means of protest which could cause any law to be re-examined."[67] This "right of censure" could be exercised by any citizen, who after collecting fifty supporting signatures, could request his primary assembly to review an existing law or consider proposing a new one.[68] These proposals would not be immediately debated in the assembly but first analyzed and refor-mulated to become what Condorcet calls a "simple proposition." Following Rousseau, Condorcet argues there should be no formal debate in primary as-semblies, but only a yes/no vote on questions that have "already been reduced to their simple component propositions":

> Let us call a proposition which may only be accepted or rejected, but not amended, a "simple proposition". It is on propositions like these that voters should be asked their opinion, and not on the reasons which make them accept or reject the various propositions. The analysis should stop there.[69]

However, despite his stance against structured deliberation and in favor of silent voting, Condorcet conceives of primary assemblies as permanent sites of deliberation, where "members can, of course, debate freely in the assembly rooms in between the proposal and resolution of a question, but these debates remain completely private."[70] Moreover, assemblies must be opened every Sunday to enable for citizens' deliberations.[71] By understanding politics as political judgment Condorcet positions assembled citizens and their

---

select candidates through two ballots: one "preparatory," in which a list of potential candidates is created, and a second, "final," ballot based on this list. The first preselection of candidates takes places in primary assemblies in which citizens put forward names of candidates—triple the number needed to fill the seats. Each assembly would send its list of candidates to the regional administration, which would make all the lists public and put together a definitive regional list with the candidates who obtained the most votes. This list is sent back to the primary assem-blies, in which the second, definitive vote is cast.

66. Condorcet, "Survey of the Principles," 199.

67. Ibid., 192.

68. Ibid., 197; *Le Girondine*, title VIII, art. 3, and title IX, arts. 5 and 6.

69. Condorcet, "On the Constitution," 161.

70. Condorcet, "Survey of the Principles," 196.

71. *Le Girondine*, title III, §V, art. 3.

"reasoned opinions" as the core site of sovereignty and legitimacy.[72] Primary assemblies, because of their capacity to aggregate particular knowledge and relate it to the general interest, would allow for a recursive relation between local and national politics and the truest expression of the general will.

To allow for primary assemblies to be self-governing, Condorcet proposed a council composed of one member for every fifty citizens registered in the primary assembly records (nine to eighteen members per assembly). In addition to keeping the voting roles up-to-date, convening the assembly in the cases determined by the constitution, and making the necessary demands to other assemblies or the regional government for the exercise of the people's right of petition and censure,[73] the council must also reduce citizen's petitions to simple propositions—the answer to these statements would allow an individual to "arrive at a true expression of his own opinion."[74] The council would be in charge of analyzing the subject and bringing all the necessary information to the assembly. This power to frame the discussion by analyzing that subject and reducing all the different opinions about it to a series of "basic propositions and their contradictories"[75] "must not be confused with giving any group of men, or even any individual, the right to suggest a subject for debate."[76] Condorcet does not give agenda-setting power to the council; its prerogative would be limited to bringing to the assembly the initiatives of citizens, presenting the "whole subject of debate and a table of all propositions in which they had to vote."[77] After being presented with a simple proposition, citizens would have eight days to deliberate on the matter and cast their vote during the next session.

Given his aversion to antiprogressive forces in society driven by "fear of innovation," what for him is "one of the most damaging scourges of the human race,"[78] Condorcet devised a constitutional plan in which legal, policy, and constituent change could originate at the neighborhood level, in any corner of the republic. Progressive reform could be put into motion organically, spreading through the network of assemblies at the district and regional levels. If a resolution passed in one assembly, this assembly would have the right convoke all other assemblies in the district to decide on the particular motion. If the majority of assemblies in the district agree to go forward with it,

---

72. Urbinati, "Condorcet's Democratic Theory of Representative Government."
73. *Le Girondine*, title I, art. 7.
74. Condorcet, "On the Constitution," 161.
75. Ibid., 159.
76. Ibid., 166.
77. Ibid., 166–67.
78. Condorcet, "Survey of the Principles," 200.

all assemblies at the regional level would decide on the matter. If they are also in agreement, then the national representative assembly must consider if the proposition is "worthy of examination." If the representative assembly agrees with the motion agreed on by a majority of primary assemblies at the regional level, it is then transformed into law. But if the will of the representative assembly (based on a simple majority of its members) contradicts that emanating from the primary assemblies in a region, all primary assemblies in the republic are called to decide on the question. If the majority of primary assemblies is in contradiction with the representative assembly, then the latter "would seem to have lost the nation's trust and must be replaced"[79] by new representatives who would carry out the general will. In this way, Condorcet builds into the lawmaking process an enforcement mechanism of the popular will. If the legislature deviates from the popular will and writes a law that does not track the people's will, it is recalled. Therefore, representatives have a strong incentive to track the will emanating from primary assemblies.

Even if the representative assembly is the ruling power, in charge of legislating and directing government, Condorcet gives the ultimate decision over any matter to primary assemblies, setting his project apart from those of elitist republicans such as James Harrington[80] and liberal republicans such as Thomas Paine.[81] In Condorcet's constitutional structure the assembled multitude has the power to oppose change and to generate it, autonomously, effectively setting the direction that government must follow. Moreover, in addition to the functions of electing representatives and repealing and initiating law through censorship procedures, Condorcet gives to primary assemblies the role of approving or rejecting drafts constitutions, as well as deciding whether to initiate a constituent process.

Proceduralizing Plebeian Constituent Power

By constitutionalizing nongovernmental political activity Condorcet's constitution sought to be more than a mere regulatory document like the American framework, which mostly contained detailed functions and limits to

79. Ibid., 197; *Le Girondine*, title VIII, arts. 22–26.

80. Even though Harrington proposed a popular assembly because without one the Senate "will not be honest," he restricted political rights to landowners and gave the "popular" assembly only ratifying power. *Political Works of James Harrington*, 772.

81. Even if Paine recognized the people as a whole has a right to abolish government and decide on the constitution, he did not conceive of a popular institution or gave any political power to citizens beyond electing representatives. *Rights of Man* (1792).

government. *Le Girondine* established also a creative institutional framework enabling the exercise of popular constituent power. In addition to the "protest power" of primary assemblies to censure government during normal politics, through binding motions for repealing and initiating legislation, Condorcet argued that for the republic to stay free and stable, the constitution needed to provide for procedures to periodically activate the constituent power. In the declaration of rights of his constitutional draft, echoing his friends Jefferson and Paine, he stated that "a generation has no right to subject its laws to future generations" and thus a people "always has the right to review, reform and change its Constitution."[82] The same as Machiavelli, for whom a periodic activation of constituent power is necessary to push back against oligarchy and protect liberty, for Condorcet the periodic revisiting of fundamental laws is also a necessary condition for the legal system to remain productive of liberty. Because no legal structure is immune to corruption, the constitution must provide for ways "to regulate the way in which a nation can establish a new constitution if citizens feel that the first poses a threat to their freedom."[83] Moreover, the appropriate procedures for activating the constituent power should take into account both the "profound indifference which often follows revolutions" and "the slow and secret abuses which eventually corrupt human institutions."[84]

Following the premise that even the "best organized constitution" will eventually become corrupted if it is not periodically reformed, Condorcet pushes for constitutionalizing the constituent power, for normalizing extraordinary politics through institutions and procedures:

> The only way to bring regular and lasting order to a society whose members have just retrieved their jealously guarded rights, and who fear that they may lose them once again, is for the citizens explicitly to adopt a constitution which contains an orderly means of correction and reform. This will also eliminate enthusiasm and exaggerated suspicion, partisan frenzy and the fear of factions, the faintheartedness which says that all disruption will destroy the State, and the fear which constantly sees tyranny in peace and order.[85]

Condorcet offers a model in which the initiation of the constituent process is not the monopoly of an institution or invoked through a single procedure.

---

82. *Le Girondine*, Déclaration des droits naturels, civils et politiques des homes, art. 33.
83. Condorcet, "Survey of the Principles," 221.
84. Ibid., 221.
85. Ibid., 225.

Le Girondine established three ways to activate the constituent process: (1) periodically through law (in intervals of twenty years), (2) by individual citizens through their primary assemblies, and (3) by the national legislature after approval of a majority of primary assemblies. Condorcet's multidimensional strategy to allow for the activation of the constituent power, which proceduralizes individual, institutional, and constitutional methods, is perhaps the most radical, comprehensive proposal ever written to integrate the constituent power into the constitutional structure.

In addition to mandating a constitutional convention to review and improve the constitution every twenty years, *Le Girondine* gave to every citizen the right "to lead the call for a Convention for the reform of the Constitution" through the same "forms and rules established for the exercise of the right of censorship."[86] With fifty signatures of its members, primary assemblies would be forced to vote on whether or not amending the constitution would be necessary and desirable. This guarantee for an individual prerogative to initiate a critique of the constitution would foster a dynamic constitutionalism in which change could be initiated at the local level through a capillary system[87] of political judgment. The question to initiate a constituent process would then spread organically through the network by triggering discussions and decisions one district at a time. If a majority of assemblies agrees, then the legislature would be required to call a national convention.[88] This extraordinary assembly would be composed of two members per region, elected in the same way as members of the legislature.[89] This would mean that each citizen would have to select and rank six candidates for the convention, which would have one year to complete a draft to send to the primary assemblies for ratification.[90]

If we take into account that for Condorcet the only requirements for citizenship are one year of residence and being twenty-one years old, giving the

---

86. *Le Girondine*, title IX, art. 5.

87. Foucault uses this concept to explain how power migrates from the margins of society to its center, transforming individuals in the process. "Prison Talk," in *Power/Knowledge*, 37–54.

88. *Le Girondine*, title IX, art. 6.

89. Each assembly would send its list of candidates to the regional administration, which would make all the lists public and put together a definitive regional list with the six candidates who obtained the most votes. This list is sent back to the primary assemblies, in which the second, definitive vote is cast. The results are sent again to the regional government and published. The two candidates with the majority of votes would be selected as members to the National Convention.

90. *Le Girondine*, title IX, art. 16.

right to initiate a constituent process to citizens is quite revolutionary in terms of its radical inclusiveness and the possible articulation of subaltern forms of political judgment this would allow for, as well as of its postnational implications. To be a resident is for Condorcet to be a citizen, and the exercise of political rights, including the right to amend the constitution, is done directly, at the local level, where references to the "national will" are connected not to the ethnic conception of the people developed under the nation-state, but to the decisions reached in a majority of primary assemblies. This majority decision is constructed locally, which allows for the integration of local contexts and conjunctures into the "national will." However, that this national will is constructed from the aggregate reasoned decisions taken in primary assemblies does not mean that Condorcet wants to "federalize the sovereign or particularize the law."[91] The people are a collective sovereign, and therefore individual citizens need to exercise their sovereign rights assembled, in a material and procedural space conducive to deliberation and decision making.[92] Generality is achieved only through a collective process of opinion formation that originates at the local level. Therefore, the people would operate not as a centralized system of command, but as a grid of political judgment in permanent flow. The *people as network* would be a subject with as many brains as assemblies, in which collective learning, reaction against domination, and social change would happen organically and independently from representative government and political parties.

The Council of Overseers as Plebeian Institution

According to Condorcet, under any system in which government legitimately makes law, the right to resist a law that is "clearly unjust," even if procedurally sound, must be confronted. For him, only the "direct majority of the people, limited only by the laws" can legitimately "judge whether this [legal] injustice is real" because the assembled people—not their representatives—are the "primary political power."[93] Only the people themselves, exercising their right to censure in their primary assemblies, are able to legitimately and properly judge if a law is unjust.

---

91. Urbinati, "Condorcet's Democratic Theory of Representative Government," 67.

92. For an analysis of Condorcet and political deliberation, see Urbinati, *Representative Democracy*, 197–205.

93. Condorcet, "Survey of the Principles," 204.

Because the probability of approximating the best judgment increases in proportion to the number of people deciding on an issue within appropriate rules of engagement,[94] decisions reached in a majority of primary assemblies would have the highest probability of being correct. It is within this argument—of popular sovereignty as a form of judgment passed on the injustice of law and the power to resist laws that enable domination—that Condorcet proposes a popular surveillance institution. This supervisory institution, "the council of national overseers," however, was not included in the final draft of *Le Girondine* and thus is not as detailed in terms of its procedures:[95]

> In the interest of uniform action and theory, the constitution needs to establish a council of national overseers in between the legislature and the citizens who must obey the law, and the public officials who must execute the laws or supervise the detailed application of general administrative measures. The council will supervise (*surveiller*) the observance and execution of the laws and arrange the details of general administrative measure, so that they can be applied. It will carry out the will of the nation (*volonté nationale*) and inform the people's representatives of anything which may require new resolutions to be made.[96]

Condorcet conceives this Council of Overseers as a liaison (*lien*) both between the citizens and the legislature, and between the legislature and the executive and administrative branches. According to Condorcet, such an office, "necessary for social order," is aimed at both *enforcement* and *surveillance*, at supervising that the will of the people "is carried out precisely, in an orderly and safe fashion."[97]

Even if Condorcet's Council of Overseers does not appear as a straightforward plebeian institution—defending the will of the people against the government of the few—but rather as an office that only claims allegiance to the law, I would argue that it should nevertheless be seen as a form of tribunician power akin to Machiavelli's Council of Provosts.[98] Following McCormick's interpretation through which plebeian institutions would provide not only

---

94. Condorcet, "An Essay on the Application of Probability Theory to Plurality Decision-Making" (1785), in *Condorcet: Foundations of Social Choice and Political Theory*, 131–38.

95. More research needs to be done on the reasons why this proposal was not included, and what Condorcet's original constitutional proposal before presumably being outvoted by the rest of the commission was.

96. Condorcet, "Survey of the Principles," 204–5.

97. Ibid., 204–5.

98. For an analysis of Machiavelli's proposal, see chapter 4.

protection against oligarchic power but also popular learning of the internal functioning of government, Condorcet's Council of Overseers is a "popular agent of elite accountability"[99] that observes and supervises elected representatives and therefore should be analyzed as part of the plebeian tradition of institutionalized tribunician power.[100]

To elaborate his popular surveillance office Condorcet's closest example was the powerful Council of Censors that his friend Benjamin Franklin had introduced in the 1776 Constitution of Pennsylvania. Article 47 established that the members of the council would be selected directly by the people and would have the duties to

> enquire whether the constitution has been preserved inviolate in every part; and whether the legislative and executive branches of government have performed their duty as guardians of the people. . . . For these purposes they shall have power to send for persons, papers, and records; they shall have authority to pass public censures, to order impeachments, and to recommend to the legislature the repealing such laws as appear to them to have been enacted contrary to the principles of the constitution.[101]

In addition to their power to subpoena and impeach, and the right to recommend the repeal of laws to the legislature, the council had the power to call a convention to amend the constitution.[102] Therefore, the censors not only would oversee that government is performing appropriately and recommend the repeal of corrupting laws but also would serve as a constituent board, calling a convention when the constitution needs an overhaul. While Condorcet agrees with Franklin that the duty of a censorial institution should be to oversee that representative government is acting in accordance with its duty, and that its members should be selected by the people, he disagrees on the prerogatives such a council should have. Condorcet gives the power to repeal and propose legislation as well as to initiate the constituent process to primary assemblies, and therefore his proposed censorial institution is narrower in

99. McCormick, *Machiavellian Democracy*, 106.

100. Even if Condorcet did not support the dual-authority model of the Roman republic because it led to constitutional crises, the censorial powers he gives to his Council of Overseers are decisively part of the tribunician tradition.

101. Constitution of Pennsylvania (1776), art. 47. The Council of Censors was in operation in Pennsylvania from 1776 to 1790 and was also adopted in Vermont from 1777 to 1869. For more information about the office, see Meader, "Council of Censors."

102. The calling of a convention required a supermajority of two-thirds. All other decisions were taken by simple majority. Constitution of Pennsylvania (1776), art. 47.

terms of the scope of its powers than the one established in Pennsylvania, but potentially more effective given its sharper focus on surveillance of representative government and closing the gap between law and its application.

Condorcet frames his Council of Overseers as an enforcer of the law, and its members as "agents of the legislature" and thus "subordinate to those with legislative power."[103] However, despite the subordination of the *members* of the council to the legislature—which "must be able to force council members to obey the law and to curb their deviations"[104]—the office itself is not the tool (*créature*) of the legislature but acts independent from it; its main task is to enforce the national will (*volonté nationale*), which emanates from primary assemblies. Moreover, members of the Council of Overseers would be elected not by the legislature but by the assembled people, since they are "officers of the people and not of the representatives."[105] Consequently, I argue Condorcet's surveillance council—selected by the people and aimed at enforcing the people's will by examining every law approved by the legislature and seeing that it is appropriately applied—should be analyzed as a plebeian institution of accountability.[106]

As a liaison between the people and the legislature, the council resembles the office of the Tribunate as an institution elected by the Plebeian Council that served as the link between plebeians and the seats of power, where law and its application were decided. The tribunes were the representatives of plebeians, and therefore acted as brokers between the ruling class and the common people as well as defenders of the people against the ruling class.

Even if from the point of view of primary assemblies Condorcet's Council of Overseers has a tribunician character, as an "agent of the legislature" (and

---

103. Condorcet, "Survey of the Principles," 206.

104. Ibid. The legislature has the right to impeach council members, but only a national jury, selected at random from the people, can decide "whether or not the accused should be dismissed from office."

105. Ibid.

106. Even if Condorcet criticized the dual-sovereignty model of Rome and chose the assembled people as the sovereign, given that assemblies without tribunes are weak, and decisions without enforcement are merely a wish, he designs a censorial office to enforce the people's will. There is still authority vested in government as well as actual power, but there is no "balance of power" between government and the plebeians. The assembled people—as opposed to the few holders of state power or the people as a whole—are the sovereign. This is the mark of plebeian constitutionalism. It is in this way that I interpret Condorcet's proposals as part of the plebeian tradition that presupposes the power of "the few"; if there were no such power, but government just implemented the common good, there would be no need for tribunes.

not of the people), overseers are conceived as an extension of the legislature: "the hand which enables the legislators to act and the eyes with which they can observe the execution of their decrees and the effects they produce."[107] In this manner, this popular censorial office is invested with the role to be the hands and eyes of the legislature in the execution of the law, and to force the executive to apply the law in a determined manner. Condorcet's council, as the agent of the legislature, could be conceived as a popular accountability office aimed at enforcing the law *against* the oligarchic tendencies of the executive organs. Seen from this perspective, the Council of Overseers is a popular anticorruption institution checking that oligarchic domination does not creep into the gap between formal rules and their material application.

To avoid the corruption of this plebeian council without undermining its strength, Condorcet proposes that half of the council should be renewed each year.[108] This high rotation would "prevent any habitual opinions or procedures being formed which would inhibit useful reforms and make everything a matter of routine."[109] In addition to preventing bureaucratic logics to become encrusted, high rotation of members would also work to avoid oligarchic takeover of the council and to provide for collective learning, not only of law but also of how the government operates.

The council acts not only as the eyes of the legislature in the process of execution of law, but also as the eyes of the people in the places of power. Like Machiavelli's provosts, who would reside in the palace to witness all proceedings, Condorcet's overseers would observe and analyze how the government implements the law. Moreover, his overseers seem more powerful than Machiavelli's provosts since they would not only observe, but also direct and enforce; as agents of the legislature they would have the institutional power to set limits and expectations for the executive branches in terms of the correct application of the law.

Seen from a plebeian perspective, Condorcet's Council of Overseers appears as a potentially strong popular accountability institution, playing the role of liaison between the people and government, and of enforcer of the people's will against the corrupting tendency of the few. While primary assemblies are conceived as sovereign organs of judgment that function as a check on representative government, the Council of Overseers is a delegate censorial institution that does not have a will of its own, but is tasked with making sure popular

---

107. Condorcet, "Survey of the Principles," 206.

108. The Council of Censors in Pennsylvania would be elected every seven years. Art. 47.

109. Condorcet, "Survey of the Principles," 205–6.

judgments get codified into law and are properly applied by the executive and administrative organs. Put together, Condorcet's "popular branch" composed of a network of primary assemblies and a surveillance council appear as a powerful counterpower to representative government, being able not only to prevent systemic corruption and the gradual decay of the republic into an indirect despotism, but also to allow for individual flourishing and social progress.

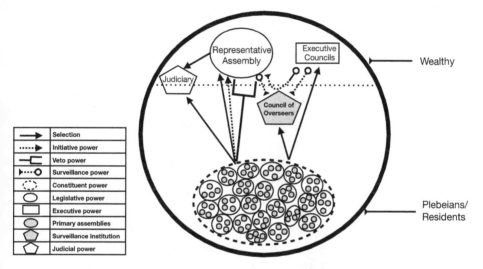

FIGURE 5.1. Simplified interpretation of Condorcet's constitutional proposal for France.

6

Luxemburg on Popular Emancipation

EVEN IF she was mislabeled as an idealist[1]—an ideological position she decried as working *against* proletarian emancipation—Rosa Luxemburg's thought is deeply materialist. From her assessment of the Social Democratic Party in Germany to revolutionary politics in Russia, she was able to unveil power relations and their trajectories, analyzing them from the impact they had on the material conditions of subordination of the working class. She comes early to the understanding that Marx and Engels's insight after the experience of the Paris Commune was correct: that the "working class cannot simply lay hold of the ready-made state machinery and wield it for its own purposes."[2] The socialist state needs to be constructed from the bottom up, apart and distinct from the bourgeois seats of power, through its own class-based, local organs of proletarian power. For Luxemburg, if the material conditions for exercising collective power do not exist, there is no possible path to socialism and thus no real freedom for the working class. To think otherwise is indeed to be clouded by "illusions" that lead to an untenable idealist position: the belief that socialism could be realized by decree.

Following Marx, for Luxemburg representative democracy is not a deficient political system, ineffective in properly channeling working-class priorities, but the political structure *of* the ruling class, and therefore unable to deliver socialism through legal reform.[3] Even if this realization made her deny the possibility of proletarian law within the capitalist system,

1. Norman Geras argues her thought has also been mischaracterized as determinism, fatalism, and spontaneism. *Legacy of Rosa Luxemburg*, 21.

2. Marx and Engels, "The Communist Manifesto," in *Marx-Engels Reader*, 470. Quoted in Luxemburg, "Our Program and the Political Situation," in *Rosa Luxemburg Reader*, 358.

3. Engels, "Socialism: Utopian and Scientific," in *Marx-Engels Reader*, 713.

something Evgeny Pashukanis would develop during the early years of the soviet regime in Russia,[4] her thought transcended critique as she focused on the conditions that were necessary for proletarian law to become a real possibility. The popular sectors needed to create their own revolutionary institutional infrastructure; without it, the path to socialism and proletarian law are foreclosed.

In this chapter I suggest that focusing on Luxemburg's critical assessment of legal reform and her proposal to incorporate councils as a foundational democratic institution could guide us in thinking about effective ways to counteract the increasing corruption and oligarchic domination developing within the contours of our constitutional democracies. In both her structural analysis of law and her endorsement of the council system she offers a materialist reading of politics that is refreshing, given the predominant nonmaterialist, abstract theory that the Left has tended to produce in the last four decades.[5] I approach Luxemburg's work through a constitutional theory lens and argue that her ideas on the futility of reform and the need to institutionalize working-class power to achieve social change are part of the plebeian materialist strand of constitutional thought that embraces conflict as productive of liberty, and sees the institutionalization of popular power as a necessary condition for emancipation.

Even if Luxemburg's primary concern was not with legal theory, a constitutional interpretation of her political philosophy gives another point of entry not only into her assessment of the revolutionary processes taking place in Russia and Germany in the first decades of the twentieth century, but also into the structure of political power she envisioned for the transition period in between the capitalist and socialist society. In what follows I first provide an analysis of Luxemburg's legal thought, and after laying out her arguments on the inadequacy of representative government to establish emancipatory, proletarian law, I focus on her support for worker's councils as the necessary material ground for a new legal system that would express a socialist instead of a capitalist society. The politics of collective power, organized and deliberative, appear through the lens of Luxemburg's thought as the only one able to guarantee emancipation, being able not only to break with the current legal expression of society but to create a new socialist one, based on the political activity of workers' councils.

4. Pashukanis, *General Theory.*
5. An example is the scholarship produced by the Frankfurt and Essex schools.

Legal Reform as Regulation of Exploitation

Luxemburg's critique in *Reform or Revolution* of Eduard Bernstein's revisionist theory of socialism gives an insight into her general critique of law, which she developed further in her final speeches, written in the aftermath of the German Revolution of 1918. She denounces not only revisionism as an opportunistic shift away from the socialist goal, but also its contribution to fostering the "illusions" and "self-deceptions" that undermine the power of the working class.[6] According to Luxemburg, revisionism "lifted the program of the socialist movement of its material base and tried to place it on an idealist base,"[7] in which the antagonism between capital and labor can be "adjusted" to attenuate exploitation by "bettering the situation of the workers and by the conservation of the middle classes."[8] This "regulation of capitalism" is certainly not the same as socialism,[9] which for her cannot emanate from the existing legality. "Socialism will not and cannot be created by decrees; nor can it be established by any government, however socialistic."[10]

According to Luxemburg, Bernstein is able to deliver this illusion of "socialism by decree" because his theory "abandons the materialist conception of history"[11] and pulls "details out of their living economic context. It treats them as *disjecta membra* (separate parts) of a lifeless machine."[12] By treating factors as separate from the structure instead of as organic links, as "indispensable gear in the mechanism of capitalist economy," Bernstein misinterprets them as "means of adaptation" able to suppress the internal contradictions of capitalism. Within revisionism the credit system, instead of a "means of destruction," is seen as a possibility for "patching up the sores of capitalism." In the same way, legal reforms, which appear as effective ways to achieve socialism from within the capitalist system, should be seen for what they really are: "surface modifications" to "reform capitalism" and forgo the socialist project.[13]

Luxemburg reminds us that legislative reform was from the beginning a bourgeois strategy, serving "to strengthen progressively the rising class till the

---

6. Luxemburg, "Our Program," in *Rosa Luxemburg Reader*, 367.

7. Luxemburg, *Reform or Revolution*, in *Essential Rosa Luxemburg*, 66.

8. Ibid., 69.

9. Similarly, the collapse of capitalism cannot be equated with socialism. For a discussion, see Geras, *Legacy of Rosa Luxemburg*, 32–42.

10. Luxemburg, "Our Program," 368.

11. Luxemburg, *Reform or Revolution*, 97.

12. Ibid., 70.

13. Ibid., 97 and 90.

latter was sufficiently strong to seize political power, to suppress the existing juridical system and to construct itself a new one."[14] The new political constitutions, born out of the bourgeois revolutions, legalized a type of class domination that "does not rest on 'acquired rights' but on *real economic relations*,"[15] and since there is no "single legal formula for the class domination of today,"[16] it is impossible to suppress it the "legislative way." While in the past, domination was expressed in "distinctly determined juridical relations" that were connected to feudal privilege, bourgeois liberalism codified equal liberty while keeping the material conditions for domination intact.[17] For Luxemburg the liberal rule of law is the "political expression of the life of a society that has already come into being,"[18] and therefore, emancipation from exploitation and domination existing within this framework cannot be achieved through the law.

For Luxemburg, labor legislation, a main goal of revisionist socialism, is a form of "social control" that is "enacted as much in the immediate interest of the capitalist class as in the interest of society in general."[19] As such, laws that are championed as socialist, as protecting workers, are "simply the regulation of exploitation."[20] But even if labor laws are not emancipatory—with much socialism as "a municipal ordinance regulating the cleaning of streets or the lighting of street lamps"[21]—this regulation of exploitation coming out of the "attempt to increase the share of the social wealth going to the working class" is as indispensable as it is marginal to the socialist cause.[22] In her analysis of the "industrial constitutionalism" promoted by revisionists in Germany, which incorporated trade unions and industrialists, she argued it is not a socialist type of constitutional project, but a mere regulation of labor relations. Even if born in the political action of the masses, the industrial constitutional project would develop a form of legality aimed at controlling labor without including

14. Ibid., 89.

15. Ibid., 90.

16. Ibid., 91.

17. Ibid.

18. Ibid., 89.

19. Ibid., 61.

20. Ibid. For an analysis of Lenin on labor law as regulation of exploitation, see Vergara, "Lenin and the Materialist Critique of Law."

21. Luxemburg, *Reform or Revolution*, 61.

22. She uses the image of Sisyphus, pushing a rock up the mountain. Luxemburg, *Reform or Revolution*, 83.

the "material standard of life as a permanent stage of well-being" as part of its core reasoning.[23]

Luxemburg's denial of the possibility of enacting proletarian, emancipatory law within the existing capitalist legality is predicated on her assessment of parliamentary government—as an elitist organ in which the interests of capital predominate—and of democratic proceduralism as a way of masking oligarchy. "In this society, the representative institutions, democratic in form, are in content the instruments of the interests of the ruling class."[24]

After the Social Democratic Party obtained a plurality in the German Parliament in 1912, and then decided to switch its position and vote in favor of the war, the "illusion of unity under the socialist banner" began to vanish. Luxemburg denounced her party not only as placating the bourgeoisie with the adoption of a "policy of compensation" and "diplomatic conciliation," but as supporting a "government representing the bourgeois counterrevolution."[25]

In a rather paradoxical move, at least from a democratic theory perspective, Luxemburg condemns the decision of the socialist government to convene a constituent national assembly. Her structural argument against setting up such a constituent body in Germany is based on the irreducible antagonism between capital and labor, the power of the few to oppress and the many to resist oppression. Because political institutions are forms of power that either reproduce capitalist society or oppose it, she condemns the decision by the government to convene a national constituent assembly because it would develop the power of the bourgeoisie (the selected few) and do nothing to advance the interest of the working class (the organized many). Luxemburg saw the National Assembly as an institution constitutive to bourgeois revolution, a symbol of the triumph of the new bourgeois social order over the feudal structure of power:

> The National Assembly is an outmoded legacy of bourgeois revolutions, an empty shell, a requisite from the time of petit-bourgeois illusions of a "united people" and of the "liberty, equality, fraternity" of the bourgeois State.[26]

According to Luxemburg, through the wielding of state power the revolutionary government was establishing a "bourgeois counter-weight to the

23. Luxemburg, "The Proletarian Woman," in *Rosa Luxemburg Reader*, 185.

24. Luxemburg, *Reform or Revolution*, 64.

25. Ibid., 68; Luxemburg, "Our Program," 367.

26. Luxemburg, "Die Nationalversammlung," https://www.marxists.org/deutsch/archiv/luxemburg/1918/11/natvers.htm.

workers' and soldiers' representatives,"[27] and thus rather than empowering the workers, it diverted "the revolution on to the track of a bourgeois revolution," which is not only unable to threaten the "capitalist class rule"[28] but also effectively works "against the proletariat and against socialism."[29] Instead of consolidating the power of working-class councils, giving constituent power to the masses, the government, following the bourgeois track of constitution making, established an institution for the selected few to decide on the rules for the new "socialist" society. This was for Luxemburg a counterrevolutionary act that was legitimized under a narrative of democracy and the fantasy of the people-as-a-whole:

> All the "people," the whole "nation" should be called to decide on the further destiny of the revolution by majority vote. This slogan is, for the open and disguised agents of the ruling classes, self-evident. We shall discuss neither *in* the national assembly nor *about* the national assembly with the guardians of the capitalists' safes.[30]

The belief that the leaders of the working class could negotiate in a bourgeois institution with the "guardians of capital" to legally suppress capitalism is for her a dangerous illusion. Proletarian law challenging the political and economic systems is impossible within the structure of representative government, which legislates to reproduce the system (for which it needs labor laws in order to *regulate* exploitation and prevent violence). Law coming out of workers' councils, on the other hand, would aim not at relatively empowering the many within the current structure, but at radically emancipating them from the domination of the few, a form of revolutionary reform that subverts the predominant structure of class domination. Different from the *minimal* program of social reform sponsored by Bernstein, the *maximal* program of the socialist society advocated by Luxemburg was aimed at the subversion of capitalism. Even if this subversion would be attempted through a new form of legality, its force would not be grounded on procedural legitimacy but on the power of the working class.

Because proletarian law can come out only from the councils, through class consciousness and the performance of emancipatory politics, the legal subversion of the system would be grounded on material conditions, backed up by the collective power of the organized masses. This is why, when proletarian

27. Luxemburg "The Socialization of Labor," in *Rosa Luxemburg Reader*, 344.
28. Ibid., 344.
29. Luxemburg, "Our Program," 367.
30. Luxemburg, "Die Nationalversammlung."

law finally arises out of the proletarian councils to challenge the economic system, and the capitalist class reacts, a civil war between the ruling forces and the organized masses would inevitably ensue. For Luxemburg a peaceful transition from capitalism to socialism is impossible, not because the working class would need to take governmental power by force (elections have already placed the SPD in a government coalition), but because of the violent response of the ruling class to proletarian, anticapitalist law. Barbarism thus comes from the counterrevolution, from the pushback of the ruling class to the radical social change initiated in the workers' councils.

Red Rosa—as her antagonists called her—did not advocate for violence; Luxemburg recognized the inevitability of bloodshed and the need to plan for it. For her, the ideal of a peaceful transition advocated by SPD leaders, "profound Marxists [who] have forgotten the ABCs of socialism," is another pernicious illusion that undermines the proletarian emancipatory movement:

> [They want] to spare themselves the revolution, the use of force, the civil war with all its horrors. Petit-bourgeois illusions! They imagine that the mightiest revolution since the beginning of mankind will develop in such a form that the various social classes will come together, engage in a pleasant, calm and "dignified" discussion with each other, and will afterwards hold a vote, perhaps even one with a famous "division". When the capitalist class sees that it is in the minority, it, as a well-disciplined parliamentary party, will declare with a sigh: There's nothing we can do! We see that we are outvoted. All right, we shall submit and hand over all our lands, factories, mines, all our fire-proof safes and our handsome profits to the workers.[31]

Given that oligarchs would never give up their wealth willingly and peacefully, proletarian authority is bound to be disavowed, and blood to be shed. Institutional popular power within a system in which the organized few run the state inevitably leads to competing authorities, an unsustainable dual-sovereignty model that ends in a constitutional crisis. It is in this moment when the power of deadly violence breaks through the constitutional scaffolding of rights and democratic institutions, negating the legitimate authority of the people to make anticapitalist law:

> These gentlemen Junkers and capitalists will remain quiet only so long as the revolutionary government is content to whitewash over capitalist wage relationships. They will be good only so long as the revolution is good, that is, long as the vital nerve, the artery of bourgeois class pile—capitalistic

31. Ibid.

private property, wage relationships, profit—are left undisturbed. If profit is called to account, if private property is to be done away with, then this is going too far. . . . Once the bourgeoisie is touched in the heart—and its heart beats from within a fire-proof safe—it will fight a life-and-death battle for its rule and will develop thousands of open and covert methods of resistance against the socialist measures.[32]

Given their class interests, ruling elites are bound to disregard legitimate popular authority, and the resulting constitutional crisis would then radicalize and accelerate the course of the revolution.

Democratic Rights and Workers' Councils

Luxemburg was a creative thinker who did not "profess" any particular ideological position other than the evidence she discovered from the historical materialist method she learned from Marx. Her prescient, sharp critique in 1904 of the "ultra-centralist" strategy pursued by Vladimir Lenin, which she further developed in her 1918 analysis of the Russian Revolution, was unpopular and relegated her to the margins of socialist thought.[33] She accused Lenin's revolutionary party of strengthening "the conservatism that springs inevitably" from social democratic parties, which tend to defend what they have gained against "further innovation at a greater scale."[34] She saw in Lenin's centralism not the creative, constituent energy of the masses, but the "sterile spirit of the night-watchman state."[35] She argued that the party's attempt to control the movement, to "oversee" the revolution instead of fostering it, would end up stifling it. According to Luxemburg, Lenin's aim at controlling the party was concerned "with *narrowing* and not with *broadening*, with *tying the movement up* and not with *drawing it together*."[36]

Fourteen years later, in her analysis of the Russian Revolution, she denounced the progression of the centralist strategy and the "cool contempt" the revolutionary government had for democratic rights such as suffrage and freedom of the press and assemblage.[37] Luxemburg argued that it was necessary

---

32. Ibid.

33. Already in the 1925 Comintern her political ideas were being demonized as part of the "Bolchevization" of socialism. Nettl, *Rosa Luxemburg*, 533, 800–801, 805–6; Geras, *Legacy of Rosa Luxemburg*, 28–29.

34. Luxemburg, "The Mass Strike," in *The Rosa Luxemburg Reader*, 255.

35. Ibid., 256.

36. Use of italics in the original. Ibid., 256.

37. Luxemburg, "The Beginning," in *Rosa Luxemburg Reader*, 294.

for these rights not only to be formally respected, but also to be backed by material conditions and exercised through political action. Her analysis of these democratic rights was informed not by liberalism,[38] but by the conclusion she drew from her critical approach to women's political rights: that formal equal rights "conform quite harmoniously with the bourgeois state."[39]

Women's political rights, because they do not "encroach upon the domination of capital," do not bring the emancipation of women from the exploitation of domestic labor or overturn the state.[40] This coexistence of formal rights and domination in the case of women came to reinforce what she had learned from Marx's analysis of individual rights: not only that formal rights are an inherently partial form of freedom but also that they contribute to the endurance of relations of domination that are presupposed even if legally abolished.[41] For rights to be emancipatory they need to be grounded on material conditions and relations of power. The same way that giving the right to vote to women does not bring their emancipation from domestic domination, giving formal political rights to the masses without actual collective political activity not only would not contribute to the emancipation of the proletariat from the capitalist state but would allow for the endurance of relations of domination while giving the appearance of liberty.

Political activity is for Luxemburg crucial for developing class consciousness among the proletariat. She argues that the active exercise of democratic rights[42] is for the proletariat indispensable not only because it renders the "conquest of power both *necessary* and *possible*,"[43] but more importantly "because only through the exercise of its democratic rights, in the struggle for democracy, can the proletariat become aware of its class interests and its historic task."[44] This does not mean that the exercise of democratic rights should be the final goal of the revolution. Even if Luxemburg sees value in parliamentary activity and trade unionism in the class awareness it promotes through party organizing, and as a means for advancing workers' interests, she sees grave danger in trading means for ends, and conceiving the party as the main goal of socialist politics.[45] When the means are "separated from the

38. For a liberal interpretation of Luxemburg, see Vollrath, "Rosa Luxemburg's Theory of Revolution." For a refutation of this liberal interpretation, see Geras, *Legacy of Rosa Luxemburg*, ch. 4.

39. Luxemburg, "The Junius Pamphlet," in *Rosa Luxemburg Reader*, 244.

40. Ibid., 244.

41. Marx, *On the Jewish Question*, 33.

42. Freedom of speech and assembly, and the right to vote.

43. Luxemburg, *Reform or Revolution*, 93.

44. Ibid.

45. Ibid., 67.

movement" and "made an end in themselves, then such activity not only does not lead to the final goal of socialism but moves in a precisely opposite direction."[46] Even if the party appears as an indispensable means to conquer the state, neither the conquering of the bourgeois state nor the maintenance of the party structure is connected to the final goal of a socialist society, which can be built only from the ground up, by the workers themselves. Consequently, actions by the party to control the movement by undermining democratic rights are ultimately self-defeating:

> To be sure, every democratic institution has its limits and shortcomings, things which it doubtless shares with all other human institutions. But the remedy which Trotsky and Lenin have found, the elimination of democracy as such, is worse than the disease it is supposed to cure; for it stops up the very living source from which alone can come the correction of all the innate shortcomings of social institutions. That source is the active, untrammeled, energetic political life of the broadest masses of the people.[47]

The "deprivation" of democratic rights under a socialist government is especially damaging for the revolution because it undermines the collective power of the proletariat and therefore the internal checking power to correct for inevitable institutional weaknesses of the political and economic systems. Luxemburg also observed in the antidemocratic tendencies of centralism the revolutionary party's contempt for local proletarian organizations. The Bolsheviks saw the soviets—the incipient revolutionary popular infrastructure that spontaneously emerged in Russia—with suspicion and designated them at first as "reactionary" because the majority of council members were peasants.[48] Even if Lenin was a strong supporter of the soviets in the aftermath of the 1905 revolution, arguing that "politically the Soviet of Workers' Deputies should be regarded as the embryo of a *provisional revolutionary government*,"[49] his embrace of centralism once in power stifled the autonomous development of the workers' councils. According to Luxemburg only the *correct* organs of the workers were conceived as valid interlocutors, and even those were being

46. Ibid. Luxemburg objected to "making a virtue out of necessity and then turning it into a veritable principle." Dunayevskaya, *Rosa Luxemburg*, 55.

47. Luxemburg, "Beginning," 302.

48. Ibid., 304. See Lenin's contempt for the peasantry and its populist petit-bourgeoise ideology in "The Economic Content of Narodism and the Criticism of It in Mr Struve's Book," in Lenin, *Collected Work*, 1, 341.

49. Lenin, "Our Tasks and the Soviet of Workers' Deputies," in *Collected Works* 10, 19. I thank Peter Hudis for pointing to Lenin's original idea of the workers' councils as being the main actors within the new governing structure.

deprived of the necessary liberties to operate autonomously. By suppressing grassroots politics, the revolutionary government, occupying the oligarchic state machinery, had established not a dictatorship of the proletariat (soviets) but a dictatorship of the selected few (party leaders) that the masses were forced to support:

> With the repression of political life in the land as a whole, life in the soviets must also become more and more crippled. Without general elections, without unrestricted freedom of press and assembly, without a free struggle of opinion, life dies out in every public institution, becomes a mere semblance of life, in which only the bureaucracy remains as the active element. Public life gradually falls asleep, a few dozen party leaders of inexhaustible energy and boundless experience direct and rule. Among them, in reality only a dozen outstanding heads do the leading and an elite of the working class is invited from time to time to meetings where they are to applaud the speeches of the leaders, and to approve proposed resolutions unanimously—at bottom, then, a clique affair—a dictatorship, to be sure, not the dictatorship of the proletariat but only the dictatorship of a handful of politicians, that is a dictatorship in the bourgeois sense.[50]

In Germany, the incipient council system also came under attack from the socialist party. Even if Luxemburg prioritized the mass strike over workers' councils in her early writings, after the SPD entered the government coalition and turned against the workers, Luxemburg goes back to the councils, conceiving them as fundamental institutions of the socialist revolution. This shift in her focus from the mass strike to the councils appears not only as a strategic move after the state machinery had been partially seized by the SPD, which would have made a mass strike more difficult to pull off, but also as a political project coming out of her critical analysis of Russian centralism and the death of public life.

To push back against the debasement of worker power and continue to oppose the war through revolutionary methods, Luxemburg founded in 1916 the Spartacus League[51] together with Karl Liebknecht, Clara Zetkin, and Franz Mehring. In a series of speeches published in the league's newspaper *Die Rote Fahne*—within the two months after she was released from jail and before being shot by the government-sponsored Freikorps[52]—Luxemburg denounced "the systematic destruction of the system of workers' and soldiers'

---

50. Luxemburg, "Beginning," 307.

51. Spartacus led the largest slave rebellion during the Roman republic (73 BC).

52. The Freikorps were a right-wing paramilitary militia. *Rosa Luxemburg Reader*, "Introduction," 29.

councils" and called for reinvigorating the council system by spreading its mode of organization to the peasantry.[53] For her, because the revolution aims "at the foundation and base of the social constitution" it needs to "work from beneath," and the duty of the revolutionary party should be to support councils as part of a revolutionary democratic constitution.[54] The path of the revolution therefore is not centralization, but the strengthening and spreading of the council system:

> All power in the hands of the working masses, in the hands of the workers' and soldiers' councils, protection of the work of revolution against its lurking enemies—this is the guiding principle of all measures to be taken by the revolutionary government.[55]

Luxemburg sees as an imperative to first dispel the illusion that to achieve socialism it is only "necessary to overthrow the old government, to set up a socialist government at the head of affairs, and then to inaugurate socialism by decree."[56] The proletarian masses need to realize that they cannot be liberated from the top, but need to emancipate themselves through political action. The "essence of socialist society" is that "the great laboring mass ceases to be a dominated mass"—a collection of "dead machines assigned their place in production by capital"—and workers become agents giving "conscious, free, and autonomous direction" to the life in common.[57] This requires a transformation of the proletariat. Because "one cannot realize socialism with lazy, frivolous, egoistic, thoughtless and indifferent human beings," individual men and women have to cultivate "inner self-discipline, intellectual maturity, moral ardor, a sense of dignity and responsibility," what Luxemburg deems "a complete inner birth of the proletarian."[58]

Socialism, which appears constitutively tied to local councils as sites of self-rule, cannot be established by decree but "can only be won by a long chain of powerful struggles, in which the proletariat, under the leadership of the Social Democracy, will learn to take hold of the rudder of society to become instead of the powerless victim of history, its conscious guide."[59] The only way for workers to undergo this transformation, from a dominated to an

---

53. Luxemburg, "Our Program," 371.

54. Ibid., 372–73.

55. Luxemburg, "Socialization of Labor," 343.

56. Luxemburg, "Our Program," 368.

57. Ibid., 350–51.

58. Luxemburg, "Socialization of Labor," 348.

59. Luxemburg, "The Russian Revolution," in *Rosa Luxemburg Reader*.

empowered class, is by exercising power in the "school of action,"[60] "through constant, vital, reciprocal contact between the masses of the people and their organs, the workers' and soldiers' councils."[61] The masses need to be educated in the art of power by wielding power, and in this process transform "themselves into the free and independent directors of this process," with the sense of "responsibility proper to active members of the collectivity":[62]

> Our motto is: In the beginning was the act. And the act must be that the workers' and soldiers' councils realize their mission and learn to become the sole public power of the whole nation.[63]

Because without the material conditions for local worker power, "the naked decrees of socialization by the highest revolutionary authorities are by themselves empty phrases,"[64] the main revolutionary task is to promote a proletarian institutional structure: the councils as constituent institutions:

> The symbol of the new socialist social order borne by the present proletarian revolution, the symbol of the class character of its true task, and of the class character of the political organ which is meant to execute this task, is: the workers' council, based on representation of the urban and rural proletariat.[65]

If the final objective of the movement is the socialist society, in which the working classes are free from domination, not being "ruled over" but ruling themselves, the immediate objective of the movement should be to "replace the inherited organs of bourgeois class rule" that rule over the working class with a working-class political infrastructure aimed at self-rule, at cultivating the proper political character and activity among the proletariat so to adequately train them to "occupy all the posts, supervise all functions, measure all official needs by the standard of its own class interests and the tasks of socialism."[66] To accomplish this, Luxemburg argues for active organizing and institution building at the local level, "down to the tiniest parish":

---

60. Luxemburg, "Our Program," 372.

61. Luxemburg, "What Does the Spartacus League Want?," in *Rosa Luxemburg Reader*, 351.

62. Ibid.

63. Luxemburg, "Our Program," 372.

64. Luxemburg, "What Does the Spartacus League Want?" 351.

65. Luxemburg, "National Assembly," https://www.marxists.org/archive/luxemburg/1918/11/20.htm.

66. Luxemburg, "What Does the Spartacus League Want?" 351.

It is a question of fighting step by step, hand-to-hand, in every province, in every city, in every village, in every municipality in order to take and transfer all the powers of the state bit by bit from the bourgeoisie to the workers and soldiers councils.[67]

Among the first necessary steps the revolutionary government should take to foster the council system[68] are (1) to improve the councils "so that the first chaotic and impulsive gestures of their formation are replaced by a conscious process of understanding the goals, tasks and methods of the revolution"; (2) to ensure that they have regularly scheduled meetings and adequate power-sharing processes; and (3) to establish a "national council of workers and soldiers in order to establish the proletariat of all Germany as a class, as a compact political power, and to make it the bulwark and impetus of the revolution."[69] The revolutionary government would have therefore the task not only to systematize and standardize the procedures of self-rule used in the councils, but also to establish a new national institution that would further construct the workers' class identity, empowering them to keep energizing the revolutionary process:

> Without the conscious will and action of the majority of the proletariat, there can be no socialism. In order to intensify this consciousness, to steel this will, to organize this action, a class organ is necessary: a national council of the urban and rural proletarians.[70]

The organized masses are for Luxemburg the agents and guardians of their emancipatory process, and therefore the duty of the revolutionary government, elected by the masses to take control of the state and wield its power, is to foster the institutional organization of the proletarian masses. The party should not be guided by centralist or revisionist strategies, but by the need to strengthen the council system.[71]

---

67. Luxemburg, "Our Program," 372.

68. For an account of the development and operation of soldiers, workers and peasants' councils, see Mitchell, *Revolution in Bavaria*.

69. Luxemburg, "Socialization of Labor," 343–44.

70. Luxemburg, "National Assembly."

71. Kautsky believed that workers councils, while a vital part of the revolutionary process, are restricted to the local and firm level, necessitating the continued existence of parliamentary forms to address overall societal needs. "To opt exclusively for the council form would be to introduce a system based on workplace and occupation, that would exalt particularist and corporatist tendencies, creating and consolidating divisively localist interests and loyalties." Salvadori, *Karl Kautsky*, 237.

Luxemburg's Transitional Constitutional Structure

Luxemburg's materialist approach made her understand that revolution, the political action that is the origin of constitution, is conditioned by the current stage of class struggle and the legal and extralegal means available to the masses. Political action, the "deed," is the starting point of the revolution, and the factors conditioning these actions become a constitutive part of it. Being not only a materialist thinker, but also very much a realist like Engels,[72] Luxemburg envisioned a period of transition between the capitalist and socialist societies, a regime in which both bourgeois and proletarian institutions would coexist. Even if she did not propose a proper constitutional structure for this transition period, her material legal thought reveals two basic elements the revolutionary constitution must have in order to enable the path to socialism: democratic rights to free speech, assembly, and suffrage to assure the conquest of representative structures, and local, autonomous working-class councils as constitutive institutions of the new socialist society. As I discussed above, democratic rights need to be not only formally respected, but also equally exercised, which would require the socialization of burdens preventing proletarians from engaging in political action. In the case of proletarian women, for example, the socialization of child care and domestic labor would be a necessary condition for their equal access to politics.[73]

According to Luxemburg, what makes the proletarian revolution radically distinct from bourgeois revolutions is the spontaneous organizing of the masses in councils, "the stamp of a proletarian socialist revolution."[74] Even if she does not mention the exercise of constituent power in this spontaneous self-constitution of the councils, this is the power workers and soldiers are actually wielding when defying the existing structures of power and setting up their own autonomous political institutions of self-rule. Consequently, the establishment of local worker councils marks the origin of a constituent revolution "from below," and therefore its fate is tied to the strength of the council system, which is supposed to replace the bourgeois ruling structure in the long run. This transitional phase, in which the new proletarian institution is added to the existing political structure, corresponds to the type of "composite" constitutionalism endorsed by Machiavelli; because it is realist, it does not seek

---

72. "Engels demonstrates, using all his knowledge as an expert in military science, that it is a pure illusion to believe that the working people could, in the existing state of military technique and of industry, and in view of the characteristics of the great cities of today, bring about and win a revolution by street fighting. Luxemburg, "Our Program," 361.

73. Luxemburg, "Junius Pamphlet."

74. Luxemburg, "Our Program," 366.

to directly abolish current oligarchic structures of power, but to add new autonomous institutions resting on plebeian authority rather than on existing legality. The mere existence of an institutional source of proletarian authority, even if not properly constitutionalized, would imply the recognition of organized proletarians as political agents, and establish the institutionalization of class conflict. The continual agonistic opposition of the councils to the liberal representative structure appears moreover as the effective cause of the revolution in this transition period, which would be completed only once proletarian institutions acquire supreme authority and decision-making power, and a new legality expresses a socialist society rather than a capitalist one.

I argue Luxemburg's transitional regime constitutes a hybrid constitutional framework in which two sources of authority—the liberal democratic order and its proceduralist justifications, and the proletarian order based on the collective activity of the councils—compete for power. This combination of legal and extralegal forms of authority within one political system should moreover be interpreted as a Marxist iteration of the republican mixed constitution, in which the legal power of the oligarchy is checked by the constituent power of the proletariat as a universal agent of emancipation. Through Luxemburg's materialist approach, the establishment and development of proletarian organs of power, far from being an idealist position, appears as the necessary material ground from which the new socialist society can begin to be collectively conceived.

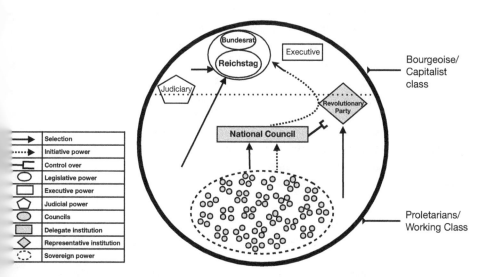

FIGURE 6.1. Interpretation of Luxemburg's ideas on a council democracy for Germany.

7

Arendt on the Republic of Parties and Councils

HANNAH ARENDT's first encounter with Rosa Luxemburg and revolutionary action was in 1919 when her mother took her to a public discussion circle about the recent uprising of the Spartacus League.[1] Luxemburg became for Arendt a role model, not only because of their shared cultural Jewish heritage and gender, but also with respect to Luxemburg's position as an ideological pariah, an outsider bound to be misunderstood and even demonized.[2] In this chapter I analyze Arendt's most controversial, understudied, and misinterpreted work, *On Revolution*, which was conceived after her engagement with Luxemburg's critical essay on the Russian Revolution.[3] Most Arendt specialists have tended to neglect or dismiss her proposal to establish a republic of councils as an anomaly in her thought—an idealist move in a rather realist thinker,[4] a critique that was also raised against Luxemburg. Through a material analysis of Arendt's thought, I conceive of her proposal for a council system not as a marginal thought experiment, but as central to her political philosophy, as inseparable from her conception of political freedom as action and her critique of the liberal republic, and in this way very much in tune with Luxemburg's own theory of political action and critical assessment of constitutional democracy.

In her review of J. P. Nettle's 1966 biography of Luxemburg, Arendt claims that Luxemburg's "insight into the nature of political action" came out of her experience of the 1905 Russian Revolution:

1. Young-Bruehl, *Hannah Arendt*, 29.

2. Shklar, "Hannah Arendt as Pariah," 371.

3. Letter from Arendt to Blumenfeld, July 31, 1956, cited in Muldoon, "Origins of Hannah Arendt's Council System," 780.

4. See, for example, Canovan, *Hannah Arendt*; Benhabib, *Reluctant Modernism of Hannah Arendt*.

The main point is that she had learned from the revolutionary workers' councils (the later *soviets*) that "good organization does not precede action but is the product of it," that "the organization of revolutionary action can and must be learnt in revolution itself, as one can only learn swimming in the water," that revolutions are "made" by nobody but break out "spontaneously," and that "the pressure for action" always comes "from below." A revolution is "great and strong as long as the Social Democrats [at the time still the only revolutionary party] don't smash it up."[5]

Arendt adhered not only to Luxemburg's basic idea that political action precedes organization, springing from the people who necessarily perform their own political emancipation, but also to her vision of the grave threat revolutionary parties posed for the councils. She argues that what made Luxemburg a real outsider within the revolutionary Left was her staunch commitment to the republic and its guarantee of democratic rights such as free speech and assembly.[6] Even if she is right about this assessment, Arendt's "republican" reading of Luxemburg makes sense only if we understand republicanism in its plebeian strand, as an ideological framework that conceives of the political action of the common people as a necessary condition for liberty. If by a republic we mean a system in which basic democratic liberties are protected and in which there are institutional spaces for the people to engage in political action, then yes, Luxemburg was very much a republican. This does not mean that Arendt is trying to deny Luxemburg's revolutionary commitments or, on the contrary, that Arendt is a closeted Marxist,[7] but that Arendt's interpretation of republican thought attempts to be purely political, stripped from socioeconomic considerations. This reduction of republican constitutional thought to a political framework of democratic rights and spaces for freedom makes it possible for it to be compatible with Luxemburg's strand of revolutionary socialism without necessarily sharing its Marxist ideological commitments, and even to be able to challenge the dominance of Marxism in the study of revolution:

> The failure of the revolutionary tradition to give any serious thought to the only new form of government born out of revolution can partly be explained by Marx's obsession with the social question and his unwillingness to pay serious attention to the questions of state and government.[8]

5. Arendt, "Heroine of Revolution." For an analysis of Luxemburg and Arendt, see Tamboukou, "Imagining and Living the Revolution."

6. Arendt, "Heroine of Revolution."

7. For an analysis of Arendt's relation between social and political, see Blättler and Marti, "Rosa Luxemburg and Hannah Arendt."

8. Arendt, *On Revolution*, 250.

Arendt claims that the council system, as a political structure, has been neglected by the Left primarily because of its "obsession with the social question" in the study of revolutions. Setting aside the issue of whether this obsession with exploitation and material necessity is reasonable, Arendt's critique of Marxist interpretations of revolutions is that they neglect what is fundamental about them: the establishment of a constitutional order where freedom can dwell. This approach to Arendt's work certainly does not solve the contradictions and paradoxes in it but certainly sheds new light on the council system as a space of freedom in which the revolutionary spirit can be preserved, a strictly political realm of appearances that needs to remain distinct from the administration of the social.

Despite Arendt's political commitments appearing as quite different from those of Luxemburg's, I argue their political philosophies are connected at the root:[9] in the understanding that political liberty is possible only in political action, and that revolutionary action is the source of political liberty.[10] Reading Arendt's constitutional proposal, as well as her critique of the modern revolutions and their outcomes through Luxemburg's "prophetic words of warning against the suppression of political freedom" in the name of revolution,[11] allows us not only to better understand Arendt's intellectual position as a pariah but also to distinguish her unique contributions to a plebeian constitutionalism in which equal access to political action and new beginnings is to be guaranteed and fostered.

Even if Arendt's project was not to advance the socialist revolution but to recuperate politics from the murky waters of the social, or not to organize the working class but to abstract the councils from their historical roots in the labor movement, I argue that her consistent support for a system of inclusive councils as an alternative form of government—from the late 1940s[12] until her last major book, *The Life of the Mind*, written in the early 1970s[13]—should be interpreted as a development of Luxemburg's political project. Arendt, picking up where

9. And thus radically, according to Marx: "To be radical is to grasp the root of the matter. But, for man, the root is man himself." *A Contribution to the Critique of Hegel's Philosophy of Right 1844*, introduction, in *The Marx-Engels Reader*, 60.

10. "The spontaneous political activity, demanded by Luxemburg against party officials, forms the essential center of Arendt's essays on revolution." Blättler and Marti, "Rosa Luxemburg and Hannah Arendt," 92.

11. Arendt, *On Revolution*, 314n82.

12. Muldoon shows how her commitments to the council system can be traced back to her experience with kibbutzim. "Origins of Hannah Arendt's Council System."

13. Left unfinished and published posthumously in 1977 by her friend and literary executor, Mary McCarthy.

Luxemburg left off, developed novel philosophical justifications for the council system, detaching it from Marxism and the primacy of necessity, and decisively connecting it to "democratic" republicanism and the primacy of politics, without in any way betraying Luxemburg's project of proletarian emancipation through political action. In this chapter I analyze Arendt's move away from the social and toward the political through her critical engagement with the French and American Revolutions, and how her particular analysis of the political nature of the councils allows for a new interpretation of the mixed constitution as a framework combining parties and councils, administration and politics.

Freedom and New Beginnings

Arendt's thought has two gravitational poles, constantly competing for primacy, but open to the possibility of synergy. On the one hand, her conception of the political as the realm of appearances, informed by the Greek political experience of the polis, is based on natality, the capacity of human beings to initiate something anew, a creative force capable of transcending the limits of the constituted reality. On the other hand, her conception of politics as the common world of institutions, informed by the Roman political experience of the republic, is based on authority, the source of stability and permanence that makes possible the preservation of freedom. This dualism between Greek and Roman political traditions—innovation and stability, power and authority—is brought to the fore and synthesized in her theory of new beginnings, as "something new [that] comes into an already existing world."[14]

Arendt's interpretation of the political is intrinsically linked to her conception of freedom as action. Following Aristotle, the political realm is also fundamentally ethical; the good life is the political life, a life of freedom marked by action in the public sphere. In the polis, to be free

> meant both not to be subject to the necessity of life or to the command of another *and* not to be in command oneself. It meant neither to rule nor to be ruled. . . . Equality, therefore, far from being connected with justice, as in modern times, was the very essence of freedom: to be free meant to be free from the inequality present in rulership and to move in a sphere where neither rule nor being ruled existed.[15]

Equality is then the precondition for freedom; without equality men's ability to act in concert for the common good is compromised. Freedom as action

---

14. Arendt, "What Is Freedom?," in *Between Past and Future*, 167.
15. Arendt, *Human Condition*, 32–33.

is reserved only for the ones who are free from the yoke of rulership,[16] and do not exercise command over others. In addition, Arendt's conception of freedom also presupposes plurality, which demands in turn the actualization of individuality, for which it is essential to be free from interference.

As Patchen Markell suggests in his interpretation of Arendt, beginning is for her an "action, whether disruptive or not, [that] involves attention and responsiveness to worldly events,"[17] and therefore "what makes a beginning a beginning for Arendt, what lends it its eruptiveness, is not its degree of departure from what preceded it, but rather our attunement to its character as an irrevocable event, which also means as an occasion for response."[18] The condition of natality, the capacity of beginning something anew, is what makes men able to engage in action, which is the political activity par excellence.

For Arendt humans differ from animals in their tendency to strive for immortality; men are capable of attaining immortality through their deeds and their collective remembrance, which gives them a "divine" nature:

> Only the best (*aristoi*), who constantly prove themselves to be the best . . . are really humans; the others, content with whatever pleasures nature will yield them, live and die like animals.[19]

Even if her embrace of excellence in politics has certainly fueled an interpretation of Arendt as a conservative, elitist thinker, I argue her realist assessment of common individuals under a system devoid of politics should not be confused with elitism:[20]

> Freedom in a positive sense is possible only among equals, and equality itself is by no means a universally valid principle but again, applicable only with limitations and even within spatial limits.

Similar to Condorcet, for whom structures of dependence make the exercise of autonomy nearly impossible, Arendt's spatial conception of freedom allows her to peg the incapacity of political action to the lack of spaces of freedom. How can one determine the capacity of individuals to be political if there are no spaces in which they can exercise freedom? An assessment of the structural conditions of domination in which the masses are atomized and deprived of political spaces, and how these conditions impede political action,

16. Those who are masters of themselves and are not dominated.

17. Markell, "Experience of Action," 65.

18. Ibid., 75.

19. Arendt, *Human Condition*, 19.

20. For an extended discussion of Arendt's elitism and relation to democracy, see Isaac, "Oases in the Desert."

is not an argument for the inherent incapacity of the masses to be political. Quite the contrary. Arendt's critique pushes her to envision a necessary political infrastructure to realize equality.

The same way that acknowledging that the majority of workers, who lack class consciousness under a capitalist system, are similar to cogs in a machine does not make Luxemburg less of a revolutionary, recognizing that without politics we are just animals—instead of *political* animals—does not make Arendt less committed to equal liberty in politics. For Arendt, as for Aristotle, politics is what makes us human and can be attained only collectively, by engaging in speech and action in the polis. Even if one could argue that valuing the aspiration for excellence is a form of elitism, because her political philosophy is not aimed at preserving the privileges of "the best," this elitism should be conceived as inclusionary since she does not conceive of any exclusion to participate in political action. She supports a self-selected political elite, an organic political class springing from popular councils that are open to all:

> The joys of public happiness and the responsibilities for public business would then become the share of those few from all walks of life who have a taste for public freedom and cannot be "happy" without it. Politically, they are the best, and it is the task of good government and the sign of a well-ordered republic to assure them of their rightful place in the public realm.[21]

Close to Luxemburg, who gave to the revolutionary government the crucial task of organizing and strengthening the council system, Arendt argues that a well-ordered republic needs to institutionalize spaces for freedom for anybody who feels drawn to politics to be able to engage in political action. Recognizing that the majority of individuals would choose not to engage in voluntary politics despite having the spaces to do so, and that therefore there would inevitably be a political elite, exposes her as a skeptical realist but hardly an elitist thinker.

Even if it is clear that Arendt's drive was to elevate politics from the realm of necessity and underscore the collective essence of political freedom, her relentless inquiry into the realm of appearances drove her work in multiple directions, sometimes obscuring extraordinary insights in topics as neglected as political foundings. Arendt's first major discovery regarding new beginnings was that plurality is at the core of the human essence. In *Origins of Totalitarianism*—thought and written during increasing domination of Stalinism and Nazism within their respective borders—Arendt encounters the quintessence of the human condition as it was gradually being destroyed by the first totalitarian

---

21. Arendt, *On Revolution*, 271.

regimes of the twentieth century. According to her, the driving force of totalitarianism reveals itself as a constant "organization" of plurality, as the elimination of what makes every human being unique and a potential agent of change,
"for to destroy individuality is to destroy spontaneity, man's power to begin
something new out of his own resources."[22]

Arendt expands this finding in *The Human Condition* and in her essays in
Between Past and Future, where plurality is defined as the condition of human
action, the prerequisite of all political life, which appears intrinsically connected to political liberty. According to her, it is the capacity of new beginnings
inherent in natality what gives us the capacity to act, to initiate something
anew, to create and reproduce liberty:

> Every act, seen from the perspective not of the agent but of the process in
> whose framework it occurs and whose automatism it interrupts, is a
> "miracle"—that is, something which could not be expected. If it is true that
> action and beginning are essentially the same, it follows that a capacity for
> performing miracles must likewise be within the range of human facul-
> ties. . . . It is in the very nature of every new beginning that it breaks into the
> world as an "infinite improbability," and yet it is precisely this infinite im-
> probable which actually constitutes the very texture of everything we call
> real. . . . The very impact of an event is never wholly explicable; its factuality
> transcends in principle all anticipation.[23]

The faculty of new beginnings is the infinite improbability that breaks into
the probable, an action that cannot be fully explained by common practices, and
that actualizes "miracles" that come to interrupt current patterns of behavior and
structures of interaction. Despite the importance she gives to the individual aspect of freedom—the liberty of the moderns or negative freedom as lack of
interference[24]—Arendt heavily leans toward a collective liberty, a freedom that
is the raison d'être of politics,[25] a freedom that presupposes liberation—
emancipation from empire, religion, oppression, necessity—and the entering
into a realm of appearances "into which each of the free men could insert himself
by word or deed."[26] Individuality and action, the highest manifestation of human
life, are possible only in the public realm allowed by political freedom, which is

22. Arendt, *Origins of Totalitarianism*, 455.

23. Arendt, "What Is Freedom?," 169.

24. Constant, "Liberty of the Ancients."

25. Arendt, "What Is Freedom?," 146.

26. Ibid., 148.

actualized through its collective performance.[27] Consequently, it is not the regularity of norms per se that undermines individuality, freedom, and the capacity for new beginnings, but "the erosion of the contexts in which events call for responses and, thus, in which it makes sense to act at all."[28]

As a republican, Arendt understands political freedom not as a good that can be acquired and maintained in degrees, but as a state of being in which one partakes through action.[29] For her, freedom as action can therefore be conceived only in absolute terms, in its exercise, within a given space. In a space in which individuals can act, freedom is both relational, because we can perceive it only in our intercourse with others through action or disclosure in the realm of appearances, and inherently limited, because the possibility of action and disclosure presupposes a politically guaranteed public realm, which "entails the recognition that no man can act alone, that men if they want to achieve something in the world must act in concert . . . [that] political freedom is always limited freedom."[30]

Even if plurality and the possibility of the improbable are part of the human condition, this does not mean that freedom, the necessary premise of plurality, is natural and should not be interfered with. In other words, action and interaction, "the patterns of engagement and responsiveness" allowed within a certain constitution, are not "accidental" but arise within a framework of "social and political practices and institutions, which structure and mediate people's experiences of the world."[31] Freedom is not natural or accidental but needs an artificial, human-made infrastructure enabling plurality and the possibility for the improbable.

Revolution as the Foundation of Freedom

Arendt recognizes that only rarely does freedom become the direct aim of political action, that only "in times of crisis or revolution" is freedom revealed through action.[32] Her consequent interest on the extraordinary politics of

27. Political freedom in the public realm has as precondition individual liberty and the right to a private life.

28. Markell, "Experience of Action," 66.

29. Liberals and neorepublicans such as Pettit think of freedom in terms of degree. An individual confronts an amount of interference and domination, which determines how free he or she is.

30. Arendt, "Willing," in Life of the Mind, 201.

31. Markell, "Experience of Action," 80.

32. Arendt, "What Is Freedom?," 146.

foundings[33] explored in *On Revolution* should then be seen not as a secondary theme inserted in a text plagued with controversial and sometimes cryptic arguments regarding the social question and the political, but as a fundamental theory, a milestone in her thinking on freedom and the necessary foundation needed for enabling political action.

Arendt begins her exploration of revolution from Aristotle's "materialistic view of history," which connected economic and political power and embraced the role of interest in politics.[34] Even if "overthrows and upheavals" against oppression were common in premodern times, Arendt follows Condorcet in arguing that to properly label a popular rebellion revolutionary, it needs to directly aim at freedom:[35] at dismantling hierarchies and achieving emancipation, and not simply at the bettering of social conditions within a system of domination. Only in modern times, she argues, is the materialist view of history able to be deployed for the direct emancipation of the masses. According to Arendt, only after social hierarchies are denaturalized and "men began to doubt that poverty is inherent in the human condition" did the "social question and the rebellion of the poor come to play a truly revolutionary role."[36] Only after the poor acquired the appropriate epistemic grounds to overturn the current hierarchy—by learning about the premodern American experience as a "society without poverty," and demanding to actualize the paradigm put forward by John Locke and Adam Smith in which labor is the source of all wealth—could a popular rebellion be properly called a revolution.[37]

Machiavelli, the "spiritual father of revolution," is for Arendt the first thinker to "visualize the rise of a purely secular realm," a realm of human affairs in need of periodic renewal.[38] Arendt follows Machiavelli and the Roman notion that all foundations are "re-establishments and re-constitutions,"[39] in arguing that new beginnings are always relative, a renovation of what exists, the irruption of something new that comes from within an existing reality to change that reality through its active engagement with it. Revolution understood as new beginning then necessarily defies the opposition between rules and the liberal interpretation of liberty as lack of interference; a new beginning is for Arendt a revolutionary political action

---

33. For an analysis of extraordinary politics and the role of constituent power, see Kalyvas, *Democracy and the Politics of the Extraordinary*.

34. Arendt, *On Revolution*, 12.

35. Condorcet, "Sur le sens du mot révolutionnaire," cited in Arendt, *On Revolution*, 19.

36. Arendt, *On Revolution*, 12 and 13.

37. Ibid., 13.

38. Ibid., 26–27.

39. See a reengagement with beginnings in "Willing," 213.

able to transform the world by precisely setting a normative structure in which the conditions for freedom as action and the possibility of the improbable are reestablished and preserved. A new beginning therefore is not defined by its degree of rupture from the present condition of the world, but by its capacity to generate and preserve juridical and physical spaces for a political freedom that is conceived as inherently limited.[40]

Having experienced directly the violence and arbitrariness of Nazism, Arendt seems to construct her theory of new beginnings against an almost inescapable original crime, searching for a peaceful new beginning, a bloodless birth of the political. However, she acknowledges that because liberation is the *conditio sine qua non* of freedom,[41] violence is inevitably present during the revolutionary experience. However, whereas violence assures liberation—the necessary first step for a potential place for politics—if it endures past this initial stage and becomes internalized, it could bring the political to its demise. Therefore, while she argues that the "aim of revolution was, and always has been, freedom,"[42] the realization of this pursuit through violence could easily turn into its opposite, the elimination of the political and the negation of plurality. Consequently, one could argue that even if violence and politics can coexist chronologically, they must not be performed within the same space. While violence could be exerted "outside" of the political realm, against an oppressive "other" from which the community must be liberated, it should not permeate the political because if violence is exerted within the realm of appearances, politics inevitably becomes mute. Persuasion and force cannot spatially coexist.

Despite the fact that both the American and the French Revolutions began with a violent liberation—from the British Empire and the French monarchy, respectively—Arendt does not dwell in the analysis of this common act of emancipation, which she states comes from the desire "to be free from oppression," but rather concentrates in their abysmal differences regarding what she calls the "foundation of freedom," the establishment of a republic as a "new, or rather rediscovered form of government."[43] While the French Revolution was for her an utter failure due to the revolutionaries' fixation with the fictions of an absolute break with the ancien régime and the sovereignty of the people-as-one, Arendt praised the American Revolution as the highest political moment of the modern age because of its acknowledgement of previous shared political practices and the cooperative essence of the constituent power it enacted.

40. Ibid., 201.
41. Ibid., 207.
42. Arendt, *On Revolution*, 1.
43. Ibid., 23.

With the death of the king and the evacuation of theology as the source of political power and authority in France, the most emblematic modern revolution destroyed the old order in the name of popular sovereignty and attempted to create ex nihilo a new body politic, "abolish[ing] the sequence of temporality,"[44] to redefine the "people" and the basic principles that would allow for the new political unity to come into existence. Arendt explains that even though this new beginning as absolute rupture from a regime based on divine royalty allowed for the creation of a secular constitutional order and popular self-determination, the price for this type of revolution was the elimination of transcendental sources of authority and the consequent groundlessness of the new legal framework:

> Those who get together to constitute a new government are themselves unconstitutional, that is, they have no authority to do what they have set out to achieve.[45]

The juridical void in which the self-authorized, arbitrary act of founding took place created the space for rightlessness and violence where the individual had no legal protection against the revolutionaries, who became the official voice of an abstract and never finalized popular will:

> The direction of the French Revolution was deflected almost from its beginning from this course of foundation through the immediacy of suffering; it was determined by the exigencies of liberation not from tyranny but from necessity, and it was actuated by the limitless immensity of both the people's misery and the pity this misery inspired. The lawlessness of the "all is permitted" sprang here still from the sentiments of the heart whose very boundlessness helped in the unleashing of a stream of boundless violence.[46]

According to Arendt, this situation of total arbitrariness that characterized the French Revolution was a consequence of the attempt to resolve the perplexity of foundations by deriving both power *and* authority from the same immanent source: the people. However, the need for a new absolute to become the fountain of legitimacy, the need for "a divine principle, for some transcendent sanction in the political realm," proved difficult to resolve and drove the revolutionaries to deify "the people" and believe that "like the absolute prince, the nation, in terms of public law, could do no wrong."[47] Yet, the

---

44. Arendt, "Willing," 208.
45. Ibid., 175–76.
46. Arendt, *On Revolution*, 82.
47. Ibid., 182.

excesses of the Terror made explicit the dangers of tyranny lurking beneath the supreme power of such a formless and unorganized subject:

> To find a new absolute to replace the absolute divine power, is insoluble because power under the condition of human plurality can never amount to omnipotence, and laws residing on human power can never be absolute.[48]

Absolute authority cannot be derived from the will of fallible human beings, and therefore laws need to remain limited and open to contestation and the improbable. According to Arendt, what made the incipient structure unstable and ultimately terminated the republican experience in France was not its openness to plurality and new beginnings, but its grounding on the will of an unorganized multitude in need of material welfare:

> The French Declaration of the Right of Man, as the Revolution came to understand it, was meant to constitute the source of all political power, to establish not the control but the foundation-stone of the body politic. The new body politic was supposed to rest upon man's natural rights, upon his rights in so far as he is nothing but a natural being, upon his right to "food, dress, and the reproduction of the species," that is, upon the right to the necessities of life. And these rights were not understood as prepolitical rights that no government and no political power has the right to touch or violate, but as the very content as well as the ultimate end of government and power.[49]

The extreme volatility of the will of the unassembled multitude could never have yielded a stable constitutional order because it "is ever-changing by definition, and that a structure built on it as its foundation is built on quicksand."[50]

The violent resistance of the oligarchy to the imposition of social rights was, on the other hand, met with the violent reaction of the Terror. Following the argument of the impossible coexistence of violence and politics within the realm of appearances, I would argue that for Arendt Robespierre betrayed the revolution by bringing the violence (and arbitrariness) that was exerted against the oppressive "other"—the king and his court—into the political sphere, through the imposition of the social question as a political project, which precluded deliberation, and the insistent search for traitors and the purging of the body politic. The material dispossession of the sans-culottes and the arbitrary

48. Ibid., 29.
49. Ibid., 99.
50. Ibid., 154.

designation of patriots and traitors by the revolutionary government—which had the task to advance the revolution while at the same time defend the nascent political project against the relentless counterrevolutionary forces— ended up imposing fear of violence rather than the *fraternité* famously declared by Robespierre in 1790.[51]

Seen under this light, the French Revolution, through its constant creation of an "objective opponent,"[52] the recognition of an internal enemy as existential "other," against which the nation's virtuous identity was permanently constructed, degenerated into a movement that sought to impose a fictional unity based on the ever-changing will of a revolutionary subject in permanent becoming. But for Arendt this degeneration of the French revolutionary experience due to the lack of proper foundations, even if was close to the totalitarian experiences of the twentieth century at the height of the Terror, was not a form of totalitarianism. It was clear to her that the aim of the French Revolution was freedom, and that the violence of the Terror was not in the essence of the movement but was instead "the reaction to a series of broken oaths and unkept promises that were the perfect political equivalent of the customary intrigues of Court society."[53] The excesses of the revolution were in part responses to a counterrevolutionary enemy that threatened the revolutionary party and therefore the securing of the republican project.[54] Violence was inevitable within a framework of lawlessness in which the revolutionary party concentrated power, and spaces of freedom were weak or nonexistent.

I would argue we should understand Arendt's controversial analysis of the French Revolution through Luxemburg's critique of Lenin's centralism after the Russian Revolution, criticism that in part inspired *On Revolution*. Neither the French Revolution nor Lenin's Soviet republic respected free speech and assembly, or fostered autonomous organs of the people, and therefore both failed at constituting appropriate foundations for freedom. While the French Revolution degenerated into the Terror and its inchoate republic was quickly overthrown, the Russian Revolution degenerated into a collectivist statism that morphed into a full-blown totalitarian regime under Stalin. While the critique of Lenin and bolshevism relegated Luxemburg to the margins of

---

51. Robespierre, *Discours Sur L'organisation Des Gardes Nationale*. Paris: Chez Buisson, 1790.

52. Arendt, *Origins of Totalitarianism*, 425.

53. Arendt, *On Revolution*, 95.

54. For a historical analysis of revolution and counterrevolution during this period in France, see Mayer, *Furies*.

socialist thought, Arendt's critique of the French Revolution made her a pariah within the intellectual Left, especially because she not only was critical of the most emblematic revolution in the popular imaginary, but also seemed to uncritically embrace the American Revolution, which yielded a constitution based not on the principles of equality, fraternity, and solidarity, but on free enterprise.

While in her critique of the French Revolution Arendt denounces the will of the multitude as an inappropriate foundation for freedom, her charitable assessment of the American founding is based on the revolutionaries' respect for individual rights and political institutions:

> The direction of the American Revolution remained committed to the foundation of freedom and the establishment of lasting institutions, and to those who acted in this direction nothing was permitted that would have been outside the range of civil law.[55]

It is only from the American founding experience that she is able to extract positive lessons for the establishment of "artificial structures that are more permanent and durable than the unpredictable actions of human beings" as the proper foundation of freedom.[56] In contrast to the French constituent attempt, Arendt praises the American revolutionaries because they acknowledged their previous political and legal practices as a common base for creating a common future, thus performing a *relative*, rather than an *absolute* beginning, as "something new [that] comes into an already existing world."[57] In addition, Arendt sees the American Revolution as the first truly *political* revolution, one that was not about the social question but fundamentally aimed at constituting a new enduring political structure. According to Arendt, when signs of conflict emerged between the American colonies and the British Empire, representatives from newly constituted bodies of the thirteen colonies were selected to assemble and discuss a possible common response. The soon-to-be revolutionaries, informally authorized by their respective self-organized communities, decided by virtual unanimity to declare independence from the British Empire and embark on the creation of a legal framework for the new body politic. As I showed in chapter 2, this narrative neglects the acute social conflict that prompted the setting up of a counterrevolutionary constitutional convention in which the legal framework was deliberated and crafted in

---

55. Arendt, *On Revolution*, 82.
56. Muldoon, "Arendt's Revolutionary Constitutionalism," 602.
57. Arendt, "What Is Freedom?," 167.

secrecy by a group of selected few. Even if Arendt's omission of conflict serves her project because it allows her to focus on the constructive elements of the founding, her sanitized assessment and strategic deployment of the American founding experience, completely detached from its sociopolitical conjuncture, not only is historically inaccurate but also obscures the particular pitfalls of the new, liberal beginning.

Arendt dismisses the materialist analysis of the American Revolution, criticizing Charles Beard's economic interpretation of the founding as a matter of "sheer" history of ideas obsessed with "unmasking [the hypocrisy] of the Founding Fathers and by the hunt for ulterior motives in the making of the Constitution."[58] She argues that it was precisely a "war upon hypocrisy" what brought the French Revolution to the Terror "as an institutional device, consciously employed to accelerate the momentum of the revolution," and that American historiography was only mimicking in paper what the French had done with blood.[59] This quest to unveil the hypocrisy of the founding, of the original "vice through which corruption becomes manifest," appeared to her more as an echo from the old world than a productive immanent critique of the liberal republic's origins.[60]

Even if applying the most charitable interpretation of Arendt's analysis of the American Revolution, as aiming to "defend the notion of political freedom against the usurpation of the public sphere by powerfully organized private interests,"[61] her rejection of an "economicist" approach to politics blinded her to the material conditions determining the constitutional convention, the Constitution, and its implementation. Arendt's attempt to rescue the politics from the managing of necessity did not leave much room for considering socioeconomic conditions during the founding or the exclusion and lack of freedom of those not present or represented in the constituent process. Nevertheless, from the relative and cooperative aspects of the American foundational experience, Arendt, in an attempt to escape the inherent arbitrariness of the founding act,[62] and against the voluntarism of popular sovereignty, elaborated a theory of new beginnings that introduced the distinction between power and authority.[63] For her, the contrast between the French and American experiences evidenced that even though the people are the source of power in

58. Arendt, *On Revolution*, 89.

59. Ibid., 90.

60. Ibid., 94.

61. Blättler and Marti, "Rosa Luxemburg and Hannah Arendt," 93.

62. Arendt, "Willing," 207.

63. For further analysis of the separation of power and authority as a form of dual constitutionalism, see Arato, "Forms of Constitution Making and Theories of Democracy."

modern republics, their will cannot be the foundation of authority for the new legal order:

> What saves the act of beginning from its own arbitrariness is that it carries its own principle within itself, or, to be more precise, that beginning and principle, *principium* and principle, are not only related to each other, but are coeval. . . . The way the beginner starts whatever he intends to do lays down the law of action for those who have joined him in order to partake in the enterprise and to bring about its accomplishment. As such, the principle inspires the deeds that are to follow and remains apparent as long as the action lasts.[64]

Through a formal argument that traces the source of authority to the principles contained in the act of founding itself, Arendt seeks to solve the perplexity of new beginnings and situate *political* action at the foundation of freedom.[65] Through this lens, the unthematized, implicit immanent principles of the constitutive act become explicit through performance, guiding the revolutionaries during the founding moment and giving stability and endurance to the constitutional project. Arendt's theory of principled action would then allow for the exercise of political freedom at the moment of founding without any external limitations and, at the same time, preclude the dangers of boundless action by conceptualizing normativity as internal to the act of foundation.[66] If the founding is done through collective political action, in which peers come together to create something new and incorporate it into their existing world, the foundations of the new constitution would maintain and reproduce this freedom by allowing for the actualization of liberty through political action.

Even though Arendt's theory gives a promising alternative to both absolute beginnings and mere evolutionary change by placing authority in the principles inherent in the act of founding, what these principles are, and how can they be recognized and correctly codified, remains undertheorized. If every act of founding has its own principles within itself, does this mean that every collective attempt at a new beginning will have the necessary authority to endure? Is the establishment of a new constitutional order enough evidence of a successful revolution? If so, can principled action be acknowledged only in retrospect, after a considerable amount of time has passed, allowing us to

---

64. Arendt, *On Revolution*, 205.

65. Political action is the performance of freedom as well as its constitutive origin.

66. For an extended analysis of performative norms, see Kalyvas, *Democracy and the Politics of the Extraordinary*, 241–44.

judge if the framework put in place by the founders managed to successfully stabilize and channel the revolutionary thrust? Even if clearly "the character of one act as a beginning hangs on its future reception,"[67] and stability and endurance would be the appropriate categories by which to assess the success of revolutionary foundings, Arendt's theory is normative, which demands bringing substantive criteria into evaluation.

Despite the absence of an unequivocal recognition of what the desirable principles are and how a successful postrevolutionary political order should look, Arendt's focus on the American Revolution suggests that the only "good" principles that would create the necessary authority for political freedom to thrive are the ones derived from mutual promise and common deliberation, and that a successful constitutional order is the one that allows for these principles to be permanently enacted. The central idea of revolution for Arendt "is the foundation of freedom, that is, the foundation of a body politic which guarantees the space where freedom can appear."[68] Thus, for a revolution to be successful, it is not only fundamental for promise and deliberation to become part of the legal structure, but it is also essential that spaces where people can meet, deliberate, and act together are recognized and legally established.

The founding act of constitution making finds its authority not in a previous legal framework or in the collective will, but in its performance, in the collective endeavor of the people who create, in action, a new constitutional framework allowing for freedom to be preserved, enlarged, and strengthened. This action, for Arendt, is first an act of mutual promise:

> Power comes into being only if and when men join themselves together for the purpose of action, and it will disappear when, for whatever reason, they disperse and desert one another. Hence, binding and promising, combining and covenanting are the means by which power is kept in existence; where and when men succeed in keeping intact the power which sprang up between them during the course of any particular act or deed, they are already in the process of foundation, of constituting a stable worldly structure to house, as it were, their combined power of action. There is an element of world-building capacity of man in the human faculty of making and keeping promises.[69]

Because there is political power only in collective action, and power can be sustained only within the appropriated structure, then the capacity to make

67. Markell, "Experience of Action," 76.

68. Arendt, *On Revolution*, 116.

69. Ibid., 166.

promises to sustain that structure is essential to the world-building capacity of humans. Promise is inherently relational, a faculty that is necessarily based on previous experiences among individuals. For a promise involving a whole community to be binding, individuals need to believe that others will respect their allegiance, and that their membership is too valuable to decide to break it. Therefore, the basic condition underpinning a mutual promise would be social trust, an informal and "invisible institution"[70] that according to Pierre Rosanvallon has three dimensions: moral, substantive, and temporal.[71] While the moral dimension of social trust would be "integrity in the broadest sense,"[72] which would translate as honesty and wholeness, its substantive aspect has to do with the concern for the common good. The temporal dimension of social trust is what allows for a promise to endure past the moment of initial allegiance, the aspect that projects past and present interpersonal relations into the future, allowing for a community to endure after its birth. Consequently, the constitutive promise is what makes the civil community possible, what allows for a diverse group of people to imagine themselves as a "'We' [that] is constituted as an identifiable entity,"[73] into the future.

If the substantive dimension of social trust is the common good, something that is socially constructed and that, at the same time, creates *the people* as an entity when acting on it, promise—the temporal dimension of trust, the projection of the present into the future—is what makes possible the endurance of the collective subject over time and the creation of a legitimate constitutional structure. However, in order for the people to yield a legal framework in which plurality and freedom can flourish, the interpersonal relations on which social trust is based must rely on a commitment to political equality, the necessary premise of the Arendtian founding principle of deliberation. As does mutual promise, which could be understood only in relation to the unity created based on already existing social trust, the principle of deliberation presupposes a realm of appearances based on political equality. Political equality, under the rule of law, is the basic condition for the creation of the *citizen*, the symbolic projection of the members of a community as legal entities, which makes possible equality in the public sphere. However, the juridical category of the citizen by itself is unable to guarantee equal liberty if the promise remains at the formal level, without yielding an adequate infrastructure to house common power.

---

70. Arrow, *Limits of Social Organization*, 26, quoted in Rosanvallon, *Counter-democracy*, 3.

71. Rosanvallon, *Counter-democracy*, 3.

72. Ibid.

73. Arendt, "Willing," 203.

In addition to political equality, deliberation also presupposes liberty understood both as the protection of individual rights and as the space for political action. Besides positive liberty—freedom as participation in the public sphere aimed at judging and deciding on common affairs—the principle of deliberation requires the negative aspect of freedom to be present at the moment of disclosure. It is in the public realm where members of the community actualize, through speech and action, their individuality, the "unique distinctness" that allows for the second birth of man in the political.[74] Therefore, while positive freedom, the acting together, is essential for the maintenance of spaces for deliberation, it is through the actualization of individuality in action that plurality is able to exist. Consequently, in addition to political equality, both positive and negative freedom must be fostered through the founding performance and codified in the constitution.

For Arendt, the spaces for freedom in a modern republic are bounded areas reserved for action, like "islands in a sea or as oases in a desert."[75] These islands of freedom surrounded by the stale waters of administration and the desert of the nonpolitical life are for Arendt not natural but rather human-made infrastructures designed to house the revolutionary spirit. Freedom as action is more demanding than the republican notions of freedom as tranquility and nondomination[76] because it requires the equal possibility of disclosure and performance of liberty, and consequently a revolutionary founding à la Arendt would differ substantially from a republican founding à la Machiavelli, in which popular political action is demanded not as an end in itself—not as a way of performing and actualizing liberty—but as a means to ward against domination. While for Machiavelli the founding of a republic justifies any means, for Arendt means and ends, new beginnings and political freedom, constituent process and constituent form, appear as intrinsically connected.

The Arendtian founding is the highest political moment, the greatest expression of freedom, which demands extraordinary engagement by individuals in collective action. Since the French Revolution, revolutionary beginnings have taken the form of spontaneous popular councils, organs that "consciously and explicitly desired the direct participation of every citizen in the public affairs of the country."[77] For Arendt, without councils, a new beginning would be unable to properly constitute freedom. Because she learned from Luxemburg that political action—the deed—is the origin of revolution, and that there is no

74. Arendt, *Human Condition*, 176.

75. Arendt, *On Revolution*, 267.

76. Machiavelli, *Discourses*, I.XVI; Montesquieu, *Spirit of the Laws*, II. XII. 2 and 1.

77. Arendt, *On Revolution*, 255.

revolution without the self-emancipatory actions of the workers themselves, the constitution of freedom therefore needs to be the result of political action of the people themselves. In contrast, Machiavelli's founding is the highest moment of *virtù* in which one man is able to seize power to make the republic anew.[78] For Machiavelli, the republican founding demands an extraordinary leader able to transcend the inherent dualism of society, a kingly power able to overcome vested interests and bring the republic back to its foundations. The founder must remain autonomous, beholden only to his own judgment. Even if the leader allies with the people, the act of founding comes out of pure will: a one-man task, a triumph of virtue over fortune, guided only by the common good.[79] While extraordinary virtuous action is required in both foundings, in Machiavelli this action is given to the new prince, the leader of the people, who concentrates all authority to establish the institutions of liberty; in Arendt the founding and the new order are intrinsically connected, the latter being the result of the particular constituent action being performed in the former.

Even if her conception of liberty and its relation to political action would make Arendt's new beginning *democratic*, in the sense that political action is an end in itself, rather than strictly republican, her reverence for institutions and procedures, and the authority vested in them, gives to her model a distinctive republican character in which power and authority are separated:

> Power springs up whenever people get together and act in concert, but it derives its legitimacy from the initial getting together rather than from any action that then may follow.[80]

By separating power and authority at the moment of founding, Arendt is able to ground the new beginning in institutions (such as the shared rules and practices of semiconstituted political communities in the case of the American Revolution), while keeping the people's constituent power open and productive of liberty. Republican authority, based on the initial foundations of the republic, is in this way able to channel the power of the people by limiting it from within. The solution against the boundlessness and instability of action during the founding moment is for Arendt found within action itself, in the act of promising:

> The remedy for unpredictability, for the chaotic uncertainty of the future, is contained in the faculty to make and keep promises. . . . Binding oneself

78. Machiavelli, *The Prince*, VI; *Discourses*, I.XXVI. For an extended analysis of Machiavelli's theory of foundings, see Vergara, "Machiavelli's Republican Constituent Power."

79. Machiavelli, *Discourses*, I.II.

80. Arendt, "On Violence," in *Crises of the Republic*, 151.

through promises, serves to set up in the ocean of uncertainty, which the future is by definition, islands of security without which not even continuity, let alone durability of any kind, would be possible in the relationships between men.[81]

While republican authority is linked to the birth of the political community, to the binding, constitutive promise to respect and augment the foundations of the republic, democratic authority is expressed in deliberation, in the way the legal structure is decided on, reproduced, and renewed. Then, from her theory of principled action, in which normativity is contained in the act of founding, one could argue that the initial promise of the political community is the source of republican authority, which in turn is conditioned by the democratic principle of deliberation. While republican authority is concerned with the relation between individuals and the political community they belong to, the duty involved with preserving and augmenting the foundations,[82] democratic authority has to do with the relation among citizens *within* the spaces of freedom, with the way political freedom is exercised.

This dual, more demanding conception of authority presupposes, in addition to social trust, rules of political engagement allowing for continued self-rule by the community and the permanent actualization of the degrees of freedom contained in the foundational political practices. In other words, for democratic-republican authority to be capable of maintaining a constitutional framework in which freedom can dwell, the political relation between individuals must be based on the principle of no-rule,[83] which is actualized in the act of deliberation, in the disclosure of oneself in the realm of appearances and the persuasion of others in relation to the definition of the common good and how to achieve it. While republican authority is necessary for the community to codify and preserve its shared practices and rules, which allows for ongoing commonality, democratic authority demands a substantive character from political institutions.

In what follows I focus on Arendt's proposal to incorporate a council system of government as a necessary condition for freedom. Following Jefferson's plan of "elementary republics," which demanded continual interaction among citizens alongside representative government, Arendt puts forward a council

---

81. Arendt, *Human Condition*, 237.

82. Arendt, "What Is Authority," in *Between Past and Future*, 121–22.

83. This principle of no-rule does not mean that there is not rule in the self-governing bodies. There is rule, but based on deliberation and persuasion, which are inimical to hierarchy and force. For an analysis of the no-rule principle, see Markell, "Rule of the People." On the relation between sovereignty and no-rule, see Arato and Cohen, "Banishing the Sovereign?"

system as an alternative form of government aimed at the continual re-introduction of freedom as action and expansion of the public sphere, so to carve political space out of the dominance of the social. I argue that we should understand Arendt's proposal as a novel interpretation of the mixed constitution, one in which the division between the few and the many is replaced by that of parties dedicated to administration, and councils dedicated to political judgment.

Parties and Councils as Mixed Constitution

Even if Arendt praises the relative new beginning of the American colonies because of its protection of civil liberties and respect for previous institutions, she strongly criticizes the exclusively representative form of government of the new liberal republic. The combination of representative institutions and individual rights, conceived as restraints on the power of government, yielded a framework in which politics was reserved for the few while the many enjoyed freedom *from* politics.[84] As a republican thinker, Arendt understands the decay of the public realm as a form of corruption associated with the pursuit of private interest against the common good. This decay is for her connected to the lack of spaces for political action and the political apathy that comes along with the neglect for the res publica and political action. Corruption is the result of the privatization of the public realm and the alienation of individuals from their political condition, "the atrophy of the space of appearances and the withering of common sense."[85] The process of estrangement from the world, the prevalence of the private, and the loss of a sense of togetherness that characterizes corrupt republics appears as intrinsically connected to a constitutional lack: the failure to institutionalize spaces of freedom where individuals could engage in political action. The American founding institutionalized a representative government selected by the people, mediated by a party system, but did not give institutional standing to the town halls and local councils that were also part of the sociopolitical revolutionary realm. The aim to institutionalize representation and not assemblies of the people in which politics could be exercised was for Arendt the beginning of the end of the republican project.

Arendt sees party and council as almost coeval, both springing from revolutions; while the councils are the organs of the people, parties are the organs of the selected elite:

84. Arendt, *On Revolution*, 272.
85. Arendt, *Human Condition*, 209.

Parties, because of their monopoly of nomination, cannot be regarded as popular organs, but they are, on the contrary, the very efficient instruments through which power of the people is curtailed and controlled.[86]

Parties not only are not representative of the popular will but also are aimed at taming the masses. Close to Cicero's assessment of the Plebeian Tribunate as an institution functional to the republic because it helped to pacify and direct the people, Arendt sees in the party a means of elite control over the citizens instead of a vehicle through which popular opinion could be formed and represented.[87] This negative conception of representation negates the benefits that Luxemburg saw on class-based representative institutions as enabling the identity of the oppressed through the clashes of the revolutionary party with state power. Since Arendt's project is not to emancipate the working class from capitalist oppression but to purge politics from necessity, she sees the representation of interest—either of the working class or of other groups in society—as nonpolitical and therefore in no way beneficial for enabling freedom—even if representative government is indeed necessary for the operation of the modern state. One could argue that in Arendt's exchange of the working class for the citizen, representation completely losses its "political" character—as partisan of the emancipation of the plebeian element. While for Luxemburg the revolutionary party's task was to give a structure to workers' councils, and in this way was an agent of emancipation, when abstracting the plebeian subject, the party becomes a mere vehicle of interest and not of freedom. In this way she accepts Schumpeter's theory of representative government as based on interest[88] and denies the political nature of representation.

Representation is for Arendt what distinguishes modern republics from democracies.[89] In a constitution based on representative government, individual citizens may wield—mainly through the vote—only negative powers, which "claim not a share in government but a safeguard against government."[90] For Arendt representative government precludes participation by the majority because it does not provide the space for public opinion to form:

> In this system the opinions of the people are indeed unascertainable for the simple reason that they are non-existent. Opinions are formed in the process of open discussion and public debate, and where no opportunity for

86. Arendt, *On Revolution*, 261.

87. For a view of representation as productive of opinion formation as connected to judgment, see Urbinati, *Representative Democracy*.

88. Schumpeter, *Capitalism, Socialism, and Democracy*.

89. Arendt, *On Revolution*, 228.

90. Ibid., 134.

the forming of opinions exists, there may be moods—moods of the masses and moods of individuals, the latter no less fickle and unreliable than the former—but no opinion.[91]

If there is no formal, instituted space for the multitude to organize and for opinion to form, there is no acting together and no freedom. Arendt's material assessment of modern democracies comes close to the critical plebeian tradition that sees representative government not as a deficient form of popular government, but as a form of oligarchy:

> That representative government has in fact become oligarchic government is true enough, though not in the classical sense of rule by the few in the interest of the few; what we today call democracy is a form of government where the few rule, at least supposedly, in the interest of the many. This government is democratic in that popular welfare and private happiness are its chief goals; but it can be called oligarchic in the sense that public happiness and public freedom have again become the privilege of the few.[92]

For Arendt representation is inimical to action, and the creation of a political system based on representative government effectively vacated action from politics in the modern world.[93] Where politics is transformed into administration, which demands the professionalization of representatives who are chosen according to nonpolitical criteria, there is no space for the people to engage in politics and actualize political freedom. Even if representative governments have democratic ideals, they are de facto oligarchies because they reserve the privilege of politics for the selected few. Interestingly, the oligarchy Arendt unveils is based not on socioeconomic privileges—the few using state power to accumulate wealth by dispossessing the many—but on political privileges; politics is a de facto monopoly of a few, while the many, deprived from spaces of freedom, are relegated to the social sphere, incapable of exercising freedom as politics through the political system and left only with extra-institutional avenues of protest to reclaim that freedom through political performance.[94]

The party system—which is supposed to aggregate citizens' wills, providing shortcuts for decision making—is, like administration and management, not only essentially nonpolitical, because its "business is dictated by necessity,"[95]

---

91. Ibid., 261.

92. Ibid.

93. Ibid., 265.

94. Arendt argued voluntary association morphed into civil disobedience. "Civil Disobedience," in *Crises of the Republic*, 102.

95. Arendt, *On Revolution*, 264.

but also an instrumentalization of the people, turning them into supporters of parties instead of political agents:

> The party, whether an extension of parliamentary faction or a creation outside parliament, has been an institution to provide parliamentary government with the required support of the people, whereby it was always understood that the people, through voting, did the supporting, while action remained the prerogative of government.[96]

Even revolutionary parties, as organs of representation, have traditionally agreed that "the end of government was the welfare of the people, and that the substance of politics was not action but administration."[97] Following Luxemburg's prescient analysis of the Russian Revolution, Arendt argues that party and councils compete for authority. The revolutionary Russian leadership, after only "halfheartedly recogniz[ing] the councils as instruments of 'revolutionary struggle,' . . . tried even in the midst of revolution to rule them from within" and saw action after the conquest of the state as "unnecessary or subversive."[98]

Arendt argues that the councils of the people "were bound to become superfluous if the spirit of the revolutionary party prevailed."[99] The party wants to execute its program, apply it on the masses without discussion by the masses, which inevitably makes the councils rebel against the party because the "average citizen's capacity to act and to form his own opinion" would be disregarded and negated. However, the rebellion of the councils against the party not only disregarded the necessity of administration but also allowed for the confusion between management and politics, which led to making councils not only political organs but also managers in common:

> If it is true that the revolutionary parties never understood to what extent the council system was identical with the emergence of a new form of government, it is no less true that the councils were incapable of understanding to what enormous extent the government machinery in modern societies must indeed perform the functions of administration. The fatal mistake of the councils has always been that they themselves did not distinguish clearly between participation in public affairs and the administration or management of things in the public interest.[100]

96. Ibid., 263.
97. Ibid., 273.
98. Ibid., 265.
99. Ibid., 256.
100. Ibid., 265–66.

For Arendt, the councils are political organs and must not engage in the administration of things, not because it is beyond their competence but because the contamination of political judgment by the social and its consequentialism is pernicious.

Because for Arendt authority is vested on law *and* institutions, it is necessary not only to codify a strong Bill of Rights, as the Americans did, but also to create spaces were freedom could be exercised. Even if it was a republic that the framers were instituting—a political system in which the people are the ultimate source of power—and its Bill of Rights was for Arendt "the most exhaustive legal bulwark for the private realm against public power,"[101] the lack of spaces of freedom in which individuals could engage in political action meant the ultimate failure of the republican project because it was unable to preserve the freedom exercised at the moment of the founding:

> This perplexity, namely, that the principle of public freedom and public happiness without which no revolution would ever have come to pass should remain the privilege of the generation of founders . . . has haunted all revolutionary thinking ever since.[102]

The moment the founders focused on representation and neglected "to incorporate the township and the town-hall meeting into the Constitution," the revolutionary spirit was lost and government became according to Arendt mere administration.[103] As the people's *political* space—the realm of appearances where *all* individuals could engage in public speech and deed—disappeared, so did the democratic principle of deliberation and political freedom itself. This is a challenge for Arendt's theory of principled action because the authority inherent in the founding act, which she praises as *political*, did not ultimately shape the constitutional framework in the way one could have expected. Even though the performed principles of the American Revolution were promise and deliberation, equal freedom as action was not institutionalized, codified, or respected as common law. Universal suffrage and equality under the law would not be able to make up for the lack of spaces of freedom, where individuals could actively engage in politics. Despite the commitment to building a house were freedom could dwell, based on promise and deliberation among equals, "the Constitution itself provided a public space only for the representatives of the people, and not for the people themselves."[104]

---

101. Ibid., 244.
102. Ibid., 224.
103. Ibid., 227.
104. Ibid., 230.

The exclusive representative character of the constituent process,[105] in which delegates from representative bodies were appointed by their peers in a closed selection process, prevented the principles of mutual promise and common deliberation being actualized through performance in the convention from yielding adequate foundations for freedom. Political freedom was exercised not by the people themselves but by their representatives; representation (and not equal political freedom) is then replicated and reproduced in the constitutional structure. Consequently, I argue that to establish adequate foundations the constituent process depends not only on the authority inherent in the principles of promise and deliberation enacted in political action, but also on the "membership" of the deliberative body; who participates seems to be crucial in the collective building of spaces of freedom. Very different from the open spaces Arendt imagined for the ideal political founding—a founding that could establish strong foundations for freedom, "both in the negative sense of liberation from oppression and in the positive sense of the establishment of Freedom as a stable, tangible reality,"[106] in which anyone could step in an engage in political action—the American constituent process was exclusionary and closed. The original exclusion based on discriminative self-selection was coupled with a formalism in the constitutional text that allowed for the cohabitation of freedom and slavery within the polity without openly establishing exclusions from citizenship in the founding document. Even if the American Constitution did not explicitly specify who "We the people" were—those who were equal and therefore entitled to liberty and the pursuit of happiness—the fact that the framers were all property-owning white males tacitly determined the characteristics of the members of the new body politic. This exclusiveness was then contested by a second liberation during the Civil War, liberation this time not from outside domination, but from slavery, the rule that had plagued the American polity since its birth.[107]

Despite the potentiality for inclusion of the constitutional document, which allowed for revolutionary legal reforms that ultimately extended citizenship to the majority of the population, freedom as spaces for action remained lost in

105. Even if I do not agree in principle that the referendum is not an adequate source of authority, I do agree with Jeffrey Lenowitz that the referendum in a constituent process led by a national assembly should not be conceived as a source of popular legitimacy. Lenowitz, "'A Trust That Cannot be Delegated.'"

106. Arendt, "Willing," 203.

107. Internal liberations and enlargements of the political community appear to be a never-ending process because membership relies on the exclusion of the "other" (nonwhites, women, youth, immigrants, etc.). Moreover, one could argue a political community is never finalized because with every new birth, there is a possibility of transformative action.

the American polity. The new legal framework "had given all power to the citizens, without giving them the opportunity of *being* republicans and of *acting* as citizens."[108] The liberal republic set up a system of constitutional liberties such that "the best it has achieved is a certain control of the rulers by those who are ruled," giving no space for participation in the political life of the republic:

> The most the citizen can hope for is to be "represented," whereby it is obvious that the only thing which can be represented and delegated is interest, or the welfare of the constituents, but neither their actions nor their opinions.[109]

Following Jefferson's plan of "elementary republics," which demanded continual interaction among citizens, Arendt puts forward with the council system an alternative form of government aimed at reintroducing freedom as action and expanding the public sphere. As Andreas Kalyvas has convincingly argued, through the establishment of councils Arendt seek to insert extraordinary politics within the constitutional structure. Infusing the analysis of councils with "her theory of constituent power and the revolutionary spirit that survives the closure of the revolutionary period,"[110] she attempts to bring together "radical change and legal continuity, the extraordinary and the ordinary."[111]

According to Arendt' reconstruction of the history of the councils, a task of both "recollection and invention as she constructs a tradition that she believes, as a historical fact, has never really existed,"[112] this type of assemblies is inherently modern. The councils are a new form of government that, at least partially, sinks its roots in the medieval towns and makes its appearance with the French Revolution.[113] Since then, different forms of councils have emerged spontaneously whenever there is a serious crisis of authority: the Paris Commune in 1871, the Russian soviets in 1905, the Bavarian Räterepublik in 1919, and the Hungarian councils in 1956. Despite its crucial role during revolutions, this spontaneous collective tradition of politics has been lost in modern democracy because it has not been properly institutionalized:

> The failure of post-revolutionary thought to remember the revolutionary spirit and to understand it conceptually was preceded by the failure of the revolution to provide it with a lasting institution.[114]

---

108. Arendt, *On Revolution*, 245.
109. Ibid., 260.
110. Kalyvas, *Democracy and the Politics of the Extraordinary*, 275.
111. Ibid., 264.
112. Muldoon, "Origins of Hannah Arendt's Council System," 786.
113. Arendt, *On Revolution*, 253.
114. Ibid., 223–24.

More than focusing on the inner workings of councils, on political action within those spaces of freedom, Arendt's assessment of these assemblies seems almost strictly constitutional. The councils are for her institutions aimed at establishing a new order, at constituting freedom:

> The councils, moreover, were always organs of order as much as organs of action, and it was indeed their aspiration to lay down the new order that brought them into conflict with the groups of professional revolutionaries, who wished to degrade them to mere executive organs of revolutionary activity. . . . [The councils] consciously and explicitly desired the direct participation of every citizen in the public affairs of the country.[115]

The councils are the organized multitude that decides to bind itself by shared rules and procedures, an institution that allows for power and freedom to be exercised, limited, and protected. They embody a particular order in which power is generated in collective political action, in which the revolutionary spirit—the capacity for new beginnings and the exercise of constituent power—is preserved and exercised. However, the council system is more than the "embodiment of constituent power in the new constitutional order."[116] Arendt saw these local assemblies not only as "the best instruments" to allow for the self-constitution of a truly political elite and as spaces open for everyone to exercise judgment on the affairs of the republic, allowing for those who want to be political to engage with others in the realm of appearances, but also as serving the purpose of "breaking up the modern mass society, with its dangerous tendency towards the formation of pseudo-political mass movements."[117]

Despite the radical democratic implications of the council system, I argue Arendt is not a radical democrat. Even though she saw as essential for freedom the preservation of the revolutionary spirit within the constituted framework, she did not intend for it to become supreme. The councils were an alternative form of government that ought to coexist with representative government, not replace it. She recognizes that what gives the new republics their stability is the party system and the recognition of the opposition as an institution in government.[118] As Arendt implicitly concedes, the same way that the Senate was the source of authority in the Roman republic, representative government based on a party system is what still would make rule legitimate and stable in

---

115. Ibid., 255.
116. Muldoon, "Arendt's Revolutionary Constitutionalism," 604.
117. Arendt, *On Revolution*, 271.
118. Ibid., 259.

modern republics. In contrast to Rome, where the power of the elite was checked by the assembled people, modern republics lack a popular institution to counterbalance parties as the expression of elite power. Thus, following a republican structure of mixed constitution, and building on Jefferson's "elementary republics," Arendt introduced a council system that she conceives as a ward-type structure in a twofold way: as *local* assemblies of the people—such as town halls—as well as a *containment* of representative government through the constant performance of freedom as action.

While we should consider Arendt's constitutional model of parties and councils to be a modern republican version of the institutionalized conflict between the elite and the people, the democratic principle inherent in the inner logic of the councils brings a new element into the analysis. I argue that the introduction of the democratic element—political action as an end in itself—into a republican mixed constitution creates a complex political system in which different conceptions of freedom and authority operate on different levels, coexisting but bound to conflict. While at the council level, deliberation is the source of authority and being free means to engage in speech and deed, at the system level, authority would reside on the republican institutional structure contained in the constitution, in which freedom is equivalent to security and balance of power. In order to preserve freedom, both as security *and* as action, party and council must interact and coexist. Without the councils, the public at large is not free; only the representatives are equals engaging in deliberation about public affairs and wielding political power. But without parties, administration and continuity of government in large nation-states seems almost an impossibility.

I argue that the conflict between parties and councils cannot be resolved by simply acknowledging the councils as bearers of constituent power.[119] For the conflicting authority of parties and councils to avoid constitutional crisis, the institutional conflict would need to be managed through a distinction and separation based, on the one hand, on a division of labor between administration and politics, and on the other hand, on their position within the constitutional structure. While the parties and representative government have as their main task to channel interest and administrate the state for the common good, the councils would be aimed at allowing for the exercise of judgment, "the most political of man's mental abilities,"[120] at allowing citizens to

---

119. For Carl Schmitt's sovereign deciding on the exception, see Kalyvas, *Democracy and the Politics of the Extraordinary*, 116, 119, and 134.

120. Arendt, "Thinking," in *Life of the Mind*, 192.

collectively "judge affirmatively or negatively the realities they are born into and by which they are also conditioned."[121]

Even if she left inconclusive her work on judgment, Arendt is clear that for her the capacity of judging is one of the "politically most important, rational faculties"[122] that, following Kant, emerges only in praxis. Judgment needs to be exercised and cannot be learned or arrived at by either deduction or induction.[123] For Arendt the "condition prerequisite for all judgment"[124] is the "deliberate withdrawal from involvement and the partiality of immediate interests"[125] in order to judge "particulars ['this is wrong'] without subsuming them under general rules."[126] Moreover, judging allows for the realization of thinking, "making it manifest in the world of appearances,"[127] and therefore the aim of the councils, as the institutionalized realms of appearance, is to enable the exercise of judgment, which in turn allows individuals to construct and discover the community and its limits. According to Linda Zerilli, for Arendt judging is an activity that is "formative of the public realm" but that is not defined "in terms of the production of a normative basis for political action."[128] Judgment is a faculty that "at once expands our sense of reality and affirms freedom."[129] Instead of setting rigid standards of validity, judging allows the imagination to be unrestrained from concepts and moral laws.

Because the object of judgment is the past,[130] the role of the councils within the constitutional structure would be to pass judgment on the actions of government. In this way, the councils would not share in administration (doing) but only pass judgment on it whenever it becomes necessary to deliberate on the particulars. The councils' judging function moreover would acquire a censorial authority from the position of these assemblies *outside* of the governmental structure. It would be their "no-rule" position that would allow for the councils to play a *negative* role in judging the outputs of government (law and policy). I argue that the realm of appearances would need to be mostly devoted to political judgment of representative government and to the role of the state in the shared world, for the councils to avoid the temptation of

121. Ibid., 71.

122. Arendt, *On Revolution*, 221.

123. Arendt, "Thinking," 215.

124. Ibid., 92.

125. Ibid., 76.

126. Ibid., 192.

127. Ibid., 193.

128. Zerilli, "'We Feel Our Freedom,'" 178–79.

129. Ibid., 178.

130. Arendt, "Thinking," 213.

directly ruling and undermining their primary censorial function. However, because judging the past is connected to thinking the future, "that is, to speculate meaningfully, about the unknown" and to "will the impossible,"[131] arguing for the councils as organs of political judgment in no way precludes the possibility of the improbable and the capacity to renew the republic from within. Even if the councils are "the institutionalized embodiment of a stabilized, pacified, and thus de-revolutionized constituent power,"[132] individuals in these councils would be able to exercise constituent power in the form of judgment, actively participating in the renewal of the republic.

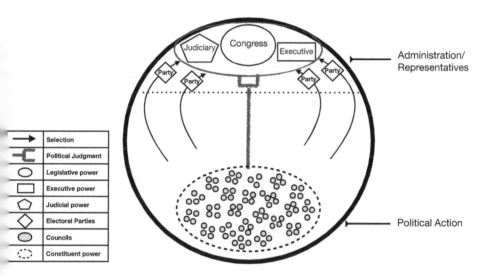

FIGURE 7.1. Interpretation of Arendt's republic of parties and councils.

131. Ibid., 71.
132. Kalyvas, *Democracy and the Politics of the Extraordinary*, 276.

PART III

Anti-oligarchic Institutions for the Twenty-First Century

8

Contemporary Plebeian Thought

GIVEN THE DEGREE of systemic corruption in liberal democracies and the increasing oppression ordinary people suffer at the hands of employers, landlords, lenders, insurance companies, and state bureaucracy, it is not surprising that the study of plebeian politics and ideology coming out of the resistance of plebeians against oligarchic power is becoming less of an oddity.[1] The first academic work to directly deal with plebeianism is Martin Breaugh's reconstruction of the intellectual history of plebeian politics in *The Plebeian Experience*, first published in 2007 in French. Breaugh traces what he calls a "plebeian principle" that resurges from time to time in history and that defines the plebeian experience as one of freedom and revolt, a refusing of "the limits of the possible present of the dominant order."[2] From the historical expression of the plebeian principle from Rome to the Paris Commune, to its philosophical roots in Machiavelli up to Rancière, Breaugh shows the discontinuous struggle for freedom of plebeians and argues for conceiving the plebian subject neither as a social category nor as an identity, but as an experience, "the passage from a subpolitical status to one of a full-fledge political subject."[3] The plebeian experience materializes only when "people excluded from the *res publica* transform themselves into political subjects able to act in concert."[4] Plebeianism is therefore an experience of self-emancipation through political action that challenges the established hierarchical order in which plebeians are subordinate subjects. Even if plebeian experiences have tended to be ephemeral

---

1. According to WorldCat, there has been no major publication in which the term "plebeian" was studied since the eighteenth century. Of course, this does not mean that the word has not been used by theorists such as Foucault and Rancière, but that having plebeianism as an object of study had not been attempted until Breaugh's *L'experience Plebeienne*.

2. Breaugh, *Plebeian Experience*, xvi.

3. Ibid., 1.

4. Ibid., 241.

because unable to "found a sustainable new political order,"[5] they have kept reappearing, irrupting spontaneously, nevertheless.

Attempting to theorize the plebeian experience within liberal democracies, Jeffrey Green argues that plebeianism is defined by a "shadow of unfairness" resulting from plutocracy, "the inescapable incursion of socioeconomic inequality into civic spaces."[6] This shadow, moreover, is a constant feature of our political systems—"a permanent mar on liberal-democratic regimes' capacity to fully realize the norms of free and equal citizenship"—even in the most "enlightened and advanced."[7] Plebeianism recognizes that "within liberal democracy *ordinary citizenship is second-class citizenship*"[8] and aims at "the identification and regulation of the most advantaged class."[9] According to Green the most significant contribution of adopting a plebeian lens to analyze liberal democracies is that it unveils the illusions of equal liberty that undergird the liberal-democratic structure:

> The premise of plebeianism is that prevailing accounts of liberal democracy today suffer from unreality insofar as they take the ordinary citizen to be (or potentially become) fully free and equal vis-à-vis citizens with significantly greater amounts of wealth, fame, and political influence. . . . Overcoming these various forms of unrealism is a chief value of a plebeian contribution to the study and practice of liberal democracy.[10]

Unlike Breaugh, who analyzed plebeian politics as a discontinuous history of emancipation, Green sees plebeianism as a permanent feature of liberal democracies, an ideology that prompts individuals not to engage in political action, but rather to remain in a place of passive-aggressive resistance vis-à-vis the oligarchy through what he calls "principled vulgarity," a mode of behavior through which plebeians transgress the "well-established norms of civility."[11] According to Green, through the recognition of "reasonable envy" originating in the contestation of the "superior power of the superrich," plebeianism could contribute to make liberal democracy's "ideas and institutions even more just."[12] While in the past plebeian ideology and politics helped establish plebeian institutions able to veto and introduce legislation as well as self-government

5. Ibid.
6. Green, *Shadow of Unfairness*, 4.
7. Ibid., 13.
8. Ibid., 9.
9. Ibid., 13.
10. Ibid., 20.
11. Ibid., 10 and 110.
12. Ibid., 13.

assemblies, for Green plebeianism today means engaging in "classism" and "rancor" to regulate the most advantaged class, and in "extrapoliticism" as "solace" for coping with an inevitable state of subordination.

Even if Green's material diagnosis of second-class citizenship is certainly within a plebeian conception of the oligarchic republic, the moral philosophy that he derives from this condition of subordination is at best partial and at worst antiplebeian. He argues that one of the purposes of plebeian theory is to "help ordinary citizens find solace in the face of the inevitable unease their second-class status will generate [in] them."[13] He proposes to embrace a modern interpretation of Epicureanism—a philosophy teaching "to live unnoticed" and "avoid politics"—understood as form of *extrapoliticism*, which conceptualizes "egalitarianism in terms of a critical indifference toward politics," but that would differ from antipoliticism and apoliticism.[14] Extrapoliticism challenges "the desirability of high political office" and offers coping mechanisms "whereby political longings temporarily might be sublimated in non-political form."[15]

Green argues that plebeian philosophy today should be understood as a form of Epicureanism, both because of the historical connection with this strand of philosophy and plebeians in the late Roman republic, and because of his own phenomenological study of the plebeian experience in contemporary liberal democracies. He argues that Epicureanism is a plebeian philosophy because it was one of the "dominant philosophical schools in late republican Rome" and "appears to have been especially popular among Roman plebeians."[16] Green's source is Cicero, who derogatorily labeled Epicureanism a "plebeian philosophy." However, that a philosophy is popular among plebeians (understood as a social category) does not mean that it is a *plebeian* philosophy. This is equivalent to saying that because liberalism today is one of the dominant political philosophies, it should be considered a philosophy of "the people." Apart from the "popularity" perspective, there is no necessary connection between Epicureanism and plebeianism—even if the majority of plebeians were indeed Epicureans.

In addition to the weak historical connection, I would argue this association between Epicureanism and plebeianism runs into a serious temporality issue, both in its initial attachment to plebeianism as well as in its transposition to current political systems. As I discussed in chapter 2, during the late Roman

13. Ibid., 66.
14. Ibid., 131.
15. Ibid., 133.
16. Ibid., 132–33.

republic the political power of plebeians was highly institutionalized in the Plebeian Council and the Tribunate, but owing to the progressive oligarchization of plebeian leadership, plebeians saw a de facto retrenchment of their political prerogatives. It is in this context—in which plebeians had acquired legislative supremacy after the Senate's preapproval of legislation was eliminated, but plebeian magistrates had ceased to constrain oligarchic power— that Epicureanism becomes popular among plebeians. It is in the summit of plebeian institutional power, where decay of plebeianism as an ideology and political praxis of emancipation seems to have begun, when the popularity of a skeptical view of public office and the detachment from politics took hold of plebeians. To render Epicureanism—a philosophy that was popular at a moment of corruption and the retreat of plebeian political ideology—as a plebeian philosophy is, to my mind, misleading given that it bears no resemblance with the plebeian principle that refuses the limits of the dominant order convincingly traced by Breaugh. Green argues that while Breaugh's interpretation of plebeianism is based on revolution, his conception of plebeianism is based on an "already embraced political regime" and thus is inherently reformist,[17] even if it is not clear how engaging in a Thoreau-type of civil disobedience in which plebeians withdraw from politics could achieve any meaningful reform.

Even if one grants that Epicureanism was indeed a plebeian philosophy that aimed at liberating plebeians from a political arena in which plebeian institutions had become oligarchic, the analogy Green makes with today's plebeian experience brings its own temporal challenges. The political situation in which second-class, ordinary citizens are today—completely lacking institutional power—has little to do with the high degree of entrenchment of plebeian power in the late Roman republic. I would argue that for theorizing plebeianism as an ideology that could be useful to bring solace to the awareness of the subordinate status of ordinary citizens today, one would have to look at the philosophy prevalent during the long conquest of political power by plebeians: from the establishment of the Tribunes of the Plebs in 494 BC up to the passing of *lex Hortensia* in 287 BC, which eliminated the Senate's veto power over plebeian law. Unfortunately, there are no surviving texts by plebeian thinkers, so the precise principles and postulates of the original plebeian philosophy that underpinned the plebeian struggle for political recognition and power in Rome cannot be retrieved. Nevertheless, it seems commonsensical that such a philosophy would not have embraced the withdrawal from politics, but on the contrary, the takeover of political power. If we compare plebeian power in

17. Ibid., 13.

Rome and in contemporary democracies, the differences are so pronounced that it seems difficult to make a meaningful "analogical reasoning"[18] and base a moral philosophy on it.

The main political power ordinary citizens have today is the right to elect representatives, and therefore, compared to the late Roman republic, there is still much political ground to be gained by plebeians, advances that in the past have resulted only from political action. A contemporary version of Epicurean- ism seems odd as an adequate plebeian philosophy because it is unlikely to produce the results that philosophical ideas achieved during the plebeian con- quest of political power. Even if the "shadow of unfairness" cannot be elimi- nated from liberal democracies, plebeianism should be aimed not only at "identifying and regulating" elites through the expression of "reasonable envy," but also at gaining political power by institutionalizing the power of plebeians. A philosophy that teaches the withdrawal from politics and the expression of reasonable envy instead clearly does not contribute to reforming the system, at least not in a direct manner.

Green's phenomenological account of the emotions and behaviors preva- lent among plebeians today seems close to what James Scott calls *infrapolitics*, the "low-profile forms of resistance"[19] against oppression that are part of the hidden transcript—the discourse of "gesture, speech, and practices" that is excluded from the public sphere[20]—once it has become public. According to Scott, when the oppressed assume the resistance of the hidden transcript as common and legitimate, the political subjectivization of the subaltern classes is possible. I would argue that "principled vulgarity" should be under- stood as providing the philosophical justifications for plebeian infrapolitics to be recognized in the open, and in this way allow for the collective conscious- ness of plebeians and the discursive reenactment of the divide between the few and the many. However, if this type of infrapolitics is combined with a withdrawal from politics, as Green suggests as solace for the awareness of sub- ordination, the result is not plebeianism—understood as the ideology and politics that aims at emancipating plebeians from oligarchic domination—but the sabotage of the process of plebeian subjectivization by discouraging and thus thwarting political action.

18. According to Green, his "analogical reasoning" can maneuver between the abstraction of purely analytical modes of thought . . . and the mere empiricism of purely historical modes of investigation." *Shadow of Unfairness*, 19.

19. James Scott, *Domination and the Arts of Resistance*, 19.

20. Ibid., 27.

Following Breaugh's plebeian principle, I argue plebeianism—as an ideology and politics aiming at the emancipation of plebeians, and not only at the constraint of elites—should rest on a political philosophy that embraces conflict as productive of liberty, such as the one proposed by Jacques Rancière. Even if Rancière does not make the explicit connection between the construction of the democratic people as "those who have no part" and the plebeian conception of the people, as those who do not rule and resist oligarchic oppression, the influence of plebeian ideology in Rancière's thought is substantive and explicit. His political philosophy was heavily influenced both by his participation in *Les révoltes logiques*—a journal aimed at "reconstructing grassroots thought" while breaking away from "proletarian metaphysics"—and by Pierre-Simon Ballanche's theorization of the "plebeian principle" in the history of the Roman republic,[21] which Rancière uses as a foundational narrative in his theory of politics as disagreement.[22] This plebeian principle, egalitarian and emancipatory, appears as intrinsically connected to democracy.

Even if influenced by Lefort in terms of his conception of democracy as being a space of power, Rancière, also a student of Althusser, rejects the connection between politics and the tendency to embody this empty place and embraces instead alterity, dissent, and equality as the principles of politics. Democracy is not a form of government or juridical framework, but a "community that is defined by the existence of a specific sphere of appearance of the people."[23] Democracy is actualized when the people, understood as those who do not take part in the oligarchic structure of power, are able to become visible, modifying the realm of the visible with their mere existence, an irruption that "splits reality and reconfigures it as double."[24] Democracy allows for an alternative image of society by providing a stage for the people to become a political subject. For Rancière democracy is not part of the oligarchic structures of power—what he calls the "police order"—but consists in the materialization of the logic of equality that is antihierarchical and conflictual:

> For the forms of democracy are nothing less than the forms in which politics is constituted as a specific mode of human being-together. Democracy is not a regime or a social way of life. It is the institution of politics itself, the system of forms of subjectification through which any order of distribution of bodies into functions corresponding to their "nature" and places

21. Breaugh, *Plebeian Experience*, 91–92.
22. Rancière, *Disagreement*, ch. 2.
23. Ibid., 99.
24. Ibid.

corresponding to their functions is undermined, thrown back on its contingency.[25]

Democratic politics are a politics of disagreement, "forms of expression that confront the logic of equality with the logic of the police order."[26] True political action is always democratic because it attacks inequality and seeks to dismantle patterns of oppression that have been naturalized through the discipline of the police logic. Because politics as disagreement has been completely foreclosed by consensus democracy—a postdemocratic regime in which there is an "absolute removal of the sphere of appearance of the people"[27]—instances of politics—popular performances of the egalitarian logic against the hierarchical logic of police—are only rare. The logic of police, which also structures and disciplines the system of political representation imposing a quantitative logic based on the counting and aggregation of individual preferences and votes, floods the public space, making politics sporadic and ephemeral, outbursts of emancipation amid the oligarchic structure of the police order.

The political act of plebeians is grounded on conflict, but not a "systemic" conflict of "interest between constituted parties of the population," "a discussion between partners," but a conflict "over the very count of those parties" that "undermines the very situation of interlocution."[28] The political dispute challenges the foundations of the system of police through a radical egalitarian logic that does not speak to the system but disrupts it through the political performance of the people, of those who do not have a part in the system but nevertheless claim it. "*Politics* means the supplementation of all qualifications by the power of the unqualified," the visible action of the people, those who are not supposed to act because ignorant and untrained.[29] Through this lens, there is no freedom without politics, and the only solace for plebeians is to *claim* a part in the political process by engaging in political action and performing their equality. I argue plebeian politics are more than mere outbursts within a dominant disciplinary logic of police, a performed malcontent of a self-constituted collective political subject, but a politics of active resistance that strategically uses institutions to change the political system from within. Plebeian institutional innovations that were later recognized and further formalized within the political power structure—the Council of the Plebs and

25. Ibid., 101.
26. Ibid.
27. Ibid., 103.
28. Ibid., 100.
29. Rancière, *Dissensus*, 53.

the Plebeian Tribunate—are based on a political philosophy centered on the institutional empowerment of "second-class citizens" within a given political structure, which necessarily means carving power away from the ruling elite.

Reviving the Tribunate

While "reasonable envy" could serve as a springboard for raising class consciousness among plebeians, plebeianism also demands effective institutional mechanisms to control ruling elites and successfully contest their domination. The first to develop the strand of plebeian thought that aims at institutionalizing plebeian power was John McCormick, who in *Machiavellian Democracy* sketched "a revived tribunate, combin[ing] elements of randomization, wealth-exclusion, and direct plebeian judgment"[30] as an institutional response "to the hegemony of elections in contemporary republics."[31] Focusing his analysis on the political structure rather than on the plebeian experience in contemporary representative democracies, McCormick argues constitutional representative regimes lack two crucial elements: extra-electoral means to control elites, and a political distinction between elites and the common people:[32]

> The aristocratic effect and the privileged access to resources and information enjoyed by magistrates in modern republics render elections inadequate mechanisms of elite accountability and responsiveness; moreover, a sociopolitical definition of "the people" that includes wealthy citizens, rather than one that sets the latter apart from or even opposed to the people, allows the wealthy to dominate common citizens in quasi-anonymous and largely uncontested ways.[33]

Not only are elections inadequate to disable oligarchic domination, but they also allow the few to exert covert domination with impunity while plebeians are left without the possibility of resisting and combating that oppression. Taking inspiration from Machiavelli's provost office, designed both to control elites and to "place 'rank-and-file' plebs in positions of political authority on a regular basis,"[34] McCormick proposes the incorporation into the US Constitution of a People's Tribunate: a collective plebeian office with the power to

---

30. McCormick, *Machiavellian Democracy*, 171.
31. Ibid., 172.
32. Ibid., 179.
33. Ibid.
34. Ibid., 173.

veto, call referenda, and initiate impeachment proceedings against public officials. This plebeian institution would be composed of fifty-one nonwealthy citizens selected by lottery, who would serve for one-year nonrenewable terms.[35] This proposal to add a plebeian institution to the constitutional framework of a representative democracy marks the origin of the theorization of a new form of mixed constitution. McCormick is therefore a twenty-first-century pioneer within the institutional strand of plebeian constitutionalism to which I also attempt to contribute. In what follows I lay out his institutional proposal and analyze the challenges that arise from wealth exclusion, mode of selection, and powers of the Tribunate.[36] I also analyze McCormick's most recent, highly controversial proposal: to establish "popularly judged political trials where public officials or private citizens, indicted for corruption or treason, face the penalty of death."[37]

Problems with Wealth Exclusions

McCormick's People's Tribunate is a political institution that excludes political and economic elites. While the exclusion of the political ruling class—defined as those who have held elected or appointed office—is not problematic because the exclusion is based on the temporary role performed by individuals, the exclusion of the wealthiest 10 percent of family households[38] raises a liberal challenge. Even if the aim of the exclusion is to redraw the boundary between the few and the many, and keep the rich from capturing plebeian institutions, introducing a class-based political institution in which representation would be attached to (the lack of) wealth, would be, at least in principle, unconstitutional because it would violate the fundamental right to equal liberty all citizens should enjoy under a liberal republic. Discrimination using suspect categories such as race, national origin, and religion is subject to strict scrutiny, which forces the state to prove a *compelling governmental interest* and to show that the use of the suspect category is *narrowly tailored* to achieve that interest. Even if the Supreme Court could agree that class is not a suspect category, because the division would be formal (10/90), giving plebeians exclusive political rights that other citizens are deprived of would infringe on

---

35. Ibid., 183. He also proposes appointment procedures for high office that combine lottery and election.

36. For an analysis of McCormick's Tribunate in comparison with participatory procedures—direct legislation, minipublics, and participatory budgeting—see Smith and Owen, "Machiavellian Democratic Innovations."

37. McCormick, "Democracy, Plutocracy and the Populist Cry of Pain," 18.

38. McCormick, *Machiavellian Democracy*, 183.

voting as a fundamental equal right. A strong argument would need to be made to claim that the exclusion of the rich from plebeian institutions is necessary, and that there is no other way to achieve the objective of the Tribunate without excluding individuals from political power based on their wealth. Perhaps the exclusion could be at least partially based on the pernicious effects of having elites present during deliberation—which speaks to the difficulties of "challenging dominant discourses that privilege elite interests when members of such elites are present in the deliberations."[39] Given that the mere presence of members of the elite could negatively affect the performance of the Tribunate, their exclusion would need to be categorical.

Even if the bending of the liberal framework to exclude the wealthy from political institutions could be construed as necessary and narrowly tailored, and therefore constitutional, and a class-based institution could be established in which the richest 10 percent of society is excluded from exercising a specific form of political power, this constitutional interpretation would give birth to a mixed constitution that does not embrace liberal principles as its overarching paradigm. In the illiberal beginnings of representative government, wealth requirements to participate in the political system, barring the poor from voting, were ubiquitous. Perhaps, after the franchise has been expanded to its maximal expression, and all discriminatory exclusions have been eliminated, the corrupted version of liberal democracies (already transforming into a new political form) could likely end with the reversal of the original gatekeeping rule with a twist: barring the wealthy from exercising political power in plebeian institutions. Although I agree that it is necessary to make the political distinction between the ruling elite and plebeians, as I argue in the next and final chapter, a class-based distinction is not the only way the division between the few and the many could be drawn.

The Precarious Legitimacy of Lottery

Regarding the mode of selection for the Tribunate, McCormick endorses lottery because it "keeps economic elites from monopolizing public offices" and materializes "the principle of equitable political participation among citizens."[40] Even if as an anticorruption mechanism lottery is certainly not infallible since plebeians could be bribed or manipulated, in terms of offering equal opportunities for participation, sortition clearly delivers. While there is no empirical evidence to support that elections "are especially capable of

39. Smith and Owen, "Machiavellian Democratic Innovations," 210.
40. McCormick, *Machiavellian Democracy*, 173.

providing good government or are significantly constrained in their behavior by retrospective voting patterns," selection by lottery *guarantees* the random distribution of offices among plebeians.[41] Selecting members to the Tribunate office by lot for short periods of time not only would make it very difficult for political corruption to become entrenched in that office but also would offer equal chances of exercising political power, and in this way it would fulfill the role that Machiavelli's provosts played in allowing common citizens to *see* and *experience* political power.

Even if lottery clearly is an equal-opportunity type of selection that seems most adequate to fill offices in plebeian institutions, the inclusion allowed by the Tribunate office sketched by McCormick would be, in real terms, marginal given the small number of tribunes selected every year. The extremely low probability of being selected to serve in office,[42] or know someone who has served and could transmit that plebeian political experience,[43] would allow only for limited political learning among plebeians and also potentially undermine the legitimacy of the office, especially if the motions pursued are controversial. Materially, the Tribunate office would be run by a group of selected few, who even if plebeian from a socioeconomic perspective, might not represent the multitude in terms of their particular worldviews. Why should an unelected office, selected at random and therefore not representative, have the authority to veto laws made by people elected by the citizenry? It seems lottery, as a procedure of selection, yields a precarious legitimacy if compared to elections, which even if faulty are deeply entrenched procedures in contemporary political systems. Moreover, discrepancies of opinion in controversial cases could easily lead to an attack on the mode of selection and calls for electing "better qualified" plebeians. In the Roman case, the establishment of a plebeian political elite was the first step toward cooptation and the undoing of the plebeian project; therefore the possibility of introducing elections to solve a legitimacy problem should be avoided at all costs.

Another challenge to the mode of selection for the Tribunate office proposed by McCormick is his endorsement of an "institutional affirmative action for common citizens,"[44] taking into account "the particular history of the United States" in which racial discrimination is systemic. He suggests to have

41. Ibid., 174.

42. In the United States, where 245.5 million people are of voting age, about 220 million people would be eligible for the Tribunate, which means that each citizen would have a 0.000023 percent probability of becoming selected through nonweighted lottery. Even if tribunician offices are also implemented at state level, the probability would still be very law.

43. After a decade, only 510 plebeians would have served in office.

44. McCormick, *Machiavellian Democracy*, 184.

a pool of citizens from which members of the Tribunate are drawn "altered to give African American and Native American citizens a greater chance of serving as tribunes."[45] Even if I sympathize with the redress of historic and current inequalities based on race, there is no reason, within the logic of the office, to give more chances of being selected to some groups of plebeians rather than others. If the intention of "weighted sorting" is to achieve equity by overrepresenting oppressed groups, who gets to decide which groups suffer more oppression and therefore are deserving of special treatment? What about the historic and current subordinate position of women, whose domestic and reproductive labor is extracted from them without compensation, who suffer pay discrimination, sexual harassment, and violence?[46] What about Hispanics, the new underclass of the American economy, who are constantly harassed by immigration police? What about Muslims, who are labeled as terrorists and are victims of hate crimes and harassment? And members of the LGBTQ community, who are targets of homophobic violence and social discrimination? The list of different types and degrees of oppression within the plebeian ranks goes on. The challenge to positively discriminate without negatively impacting other oppressed groups is one of the reasons why the US Supreme Court ruled in 1978 as unconstitutional the use of racial quotas in university admission processes: discriminating negatively or positively based on race violates the equal protection clause of the Fourteenth Amendment.[47] While the goal of achieving diversity in the classroom is legitimate, special admission procedures or quotas in which race is a *required* category are not.

"Weighted sorting" brings an element of arbitrariness into lottery that could also undermine the legitimacy of the office. Deciding on which social group would deserve higher chances to become selected to exercise political power is in itself a complicated political question that could unnecessarily intensify racial division among plebeians. Moreover, individuals from ethnic minorities and other oppressed groups are not necessarily in support of progressive politics that would positively impact second-class citizens. The example of Justice Clarence Thomas—the only African American member of the Supreme Court—who is against any form of affirmative action (even if he was himself a beneficiary of it) is the most visible and paradoxical case. Even if McCormick states that a "a veto exercised by the American Tribunate ought

45. Ibid.

46. As Graham Smith has pointed out, "it is not clear whether a government that gave special governing powers to the less affluent would do more to promote transformations in those practices." Smith, "Machiavellian Democracy," 243.

47. *University of California Regents v. Bakke*, 1978.

to block oligarchically favorable as opposed to popularly progressive policy initiatives,"[48] there is no guarantee that the office would pursue a progressive agenda or a plebeian one. If owing to random selection the Tribunate ends up with a majority of middle- and working-class racists, for example, or a majority of conservatives wanting to restrict women's reproductive rights and discriminate against LGBTQ citizens, there is no mechanism to assure that the Tribunate would not be used for nonplebeian, discriminatory ends. Given that in terms of the degree of identification individuals experience, class is perhaps the weakest and most difficult identity to maintain,[49] I argue a plebeian infrastructure needs to have procedures enabling actions pursuing plebeian, emancipatory ends and limiting attempts to use plebeian power to support the subjugation of one group to another. I argue plebeian law, even if aimed at restraining the power of the wealthy, should not contain the seeds of domination within it, since laws are always in need of interpretation and application, there to be deployed and exploited in social and political struggle in an uncertain future.

The Limits of Limited Powers

Regarding the constitutional powers of the People's Tribunate, McCormick follows a gradualist strategy that attempts to lower the threat posed by the new plebeian institution. Following the example of the gradual expansion of plebeian institutional power after the establishment of the Tribunate in Rome, and Machiavelli's support for the gradual expansion of plebeian power in Florence, McCormick proposes a quantitative limit to plebeian veto power in terms of the number of items that could be vetoed at any time. Upon a majority vote, the Tribunate has the prerogative to veto one law, one executive order, and one Supreme Court decision every year. McCormick's decision to restrict the amount of times the veto power can be exercised appears as strategically in tune with Machiavelli's concessions toward the powerful few in his constitutional proposal for Florence.[50] The same way that Machiavelli attempts to put a plebeian foot in the oligarchic door of power, which eventually would allow for plebeians to finally push the door open, by lowering the threat to the

---

48. McCormick, *Machiavellian Democracy*, 186.

49. See Aslanidis, "Populism as a Collective Action Master Frame for Transnational Mobilization." Recognizing the weakness of class identity vis-à-vis other stronger identifications based on race, religion, and national origin makes enabling ways of fostering plebeian identity a central task of plebeianism.

50. Machiavelli, *Discursus on Florentine Affairs*, cited in *Machiavellian Democracy*, 124.

security of the few,[51] McCormick proposes a Tribunate that has power to grow out of an unnecessary limitation.

Even if strategically this is a sound proposal, in tune with historic plebeian self-limitation, this procedural limit could open the possibility for manipulation from representative government and render the power of the office null. As was discussed in a symposium on *Machiavellian Democracy,* in *Good Society,*[52] Congress could pass controversial mock legislation anticipating a tribunician veto, and then push through antiplebeian legislation, effectively neutralizing plebeian power. I argue that in addition to the possibility of "gaming the system" and rendering plebeian power irrelevant, quantitative limitations would also needlessly restrict the anti-oligarchic prerogatives of the plebeian office, setting a procedural precedent that is likely to stand opposed to plebeian reforms. It could be the case that several pieces of legislation, executive orders, and court decisions need to be repealed at the same time to meaningfully dismantle structures of oppression and achieve social change.

In addition to the restriction placed on the *negative* power of the Tribunate office, McCormick also limits its *positive* power to initiate law or policy through a national referendum to only once per year, a restriction that does not seem as problematic as the limits on the veto/repeal, since it is unlikely that the office could propose more than one issue per year. If the referendum wins a majority, the Tribunate's legal project would become a nationally binding plebeian law. However, in a rather unplebeian move toward legislative supremacy, McCormick gives the power to overturn a national referendum to Congress if supermajorities in both chambers "declare the statute to be unconstitutional."[53] This legislative supremacy in which Congress is the final sovereign interpreter of the constitution positions the modern Tribunate in a *subordinate* position vis-à-vis representative government, equivalent to the position the Roman Tribunate enjoyed before *lex Hortensia* eliminated the senatorial veto on plebeian legislation, or to the position of the representatives of the commons in Montesquieu's model in which the Senate retains veto over legislation coming out of the lower house. This legislative veto power over plebeian law is especially troubling given that McCormick also gives the legal power to expand the basic powers of the Tribunate to a supermajority in the House of

---

51. McCormick, *Machiavellian Democracy,* 124.

52. *Good Society* 10, no. 2 (2011).

53. Ibid., 184. Even if this does not preclude further transformation, giving the power to veto plebeian law to the legislative would certainly cause a constitutional crisis in which institutional mechanisms to channel class conflict would be exhausted. For McCormick's response to this critique, see "Machiavellian Democracy in the Good Society."

Representatives. These provisions would render the Tribunate innocuous if Congress turns out to be in the grip of oligarchy. If plebeian law could be vetoed by representatives of oligarchy, and the power to expand plebeian power and override the veto are to be granted by the same representatives, then the Tribunate could be procedurally disarmed and effectively neutralized by institutionalized oligarchic power.

Corruption, Capital Punishment, and Popular Judgment

To institutionalize the surveillance power of the Tribunate, McCormick gives the office the prerogative, upon a three-fourths majority, to initiate impeachment proceedings against one public official in each branch of government; impeachment procedures and decision making would be directed by the Senate according to the Constitution. Therefore, McCormick gives to the Tribunate the power to exercise a prerogative that is today monopolized by the House of Representatives. This prerogative, however, is only to initiate proceedings and not to investigate and pass judgment. Even if initiating impeachment procedures in cases of political corruption is a great power to wield, it could be the case that impeachment cases brought up by the Tribunate would be tried in the Senate, and then dismissed. Given the increasing difficulty to materially prove political corruption, the Senate could easily let corrupt officials off the hook, rendering the Tribunate impotent as an anticorruption office.

Perhaps because aware of the limitation of impeachment procedures to effectively fight corruption, McCormick has more recently proposed another institutional innovation that relates to Machiavelli's *avenging power* aimed at instilling the same fear of punishment to those who "had done wrong" as it was experienced during the founding: popular trials empowered to decide on corruption cases in which death is the ultimate penalty. Such popular trials would be modeled based on the "capital trials by large citizen juries like those that convicted Socrates in Athens and Coriolanus in Rome."[54] Even if progressive liberals have moved away from capital punishment, especially given discriminatory sentencing and evidence of *cruel and unusual punishment* in the way in which criminals are killed,[55] McCormick follows Machiavelli's insight that the fear of capital punishment is the only way of "deterring

---

54. McCormick, "Democracy, Plutocracy and the Populist Cry of Pain," 18.

55. See, for example, Bernard Harcourt, "The Barbarism of Alabama's Botched Execution," *New York Review of Books*, March 13, 2018, https://www.nybooks.com/daily/2018/03/13/the-barbarism-of-alabamas-botched-execution/.

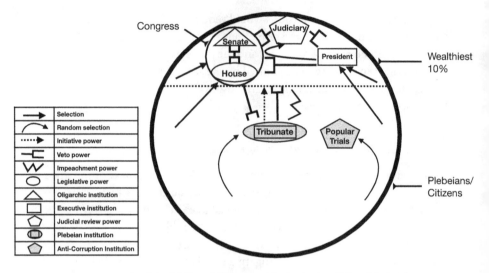

FIGURE 8.1. John McCormick's proposal for institutionalizing plebeian power in the United States.

socio-economic and political elites from steering public policy toward their own private, self-enrichment."[56] According to McCormick, imprisonment and banishment are inadequate forms of political punishment given that wealthy citizens circumvent penalties by using "their considerable resources to gain unwarranted pardons, to bust out of jail, or to return prematurely from exile."[57] Given the severity of punishing corruption with the death penalty, for McCormick the correct application demands additional "institutional modes" in which a large number of common citizens decide "over the lives of elites indicted for political crimes."[58] The only real deterrence for corruption are mass public trials in which death is the ultimate penalty.

Even if McCormick's method for adjudicating cases of political corruption is certainly unorthodox, it could be accommodated within current constitutional provisions either by defining corruption as a form of treason and oligarchic domination as a form of war against the republic, or by amending the Constitution to give public juries the power to decide on impeachment cases, which today is prohibited by article III, section II. What is more difficult to accommodate within the liberal paradigm is McCormick's suggestion to apply a form of *penal reparation* by "exempting the poor from the threat of

56. McCormick, "Democracy, Plutocracy and the Populist Cry of Pain," 19.
57. Ibid.
58. Ibid.

execution"—given that individuals from lower classes are currently overrepresented in death row—and reserving capital punishment only "for wealthy citizens or public officials found guilty of political or economic corruption."[59] First, to consider the amount of wealth one has in determining the punishment one receives in court would be in principle a violation of the equal protection clause, since every citizen should be given equal protection of the laws regardless of his or her socioeconomic status. And second, exempting the poor from execution in cases of corruption would place a pernicious incentive to bribe plebeians into corruption schemes, given the lesser penalty they risk if caught.[60] If corruption is conceived as treason to the republic because it is an existential threat to the liberty of plebeians, then it should not matter what the socioeconomic background is of the person accused of enabling oligarchic domination.

Plebeian Representation and the Challenge of Competing Authorities

Following the path charted by McCormick for the United States, Lawrence Hamilton sets out to rethink political freedom within a South African republic still dealing with the aftermath of apartheid as his "contextual and imaginative context." Moving away from a formal conception of freedom and toward a realist, material perspective based on the current praxis of political power, Hamilton wants to "deal comprehensively with the question of whether South Africans are now free":[61]

> States of domination are best overcome in practice by means of institutions of participation and power that take seriously the partisan nature of needs, interests and states of domination; and . . . therefore it is necessary to propose political institutions that act as counters to existing economic and political power balances in society and associated states of domination.[62]

Attempting to lay out a philosophical justification for incorporating class-based institutions, Hamilton argues that, given the proper procedural and institutional infrastructure, "freedom is power through representation"[63] because representatives have the power to "advance the needs and interests of

---

59. Ibid., 20.

60. This is similar to what happens with gangs that use children to sell drugs because they cannot be tried as adults and thus do not risk jail time.

61. L. Hamilton, *Freedom Is Power*, 1.

62. Ibid., 12.

63. Ibid., 193.

the citizens and reduce states of domination," and citizens have the power to restrain their representatives:

> *Representation enables the two main forms of power necessary for freedom*: the power of representatives to determine the general trajectory of a state's macroeconomic path and thus the power of its citizens, and the power of the citizens to control representatives in positive and negative ways.[64]

Following the Machiavellian idea that institutionalized conflict is productive of liberty, Hamilton argues that the freedom of individuals is better understood in relation to the group they are part of, and the power that the representatives of the group have to shape government policy:

> Given the complexity, division of labour and interdependence characteristic of modern conditions—freedom as power is not normally a matter simply of individual power but of the power of group representatives and their power to influence political representatives, especially in the determination of macroeconomic policy.[65]

With the aim of enabling usually dominated groups to exert power through their exclusive representatives to influence government, Hamilton proposes four institutional arrangements—two nonplebeian (a network of district assemblies and a conciliar system) and two plebeian (a Tribune office and an electoral procedure/quota)—as well as a popular constituent process. Hamilton argues a new popular infrastructure based on his institutional proposal would help "keep states of domination to a minimum," allowing for better identification of common interests and garnering of "support for partisan interests of normally powerless groups."[66]

The first two institutions Hamilton proposes—district assemblies and a conciliar system—are not class-based, partisan institutions but rather institutions that are local and inclusive. Hamilton envisions a network of district assemblies, not as decision-making institutions but rather conceived mainly as aggregators of local knowledge, as spaces in which citizens could articulate and evaluate needs and interest. District assemblies would also be a forum for the "presentation" of amendments to existing legislation and for voting on proposals coming from other assemblies, even if decisions reached in these assemblies do not appear to be binding or demand any active response from

---

64. Ibid.
65. Ibid., 197.
66. Ibid., 201.

government.[67] From each district assembly one counselor would be selected by lot for a two-year period to serve in a conciliar system: a group of local delegates to the national assembly aimed at *advising* representatives on local needs and interests.[68] Even if both district assemblies and the conciliar system have only nonbinding, consulting power vis-à-vis representative government, they are thought of as institutions that would allow for bridging the gap between representatives and their constituents, but without restricting the freedom representatives need to adequately advance the vital interests of the people.[69] Needs and interests would be first discerned and aggregated in district assemblies, then communicated by the counselors to representative officials, who then would have the freedom to decide which needs and interests to pursue at any given time. This first nonplebeian part of Hamilton's model is perfectly compatible with a liberal constitutional framework, a complement to the existing representative structure, even if its exclusively consulting power would have to be met with political will by representative government to achieve meaningful reform.

Hamilton also proposes two plebeian institutional arrangements: an "updated tribune of the plebs" and a plebeian election procedure/quota for the national assembly. Similar to McCormick's Tribunate, Hamilton's Tribune would be a class-based institution composed of representatives selected by lot from "dominated groups and classes in society," defined "either by a net-household-worth ceiling or associated measures."[70] This collective office would have two powers: to propose and veto/repeal legislation, and to impeach national representatives. Like McCormick, Hamilton places restrictions on the exercise of plebeian power by suggesting "strict and low" limits on the number of vetoes and impeachments that could be carried out every year.[71]

The second plebeian arrangement, aimed to "offset the potentially merely reactive character" of the Tribune, would be a "partisan, separate and independent electoral procedure" by which "the least powerful groups or classes in society" would elect 25 percent of the national assembly, "alongside the normal, open party-dominated processes of electing representatives within most existing representative democracies."[72] In effect, this partisan procedure would carve a supposedly "plebeian quarter" out of the national legislature.

---

67. Ibid., 202.
68. Ibid., 202–3.
69. For an analysis on freedom and representation, see chapter 5.
70. L. Hamilton, *Freedom Is Power*, 204.
71. Ibid.
72. Ibid.

Similarly to the introduction of electoral quotas for women and indigenous people, this partisan procedure would introduce a class-based quota that would presumably not only require that representatives be from plebeian origins but also require that only plebeians elect them. Even if electoral quotas would be unconstitutional in the United States, they are perfectly legal in other democracies around the world, which provides international legal precedents and empirical evidence for supporting them to solve class-based inequalities.[73] However, the effectiveness of having a plebeian section in the legislature, in terms of the advancement of issues specific to oppressed groups, is questionable. Not because 90 percent of citizens lack privileges and therefore share an experience of second-class citizenship will they necessarily challenge class domination if elected, or elect a representative that would on their behalf. To guarantee the plebeian character of these reserved seats, special rules would need to be put in place to strengthen the partisan character of this "plebeian quarter" by, for example, limiting the motions that could be initiated by these plebeian representatives to only plebeian-specific proposals.

Even if having plebeian quotas in the legislature could potentially be accommodated within the liberal framework, what would make for a harder sell in any constitutional democracy is the fact that some social groups would have the right to elect more representatives than others, which would constitute a violation of the principle of equal suffrage. To have reserved seats in Congress for plebeians to assure their adequate representation is not the same as allowing plebeian citizens to vote twice to select two representatives—one plebeian and one ordinary—instead of one representative like the other 10 percent of citizens. Moreover, even if the liberal challenge of attaching some political rights to only a part of the citizenry—to the exclusion of others—were overcome, this proposal would give the legislative body a dual source of authorization coming from the people-as-plebs and the people-as-a-whole, which could result in voters being represented by different officials taking opposing political stances. This added complexity could dilute political responsibility and accountability.

The most challenging issue raised by Hamilton's proposal for incorporating a plebeian quota to the legislative power is that it creates competing authorities between the Tribune and the plebeian representatives.[74] What would

73. For a review of gender quotas in Latin America, see Zetterberg, "Do Gender Quotas Foster Women's Political Engagement?"; Htun, "Is Gender Like Ethnicity?"

74. Having two plebeian institutions claiming to represent plebeians is different from having competing positions within a single plebeian institution like in the Roman Tribunate, where tribunes could veto each other's motions.

happen if plebeian representatives in the legislature were to propose and pass a law that is then vetoed by the Tribune? Or if the Tribune were to proposes a law that is then not supported by plebeian representatives? Should the veto of the Tribune—an office composed of randomly selected plebeian citizens to advance plebeian interests—be more authoritative than the vote of plebeian representatives who have also been elected to defend plebeian interests? This fundamental problem of competing authorities that comes along with the adding of participatory decision-making institutional arrangements such as citizen assemblies, public juries, and direct democratic procedures into constitutional democracies, needs to be accounted for when deciding between the different options available to be included in a plebeian republic. Even if participatory democratic theory and practice strives to increase participation by multiplying the instances of deliberation and decision, I argue participatory addendums could be compatible only if kept, as Hamilton suggests, at the consulting level, in which having a plurality of opinions and interests is beneficial. However, from the plebeian point of view, having multiple loci of decision making would blur the sharp distinction that should be drawn between the few and the many and would also dilute the authority of plebeian institutions. In a plebeian republic, the authority of plebeians, as a part of the people that stands opposed to the ruling elite, should be unitary and must be final—even if decisions could be reached by plebeians in a decentralized manner and certainly be reconsidered.

The final feature of Hamilton's constitutional proposal is a participatory constituent process in which citizens approve through a plebiscite a new constitution. The vote would be preceded by

> a month-long carnival of citizenship—a public holiday—in which all citizens would have equal formal freedom and power to assess existing social, economic and political institutional matrices and their effects on the determination and satisfaction of vital and agency needs.[75]

The constituent power, which could also be activated by any citizen through a "right of constitutional revision," would also have "*procedural* safeguards giving priority to the satisfaction of *vital* needs."[76] Hamilton's proposals for periodic constituent change attempt to institutionalize popular constituent power, but its provisions are so vague and partial that it is not clear how plebeians could participate effectively and not be mere receipts of information; or if the role of plebeians in the process would be merely advisory, like the role citizens

75. L. Hamilton, *Freedom Is Power*, 204.
76. Ibid., 205.

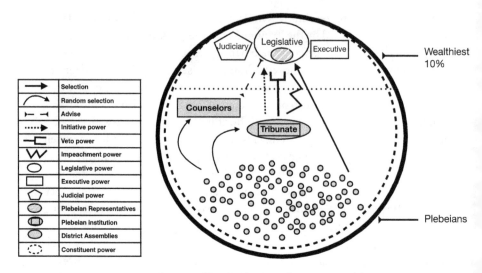

→	Selection
⌒↗	Random selection
⊢ ⊣	Advise
····▶	Initiative power
⊣⊏	Veto power
⋎	Impeachment power
◯	Legislative power
▢	Executive power
⬠	Judicial power
◐	Plebeian Representatives
⬓	Plebeian institution
⬭	District Assemblies
⟨ ⟩	Constituent power

FIGURE 8.2. Lawrence Hamilton's proposal to empower plebeians through representative institutions.

would play in district assemblies, or binding, being able to introduce and veto constitutional provisions through the tribune. As I argued in chapters 2 and 3, the issue of who is the bearer of the final decision-making power in a given constitutional arrangement—the few or the many—is of crucial importance to properly classify a mixed constitution as plebeian.

9

Constitutionalizing the Power
of Those Who Do Not Rule

IT IS IN TIMES of crisis when political imagination is needed most—even if thinking outside of the constitutional box may seem for some simply ridiculous or too extremist. This final chapter aims at contributing to the ideas and proposals I have analyzed in the previous chapters and in this way pays tribute to those who dare to boldly think of how to institutionalize the power of the many—even if this brought them the contempt of those in power. Machiavelli was demonized as the teacher of evil; Condorcet was persecuted for treason and died in prison; and Luxemburg was shot to death, and her work was vilified and marginalized. While the three of them wrote in moments of revolutionary upheaval, and thus the consequences for their intellectual deviance was more severely punished, Arendt's proposal for a system of councils was written in a moment of relative expansion of individual rights and analyzed after representative democracy had become "the only game in town" and thus was not viciously attacked but simply dismissed as a utopia, the product of a lack of realism on her part. Given our current political conjuncture, I argue there is a possibility to move away from ridicule and dismissal, and toward a renewed, serious engagement with the idea of giving institutional form to the power to the people, the plebeian constituent power that Machiavelli identified as crucial for keeping a republic free from oligarchic domination.

My proposal for constitutionalizing this power of those who do not rule is aimed at establishing a mixed constitution in which the people, understood as the assembled *many*, are the guardians of liberty. Only when the *many* have the final decision in what is considered oppressive and unjust, and have a collective institution to push back against discriminatory laws and policies, does their active resistance work to protect and enhance liberty. The juridical infrastructure I propose is meant as a contribution to the plebeian constitutional strand I have identified here, taking core elements from proposals and insights for institutionalizing popular power from Machiavelli, Condorcet, Luxemburg, Arendt, and contemporary thinkers of the subject like John McCormick and Lawrence Hamilton. I articulate these proposals aimed at addressing not only the liberal challenges raised by the introduction of class-based institutions but also the demands posed by a strong commitment to gender equality and the urgent challenge to manage increased migration due to material deprivation, violence, and environmental catastrophe.

The proposal is informed by Machiavelli's political philosophy, which is premised on the socio-ontological divide between the powerful *few* and the *many*, and the liberty-producing qualities of their conflict. A free republic demands plebian institutions. This new political infrastructure for the common people needs to allow for the exercise of a constituent power able to create laws and institutions aimed at liberty, as well as to punish those who, by engaging in political corruption, have betrayed the republic. I propose a way to institutionalize this dual constituent power following Machiavelli's "composite" approach to constitutionalism, which seeks to add new institutions and procedures while maintaining old forms and methods for the sake of stability. Consequently, despite these institutions having a rationale external to the current political framework, they are nonetheless designed to conform to the basic principles of the liberal structure existent in our current democratic constitutions. This "add on"method, however, would certainly not guarantee a conflict-free accommodation process. I argue that, the same as the introduction of a foreign object into a body could be accepted or rejected, plebeian institutions have a higher probability of acceptance by the liberal order if they are able to create as few antiplebeian bodies as possible. And the same way that a necessary medical treatment could cause a strong reaction before it is able to stabilize the body, enabling the healing process, plebeian institutions are likely to produce a strong reaction from oligarchy before they are able to effectively deal with its excesses.

Regardless, the successful establishment of plebeian institutions requires either a state of hegemony favorable for the introduction of a plebian political subject or a state of crisis in which a plebeian subject disrupts the political scene demanding a new constitutional order.[1] Despite free and fair elections,

---

1. Interestingly enough, in the current conjuncture, the three first neoliberal experiments, Chile, the United States, and the UK, are in crisis, facing plebeian challenges to the hegemony imposed during the last decade and a half of the Cold War. In the UK, Labour leader Jeremy Corbyn's government "for the many, not the few" was defeated at the ballot box, in great part because of the controversy around Brexit—the withdrawal of the UK from the European Union. In the United States the "political revolution" of Bernie Sanders could still win a majority and potentially change the existing hegemony through the electoral system. In Chile, a

establishing a counterhegemonic project of the *many* has proven difficult. Popular uprisings could potentially open a space for a redistribution of political power and institutional innovation from below—if they are able to survive state repression and achieve lasting organization.

In what follows I first give arguments for dividing the *few* and the *many* based on the position they occupy in the political system instead of along class lines, then introduce a sketch for a "Plebeian Branch" composed of two institutions: a sovereign network of local councils aimed at censoring governmental actions and renewing the republic, and a Tribunate office aimed both at enforcing the will coming out of the councils and at fighting corruption.

Separating the Few from the Many

Dividing the *few* and the *many* based on income or wealth would certainly be effective in making it easier for the people to scrutinize elites and punish them when they are self-serving. It would also promote the construction of a class-based identity among plebeians *against* wealthy elites, with long-lasting effects in the public imaginary. However, the division based on wealth carries within itself problems that are to be avoided if one wants to remain within the basic liberal structure of formal political equality. Even if establishing an updated version of the class-based political institutions in the Roman and Florentine republics would definitely have a positive effect in our representative democracies, I argue the political division between the few and the many should be done based on political power rather than wealth. Although the powerful few are almost always wealthy, it is not necessarily wealth what defines their oligarchic *umore* (appetite to oppress), but rather their power to *exercise* domination *over* ordinary people. Domination can be exerted in many ways, and even if money is a required resource to exert domination at a grand scale, the power to dominate is distinct from the amount of money a person possesses. This is true, even if all wealth is a social product and thus created through direct and indirect modes of exploitation.[2] Although wealth and the ability to dominate others are certainly related, there are individuals who oppress regardless of wealth (e.g., in a patriarchal system men subordinate women regardless of

disruptive plebeian subject took the streets in the popular uprising of October 18, 2019, to push back extra-institutionally against the neoliberal model, forcing the government to initiate a constituent process. On Chile, see my article "Chile Can Be a Laboratory of Popular Democracy," *Jacobin*, November 23, 2019, https://www.jacobinmag.com/2019/11/chile-protests -pinochet-constitution-neoliberalism.

2. Reproductive labor based on the indiscriminate exploitation of women is at the base of all social wealth. See Federici, *Caliban and the Witch*.

class) and others who are wealthy but choose to not directly oppress others (e.g., wealth-conscious benefactors of the poor). I argue that domination becomes a possibility only in *positions* of power, and therefore the division between the powerful few and the many needs to be not along class lines but rather political borders, separating individuals who are able to exert power at a large scale given the role they occupy in society from the rest.

I argue that a division based on the *governing position* of the few instead of how much money they have is less arbitrary and reifying of class. While excluding the richest 10 percent cannot overcome the arbitrariness of cutoffs for wealth requirements (e.g., one year a person could be rich enough to be excluded from the many, and the next unwealthy enough to be included), excluding those who have the ability to formally exert power *over* others and unduly influence the creation of law and policy—for example, public officials and their staff, lobbyists, judges, military commanders, and religious leaders—would establish a strictly *political* division between those who rule and those who do not. This gives an opportunity to members of the elites to become partisans of the people without the need to become "poor enough." Excluding only the *powerful* few should give plebeian institutions enough protection against direct oligarchic domination, since wealthy individuals eligible to participate in plebeian institutions are so few that their influence in terms of promoting oligarchic interests would be marginal. The argument barring elites because they would negatively influence deliberation within plebeian institutions is a sound one; however, the amount of money a member of the elites has does not necessarily track the capacity to persuade others in favor of supporting oligarchic interests. Moreover, alienating progressive elites—especially the new generations of political subjects who need to be socialized into politics—from becoming plebeian partisans would be, in my view, not only a strategic mistake but also against equal political rights. Nobody chooses to be born into a wealthy family or in a low-income one, and thus allocating political rights based on wealth would reify class differences in a way that could have detrimental effects for plebeian objectives.

Exclusions cause resentment if they are not self-exclusions—giving away wealth just to be eligible to participate in plebeian institutions requires an a priori extraordinary commitment to the plebeian cause, something that is not likely to come naturally to those born into wealth. Consequently, the wealthy are likely to resent the exclusion and therefore unlikely to support the introduction of plebeian institutions. Imposing wealth restrictions to participate in plebeian institutions seems unnecessarily contentious—even if this controversy would certainly prove beneficial to the plebeian cause, allowing for a stronger class consciousness to emerge among plebeians. As Rosa Luxemburg argues, working-class political experiences—even if unable to establish a free society—are crucial because they allow for the workers to become a political subject and accumulate experience to be able to achieve the desired transformation in the future.

The People as Network

Building on Condorcet's institutional proposal for establishing primary assemblies and Arendt's philosophical distinction between administration and politics, I propose to conceive the people-as-plebs as the assembled many who engage in political action: a sovereign network of local assemblies that makes decisions based on the aggregation of decentralized and autonomous collective judgments. Similar to the neurobiological structure of plants, in which there are "brains" in every root, local assemblies would operate as a bounded system, gathering information, processing it, and sending political signals through the network. And the same as a plant "decides" in precisely what direction to deploy its roots or leaves after gathering responses to the environment from its sentient parts,[3] the people-as-network would decide to initiate or oppose political actions based on local responses to domination spreading through the decentralized system. Approved motions would work as a "signaling" mechanism to bring awareness of domination to the network and prompt a response to it.[4]

This is different from a federation, in which diverse units with specific interests operate under an alliance. Assemblies in a network are stand-alone units but equal constitutive parts of a whole. Moreover, as a plebeian structure embodying the most proximate will of those who "do not rule," the collective decision in local assemblies would have legal power over representative government and its command structures. The people-as-network would constitute an institutional popular sovereign—and not an unorganized multitude in slumber[5]—with the strongest authority to judge the domination coming from the powerful few.

While as a *plebeian* institution the network of assemblies would fulfill the *functional* role of checking systemic corruption and resisting oligarchic domination, the internal organization of assemblies needs to be *democratic* and foster political action in order to achieve liberty for plebeians. Following

3. Michael Pollan, "The Intelligent Plant," *New Yorker*, December 15, 2013, https://www .newyorker.com/magazine/2013/12/23/the-intelligent-plant.

4. Plants of a same species signal each other to alert of pests by producing chemicals that work as neurotransmitters.

5. Tuck, *Sleeping Sovereign*.

Luxemburg's insights on the need for the self-emancipation of the workers through political action, and Arendt's argument for a space in which individuals can engage in action and new beginnings as a necessary condition for political liberty, each assembly would constitute a material political space, open to all those residents who do not rule. This realm of appearances, grounded on equality and aimed at the disclosure of opinions about life in common, would enable political discussions of what is just and unjust—what Plato and Aristotle deemed as the core of political rhetoric and action.[6] Given that political liberty is inherently limited, speech would need to be bounded within rules of engagement aimed at enabling the exchange of facts and opinions, and discouraging the use of discriminatory speech so to avoid bringing violence into the realm of appearances. Therefore, for political speech to be emancipatory and productive of liberty and not a vehicle for supremacist ends, its exercise would need to be adequately limited by antidiscriminatory provisions (see II.E.2 of "Plebeian Branch" proposal below).

Since political freedom is exercised not only by disclosing opinions, but also by acting together, individuals aggregated in the network of assemblies would have the power to decide collectively, not only to propose and repeal any decision from any branch of government they consider unjust and a means of domination, but also to exercise constituent power and revise the constitutional framework. Consequently, the juridical infrastructure of plebeian assemblies would need to enable not only "ordinary" political action by plebeians, but also the possibility of new beginnings to renew the republic from the ground up. Therefore, the proposal contains specific provisions for a constituent process to be initiated and ratified by the network of assemblies (IV and V).

Following Condorcet's radical inclusiveness, every adult residing for one year in a particular district would be eligible to attend and vote in his or her local assembly, regardless of citizenship status. Since plebeians constitute a political subject determined by its "no-rule" position in the constitutional structure, the institutionalization of plebeian power should not conform to current juridical boundaries separating citizens from immigrants but integrate newcomers through political equality instead of reserving politics only to citizens and in this way continue with the political apartheid between citizens and noncitizens. Against increasingly reifying the citizenship boundary between natives and nonnatives, radical inclusiveness based on residence—the

---

6. In Plato's *Gorgias*, deciding what is just and unjust is the aim of political rhetoric, and in Aristotle's *Politics* it is what defines our collective human nature.

material occupancy of space—aims instead at redrawing the political boundary between the few and the many.

If each assembly has in average six hundred active members (Condorcet recommends between 450 and 900) this would mean that there would be several assemblies even in small towns, which would enable assemblies to effectively channel diversity even *within* specific communities, allowing for a more engaged, less polarized citizenry, especially in regions divided across ethnic and religious lines.[7] If such a system of local assemblies were to be implemented in the state of New York, for example, in which there are 51.5 million individuals of voting age, there would be about 85,800 assemblies in the entire state. Manhattan, one of the most populous counties, with about one million voting-age residents, would have about 1,660 assemblies.

Where my proposal departs from Condorcet's model is in the method proposed for the assemblies' self-governance: he proposed a Council with elected members. To avoid the corrupting effects associated with elections and campaign finance—which Condorcet was unable to foresee and are so ubiquitous today—I argue the members of the self-governing structure of local assemblies should be selected by lottery. Following the experience of the ancient Greek Boule (βουλή), the agenda-setting council for the sovereign assembly (ἐκκλησία), members to the self-government councils would be selected by lot for a year, from a pool of volunteers, in a rotating basis to allow for institutional learning (II.C.5–10).[8] The main task of these councils would be to put together the agenda for meetings, effectively enable the exposition of topics, and enforce antidiscriminatory rules of engagement. Regarding the size of this Council, Condorcet recommends one Council member for every fifty assembly members. I would add this number needs to be an odd number to avoid gridlock. Councils thus would be composed of nine to nineteen members depending on district size. One third of the Council would be renewed every four months to enable collective learning. After serving for one term, citizens may not volunteer again for this office for fifteen years, which means that in one decade about one-fourth of assembly members would have served in the Council. This would allow every plebeian to serve in the Council one to four times in his or her lifetime. To allow for equal access, Council members would

---

7. Even if Jane Mansbridge has shown with her research on the town meetings in Shelby that there can also be intimidation and exclusion within consensus-building practices, shattering the illusion of equal deliberation, these problems can be dealt with through adequate rules of engagement and material support. Moreover, the assemblies I am proposing are not aimed at consensus but at channeling conflict. *Beyond Adversary Democracy*.

8. For a historical analysis of these Greek institutions, see Ober, *Democracy and Knowledge*; Ober, *Demopolis*.

receive a salary equivalent to the mean annual income in the district and would have their jobs back after their service.

Another departure from Condorcet's plan is that assemblies should not be convoked in a reactive manner, triggered by proposals coming from the citizens or the government. I argue this reactive mode of assemblage would mean that meetings could be either overwhelmingly frequent or too sporadic to serve as a proper way to politically educate its members. Given the busy lifestyles of twenty-first-century individuals, I argue meetings should be periodic, prescribed by law, and convoked only three times per year. Meetings are to be held on a national political holiday, and assembly goers are to be paid on an hourly basis for their participation with a special tax levied for covering the operational costs of plebeian institutions.[9] To assure gender equality, in addition to a civic payment for attendance, food and child care must be provided.

"Signaling" among assemblies would also follow Condorcet's proposal in which motions approved in one assembly are considered in other assemblies in the district. If one-third of assemblies in a district agree to a motion, then the proposal is considered by all the assemblies at the city/county level. If the issue were exclusively a city/county one, a decision by a majority of assemblies constitutes the will of the people at that level of political organization. This mechanism would be replicated at the state/region and national levels. In this way, political action aimed at resisting oppression and initiating change could arise in any part of the network of political judgment, giving individuals the institutional power to defend liberty against systemic corruption and oligarchic domination.

If, for example, a county such as Manhattan were to be divided into eight districts, containing about two hundred assemblies each, a motion passed in one assembly would prompt the other 199 assemblies in the district to consider analyzing the issue in the next assembly meeting. If one-third of these assemblies agree with the motion, then it would be added to the agenda of all the assemblies in Manhattan for the following meeting. If a majority of assemblies in Manhattan agrees to the motion, it is to be sent to the city Tribunate office, which presents it to the appropriate branch of city government and oversees its appropriate enforcement. The whole process, to have a motion

---

9. The civic pay for attendance should be pegged to an hourly rate, e.g., minimum wage, or based on GDP per capita and forty-hour week, or portion of universal basic income. If the state is going to end up paying people a universal basic income, I argue it would be better to link at least part of the UBI to active membership in political assemblies; unconditional UBI would just subsidize consumers for the market.

passed at each level of government, could take as little as four months if enough assemblies begin the process of inquiry simultaneously in the first meeting, and then a majority of assemblies votes in favor of the motion during the second meeting, or twelve months if the motion begins in a single assembly and follows the ordinary signaling mechanism. If the motion were one concerning state government, the motion is put in the agenda of all assemblies in every county, adding four months to the process. If the motion were one concerning the federal government, it is put in the agenda of the assemblies in every state, adding at least four more months. Consequently, a motion under federal jurisdiction could be approved by a majority of assemblies in four to twenty months.

The Tribunate as Enforcer and Anticorruption Office

The proposal also sketches a Tribunate office that would be subordinate to the network of assemblies, combining features of Machiavelli's provost office and Condorcet's Council of Overseers, with the impeachment prerogative of McCormick's Tribunate and public trials for political corruption. In its role of overseer and enforcer, the Tribunate would makes sure mandates coming out of the network of assemblies are properly and promptly carried out.[10] In its anticorruption function, the Tribunate investigates complaints of political corruption, having the power to initiate impeachment and prosecution procedures according to the constitution, and recommending a penalty. If the verdict of the appropriate branch of government in charge of impeachment or prosecution is not in line with the recommendation of the Tribunate, then the case is decided in a public trial in which all the members of the Tribunate pass judgment. The decision by the Tribunate is final.

To enforce the will of assemblies and persecute political corruption at every level of government, I propose offices of the Tribunate at the city/county and state/region levels, as well as the national level. Offices at the city/county level would each have nine members selected by lot from plebeian residents, while the state/region and national offices would have twenty-seven members selected in the same manner. To allow for collective learning and avoid corruption, tribunes would serve for one year, and one-third of the posts would be

---

10. The same as Rousseau's censorial tribunal, the plebeian Tribunate would only "declare" the judgment of assemblies. *Social Contract*, IV.7. The radical difference is that while the censorial tribunal declares the opinion of the people, which is "derived from its constitution," the Tribunate would declare the decisions reached in a majority of assemblies of the people. There is nothing to be derived since the will is declared and only in need of enforcement.

renewed every four months. If such a plebeian institution were to be implemented in the state of New York, there would be sixty-two county-level offices staffed with a total of 558 plebeian members, and one state office with twenty-seven plebeian members, who would serve for one-year terms. In cases of political corruption in which there is discrepancy between the recommendations by the local Tribunate office and the relevant branch of government, all members of the Tribunate would pass final judgment.

Finally, following Machiavelli's insight that for plebeians to live in liberty they need not only good laws, but also weapons to defend the republic against oligarchic takeover, the proposal reinforces the legal power of the Tribunate to command the different branches of government with the constitutional prerogative to direct the forces of order if necessary. While the Roman tribunes had only the threat of popular mobilization to force the Senate and the magistrates to enforce plebeian law, the modern Tribunate would have the constitutional power to command the state's forces of order to back up plebeian decisions that the ruling elite would prefer to disregard. Instead of resolving a constitutional crisis in which a part of the government disregards plebeian authority, which prompts the killing of the tribunes as it happened in Rome, the proposal attempts to resolve a potential crisis by transferring the command over the forces of order to the Tribunate in cases the government decides to disregard plebeian authority.

In what follows I provide a juridical sketch for a Plebeian Branch aimed at constitutionalizing the power of the people as way to adequately counter systemic corruption and oligarchic domination. The sketch has five parts. Part I offers a preamble with general considerations framing the institutions. Part II establishes the network of local assemblies and details their functions, membership, organization, and procedures. Part III establishes the office of the Tribunate and details its functions, membership, and organization. Finally, while part IV establishes the mechanisms to initiate constituent processes, and the procedures involved in revising and ratifying draft constitutions, part V sketches a founding constituent process with the necessary steps to establish a plebeian republic.

The Plebeian Branch

I. General Considerations

1. Plebeian institutions allowing for the direct participation of all adult residents in deliberation and public judgment are foundational to free government; equal liberty for all residents cannot be guaranteed without them.

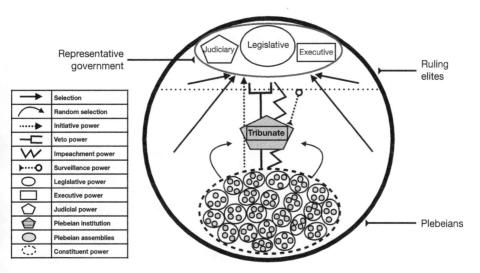

FIGURE 9.1. Proposal for constitutionalizing plebeian power.

2. The Plebeian Branch is to be composed of two basic institutions:
    a. A decentralized network of local assemblies of residents (see section II).
    b. A Tribunate—an office aimed at enforcing motions approved by the network of assemblies, and at fighting political corruption (see section III).
3. The total aggregation of local assemblies is the sovereign subject of the republic; a decision reached in the majority of assemblies is the legitimate will of the people, and all branches of government must yield to it and properly enforce it.
4. The Plebeian Branch is to be funded by a national tax collected for the sole and direct purpose of funding all the costs associated with the operations of local assemblies and Tribunate offices, and their appropriate exercise of constitutional powers.
5. All branches of government—Executive, Legislative, and Judicial—are to obey decisions reached by the Plebeian Branch.

II. Local Assemblies

A. Functions

1. Residents meet in local assemblies to deliberate on issues that affect the general interest of a district, city, county, or state, or the republic as a whole.

2. Members vote to:
   a. Initiate, veto, or repeal laws, policies, executive actions, judicial decisions, and appointments for public office;
   b. Initiate a constituent process;
   c. Propose amendments to the Constitution;
   d. Accept or reject a draft Constitution.

B. Membership
   1. Any adult person may register to be a member of a local assembly in any district if three conditions are fulfilled:
      a. Must have one-year residence in the district without interruption;
      b. Must not occupy a position of political, judicial, cultural or religious authority—including all public officials serving in political posts and their staff, judges, and religious leaders;
      c. Must not occupy a position as lobbyist advocating for wealthy individuals or corporations.
   2. Membership in a local assembly is to be temporarily lost by:
      a. Residence in another district for more than six months;
      b. Use of discriminatory speech or violent behavior in the assembly (see II.E.3);
      c. Occupying a position of political, judicial, cultural, or religious authority;
      d. Becoming a lobbyist or advocate for wealthy individuals or corporations.
   3. Any person who is absent for more than a year from the district is to regain voting in that district after three months.
   4. All members have the right to vote in all resolutions passed in their respective local assembly and are eligible for holding office in the Plebeian Branch in a rotating basis.
   5. No person is to vote for the same motion in more than one local assembly.
   6. Members have the right to propose a motion to be voted in their local assembly after collecting signatures from 10 percent of assembly members in support of the motion.

C. Organization
   1. Local assemblies are to be established throughout the republic according to residential districts or neighborhoods. Districts are to be set up in such a way that none of them have less than 450 eligible members, or more than 600.
   2. Local assemblies are to be grouped by neighborhood, city/county, and state/region.

3. Local assemblies are to meet three times a year in national political holidays for ordinary sessions. On the day of the meeting, communal meals as well as child care are to be provided, paid with public funds set aside for the operations of the Plebeian Branch.

4. Attendance at assembly meetings is voluntary and is to be compensated based on a predetermined hourly rate above the national minimum wage, using the public funds set aside for the operations of the Plebeian Branch.

5. Each local assembly is to be governed by a council selected by lottery from a pool of volunteers taken from the registered members of local assemblies. The council is to be composed of one councilperson per every fifty registered members in the assembly rolls. To avoid gridlock, the number of council members is to be an odd number. Councils thus are to be composed of nine to thirteen members depending on district size. Members are to serve as council president, leading and mediating meetings, in a rotating basis.

6. Members of the council are to be compensated for their service with a salary equivalent to the median wage in their district using public funds set aside for the operation of the Plebeian Branch, and guaranteed the return to their jobs once service is concluded.

7. Members of the council are to serve in their posts for one year. To allow for collective learning, one-third of the council is to be renewed every four months, before each general meeting of local assemblies.

8. After serving for one term, citizens may not volunteer again to serve in the council for ten years.

9. Duties of the council:
   a. Keep the register of members up to date;
   b. Convene the local assemblies in cases determined by the Constitution;
   c. Open and mediate member-exclusive forums in which members can raise concerns and proposals;
   d. Present an agenda for meetings based on the systematization of concerns and petitions coming from the members of the assembly, and motions passed in other assemblies;
   e. Gather and provide adequate information for deliberation;
   f. Enforce rules of engagement to enable adequate interaction in the assembly geared toward achieving a well-informed, deliberated decision;
   g. Present approved motions to other local assemblies and register them with the Tribunate office.

10. Within the duration of their service, council members must remain neutral during local assembly meetings. Council members are not to use their office to offer publicly their own judgment on any issue. They shall exercise their individual right to vote according to their own judgment, regardless.

D. Deliberation and Voting

1. After local assemblies are convened, their respective councils are to introduce subjects for deliberation, reduced to simple propositions, asking members to decide if they merit further discussion.

2. Local assemblies are to vote to accept or reject the further discussion of proposals. Proposals for deliberation are accepted with a simple majority of members present.

3. If a proposal is accepted for further discussion, during the adjournment each council is to enable deliberation by opening a member-exclusive media platform and also enable an exchange of opinions among members once a week in the assemblies' meeting spaces. Deliberation is to conform to basic rules of engagement (see II.E.2).

4. Local assemblies' meeting spaces are to be open every Sunday of the year for informal discussion. At least one council member is to be present to enable discussion and maintain order. Food and child care are to be provided, paid using public funds set aside for the Plebeian Branch.

5. Members interested in presenting their view to their local assembly on the issue to be deliberated are to send statements to the council, which aggregates these statements and structures a discussion to be held in the next meeting based on these statements. The structured discussion is to include as many different opinions as possible considering time constraints.

6. To ensure adequate information, in the following ordinary assembly meeting the council is to first recall the object of deliberation and then present facts, testimonies, and expert opinions whenever pertinent.

7. After adequate information has been provided, the council is to allot time for exchange of opinions and to moderate a structured discussion. To avoid reproducing patterns of inequality and domination in the deliberation, priority for speaking to the assembly is to be given to women, members of minorities, and first-time speakers.

8. After the presentation of evidence and opinion, the council is to present the issue as a simple proposition for members to vote yes or no.

9. A break of no less than fifteen minutes for informal discussion and caucusing is to precede every vote.

10. All votes are public except for the ones directed at disciplining members because of their use of discriminatory speech or violent behavior (see II.E.3).

11. All motions approved in local assemblies are decided by simple majority.

12. If the result of the vote is to support a motion, the issue is to be considered in the next meeting by all local assemblies in the city/county.

13. If an issue is a city/county one, a simple majority of local assemblies in support of a motion is to be understood as equivalent to the will of the people of that city/county. The decision is to be communicated to the local Tribunate office, which is to present it to the appropriate public office for enforcement.

14. If an issue was under the jurisdiction of state/regional authority, one-third of local assemblies in a city/county supporting a motion prompts the issue for consideration in all assemblies in that state/region. If at the state/region level one-third of local assemblies supports the motion of a national concern, it is to be put for consideration in all local assemblies in the republic.

15. A simple majority of local assemblies at the city/county and state/region is understood to be the will of the people at that particular level of organization.

16. If a majority of local assemblies in the republic approves a motion, this decision constitutes the will of the people, and the motion is to be presented by the Tribunate to the appropriate public office for enforcement.

17. If a majority of local assemblies in the republic approves to veto or repeal a law, the Legislative body is to be renewed: legislators who voted in favor of the vetoed or repealed law are to step down if still in office and their seats are to be up for election in the next cycle according to the Constitution.

18. If a majority of local assemblies in the republic approves to veto or repeal a policy, the elected public official(s) who approved that policy are to step down, and their positions are to be filled according to the Constitution.

19. If a majority of local assemblies in the republic approves to veto a judicial decision, the judges who approved that decision are to step down and their positions filled according to the Constitution.

20. If a majority of local assemblies in the republic approves to veto an appointment for public office, the persons who approved that appointment are to step down and their positions filled according to the Constitution.

21. The Executive, Legislative, and Judicial Branches may consult local assemblies on issues that interest the entire republic. If the issue is urgent, an extraordinary meeting of local assemblies may be convoked by the Tribunate after a formal request from government.

22. If there are concerns regarding the legitimacy of voting processes within local assemblies, these are to be addressed to the national Tribunate office.

E. Rules for Internal Order

1. The enforcement of order in local assemblies belongs essentially and exclusively to each assembly and is to be exercised by the council.

2. The use of discriminatory speech, symbols, images, and actions aimed at demeaning individuals or groups based on their race, ethnicity, religion, gender, sexual orientation, disability, or place of birth is to be prohibited.

3. The council is to call back to order, give warnings, and censor members who engage in discriminatory speech or violent behavior. The council is to recommend to the assembly in such cases a penalty of temporary exclusion. The local assembly is to approve or reject the penalty with a simple majority. Ballots in cases of temporary exclusion are secret so to avoid personal retaliation.

4. In the case of assault and serious excesses, the council may, after authorization from the local assembly, issue warrants against the accused.

5. Weapons are prohibited in Primary Assemblies.

III. Tribunate

A. Functions

1. As exclusive delegate of the people, the Tribunate is to oversee that the will of the people—equivalent to a decision by a majority of local assemblies in a certain city/county, state/region, or in the whole republic—is carried out properly.

2. As a surveillance office, the Tribunate is to oversee government to thwart corruption.
3. Duties of the Tribunate:
   a. Present approved motions to initiate, veto, and repeal laws, policies, executive actions, judicial decisions, and appointments for public office to the appropriate branch of government;
   b. Scrutinize the enforcement of the will of the people;
   c. Investigate cases of political corruption and initiate prosecution proceedings;
   d. Initiate impeachment procedures of public officials;
   e. Give final judgment on cases of political corruption when required;
   f. Analyze procedural issues arising from local assemblies;
   g. Initiate a constituent process by convoking constituent local assemblies.
4. Members of local assemblies have the right to present cases of abuse of power and violation of the law to the appropriate Tribunate office; cases are to be investigated and a report is to be sent back to the member(s) who submitted the case. If two-thirds of the pertinent Tribunate office agrees there is enough evidence of political corruption, the Tribunate is to recommend a penalty, and the case is to be prosecuted in open court or according to the Constitution.
5. If the verdict reached by the courts or other institutions sanctioned by the Constitution contradict the Tribunate's recommendation, the case would be decided in a public trial in which all members of the Tribunate are to participate in passing judgment. A two-thirds majority decision by the Tribunate invalidates the previous judgment.
6. If public officials disregard the mandates emanating from the Tribunate, they are to be stripped from their office and forced to resign their posts immediately. Any public official who is noncompliant is to be physically removed by the forces of order, put under arrest, and tried for treason.
7. The Tribunate is to direct the national police if necessary to enforce decisions reached by the Plebeian Branch in cases of noncompliance, overriding the authority of the Executive over the forces of order.

B. Membership
   1. Any member of a local assembly is eligible to serve in the Tribunate. Selection is to be done by lottery from a pool of volunteer members.
   2. Members of the Tribunate are to serve in their posts for one year. To allow for collective learning and avoid corruption, one-third of

the Tribunate is to be renewed every four months, before each general meeting of local assemblies.

3. After serving for one term, members are not eligible to serve in the Tribunate for fifteen years.

4. Members of the Tribunate are to be compensated for their service with a salary equivalent to the median wage in their state using public funds set aside for the operation of the Plebeian Branch.

5. Members serving in the Tribunate must give up their position immediately if any of the requirements for membership in local assemblies prescribed in II.B.1 and II.B.2 are not met. Vacant positions are to be filled before the next ordinary meeting of local assemblies.

6. Members of the Tribunate who have completed their term may be indicted on corruption charges by a two-thirds vote in the renewed Tribunate office.

C. Organization

1. Tribunate offices are to be established at each level of government—city/county, state/region, and federal/national levels.

2. Each office at city/county level is to be composed of nine members selected by lottery from a pool of volunteers.

3. At each level, offices are to have jurisdiction over the corresponding government and public officials serving in that government at that level.

4. Tribunate offices at the state and national levels are to be composed of twenty-seven members each, selected by lottery from a pool of volunteers. The offices are to be further divided into three committees dedicated to dealing with challenges posed by government, corruption, and procedures.

IV. Constituent Process

A. General Considerations

1. The constituent process is aimed at reviewing and improving the constitution of the republic.

2. Modifications to the constitutional structure can neither eliminate the foundational network of local assemblies nor go against the principle of equal liberty.

3. Every generation has the right to analyze and improve the basic structure of the society in which they live.

4. Any member of a local assembly has the right to initiate a constituent process, after gathering fifty signatures from other members
   in their local assembly supporting the motion. The process is
   the same as for any other motion initiated in local assemblies
   (see II.D).
5. The constituent process is to be funded by an extraordinary tax
   levied specifically for this purpose. Allocation of funding is to be
   managed by the Tribunate.

B. Initiation and Processes
   1. The constituent process is to be initiated periodically, in the
      seventeenth year after the acceptance of the current constitution, or
      when a majority of local assemblies in the republic demands it.
   2. The constituent process is to go through three basic stages:
      a. Propositional—constituent local assemblies are to be convoked
         by the Tribunate to review the Constitution and propose
         amendments.
      b. Redaction—proposed amendments are consolidated and redacted
         in a National Convention convoked by the Executive Branch and
         elected by the people at large.
      c. Approval—amendments are voted in constituent local assemblies.
   3. After the last ordinary meeting of local assemblies in the seven-
      teenth year after the acceptance of the current constitution, or
      if a majority of local assemblies approves it, the Tribunate is to
      initiate a constituent process by convoking constituent local
      assemblies. Four meetings are to be scheduled in the first month of
      the eighteenth year after the acceptance of the current constitution.
      Meetings are to be held once a month within that year.
   4. Each constituent local assembly is to follow the basic organization
      of ordinary local assemblies and be governed by a council selected by
      lottery from a pool of volunteers taken from the registered members.
      The council is to be composed of one councilperson per every fifty
      registered members in the Assembly rolls. To avoid gridlock, the
      number of council members is to be an odd number. Councils thus
      are to be composed of nine to thirteen members depending on district
      size. One of the members is to serve as president of the council.
   5. Members of the council are to be compensated for their service
      with a salary equivalent to the median wage in their state, using
      public funds set aside for the operation of the Plebeian Branch.
   6. Members are to serve in their posts for four months. This post can
      only be held once in a lifetime.

7. Duties of the Council:
   a. Open and moderate a member-exclusive forum for concerns and proposals;
   b. Prepare and present a presentation of current constitutional framework;
   c. Present a series of simple propositions for amendments based on concerns and proposals coming from members, or motions passed in other assemblies;
   d. Gather and provide adequate information for deliberation;
   e. Enforce rules of engagement to enable adequate interaction in the assembly geared toward achieving a well-informed, deliberated decision;
   f. Present approved motions to other local assemblies and register them with the Tribunate office.
8. Within the duration of their service, council members must remain neutral during assembly meetings. Council members are not to use their office to offer publicly their own judgment on any issue. They shall exercise their individual right to vote according to their own judgment, regardless.
9. All motions approved in local assemblies are to be gathered and systematized by the national office of the Tribunate.
10. The Executive Branch is to convoke a National Convention in the first month of the nineteenth year after the acceptance of the current constitution, or when prompted by the Tribunate after a motion is accepted by a majority of local assemblies.
11. Each state of the republic is to select by popular vote three individuals to the National Convention.
12. The National Convention is to redact the proposals coming out of local assemblies into amendments to the Constitution.
13. All meetings of the National Convention are to be public, and detailed minutes are to be kept in a public record.
14. Members elected to the National Convention are prohibited from incorporating new proposals; they are to channel, as accurately as possible, popular judgment into constitutional form.
15. The National Convention is to present a draft constitution to the Tribunate in two months' time.
16. Upon receiving a draft constitution from the National Convention, composed according to the constituent process rules specified above, the Tribunate is to convoke a general meeting of constituent local assemblies to reflect and vote on the amended constitutional framework.

17. A new constitution is to be approved or rejected in a general meeting of constituent local assemblies. The document is to be approved by a simple majority of local assemblies in the republic.
18. If the new constitution abolishes or disables local assemblies, or contains provisions undermining the principle of equal liberty, even if approved by a majority of local assemblies, is to be considered null and void; such a constitution is not a free republic.
19. If the draft constitution is approved by a majority of local assemblies, it is to be implemented in the first month of the nineteenth year after the acceptance of the current constitution.
20. If the draft constitution is rejected, the National Convention has to present within one month's time a revised draft to the Tribunate, which is to convoke an extraordinary meeting of constituent local assemblies to vote on the new draft.
21. If the draft constitution is rejected a second time, the National Convention is to be immediately dissolved. The Executive is to call elections for a new National Convention, which is to present a new draft constitution to the Tribunate within three months' time. The constituent process is to unfold following articles 10 and 11 of this section.

V. Foundational Constituent Process

A. General Considerations
   1. The constituent process is aimed at establishing a new constitution that gives institutional structure to a network of local assemblies and the Tribunate.
   2. The new document must respect the principles of equality liberty and human dignity.
   3. The constituent process is to be financed by an extraordinary tax collected specifically for this purpose.

B. Initiation and Processes
   1. The constituent process begins after local assemblies have been established at the national level in accordance with sections II.B and C.
   2. The constituent process must go through three basic stages:
      a. Proposals: Constituent local assemblies are convened to propose basic principles and rights to frame the constitutional document. The documents emanating from each assembly are to be

systematized in regional and national Councils into a plebeian declaration of rights.

    b. Drafting: The new constitution is to be written, framed by this declaration, by a National Constituent Convention convened by the Executive Power and elected by the people at large.

    c. Approval: The new constitution is ratified or rejected in constituent local assemblies.

3. The first stage will be held in four meetings within a calendar year.

4. Each constituent local assembly is to follow the basic organization of ordinary local assemblies and be governed by a council selected by lottery from a pool of volunteers taken from the registered members. The council is to be composed of one councilperson per every fifty registered members in the assembly rolls. To avoid gridlock, the number of council members is to be an odd number. Councils thus are to be composed of nine to thirteen members depending on district size. One of the members is to serve as president of the council.

5. Members of the council are to be compensated for their service with a salary equivalent to the median wage in their state, using public funds set aside for the operation of the Plebeian Branch.

6. Members are to serve in their posts for four months. This post can only be held once in a lifetime.

7. Duties of the Council:

    a. Open and moderate a member-exclusive forum for concerns and proposals;

    b. Prepare and present a presentation of current and alternative constitutional frameworks;

    c. Present a series of simple propositions for articles based on concerns and proposals coming from members, or motions passed in other assemblies;

    d. Gather and provide adequate information for deliberation;

    e. Enforce rules of engagement to enable adequate interaction in the assembly geared toward achieving a well-informed, deliberated decision;

    f. Present approved motions to other local assemblies.

8. Within the duration of their service, council members must remain neutral during assembly meetings. Council members are not to use their office to offer publicly their own judgment on any issue. They shall exercise their individual right to vote according to their own judgment, regardless.

9. After the four meetings of the constituent local assemblies, twenty-one delegates will be selected for regional councils, which are to systematize the motions passed in local assemblies, and twenty-one delegates for a national council in charge of consolidating the proposals systematized by the regional assemblies in a document. Delegates will be chosen by lot from a pool of volunteers. The regional councils must submit the proposals to the national council in sixty days, and the national council must submit a final document in thirty days.

10. Members of the councils must be compensated for their service with a salary equivalent to the average salary in their state, using public funds for the operation of the plebeian institutions.

11. The Executive Power will convene elections for a National Constituent Convention once the national council has produced a declaration of basic principles and rights.

12. Each region of the republic will select by popular vote three people for the National Constituent Convention.

13. The National Constituent Convention must draft a constitution in accordance with the declaration issued by the constituent local assemblies.

14. All meetings of the National Constituent Convention must be public, and detailed minutes must be kept in a public register.

15. The members elected to the National Constituent Convention are prohibited from incorporating new proposals contravening the declaration of principles and rights; they must channel, as accurately as possible, the popular judgment into constitutional form.

16. The National Constituent Convention is to present a draft constitution within six months.

17. Upon receiving a draft constitution from the National Convention, composed according to the constituent process rules specified above, the constituent local assemblies are to reflect and vote on the new constitutional framework.

18. A new constitution is to be approved or rejected in a general meeting of constituent local assemblies. The document is to be approved by a simple majority of local assemblies in the republic.

19. If the new constitution does not establish local assemblies, or contains provisions undermining the principles of equal liberty and human dignity, even if approved by a majority of local assemblies, it is to be considered null and void; such a constitution is not a free republic.

20. If the draft constitution is approved by a majority of local assemblies, it is to be implemented immediately.

21. If the draft constitution is rejected, the National Convention has to present within one month's time a revised draft. An extraordinary meeting of constituent local assemblies is to be convoked to vote on the new draft.

22. If the draft constitution is rejected a second time, the National Convention is to be immediately dissolved. The Executive is to call elections for a new National Convention, which is to present a new draft constitution within three months' time. The constituent process is to unfold following articles 11 and 12 of this section.

Epilogue

WHAT IS TO BE DONE?

THE FAMOUS political pamphlet that Vladimir Lenin published in 1902, *What Is to Be Done?*, charted the Marxist way forward for the brewing revolutions in Russia. Advocating to focus on developing a vanguard party instead of organizing the workers, Lenin chose a centralist strategy for a seizure of power that was effective in taking control of the state but did not yield the free society that many young revolutionaries had in mind. After the institutionalization of the revolutionary class and the brutality of Stalinism, the answer to the question *What is to be done today to realize equal liberty?* needs to avoid this ultimately failed centralist path in which the revolutionary party imposed a top-down project, "emancipating" from above the working classes, who could do no more than pledge their allegiance to the soviet state.

The original book from which Lenin took the title of his pamphlet offers instead a grassroots strategy. Nikolay Chernyshevsky's 1863 novel *What Is to Be Done?*, written after the emancipation of the serfs in Russia, became an instant classic and influenced generations of revolutionaries with its egalitarian ethos, feminist critique, and communal means to achieve freedom. This inspiration for social change, however, had no institutional projection. After surveying utopian socialist solutions, Chernyshevsky dismissed them all and did not answer the question positively.[1] This father of Russian populism,[2] the dominant ideological current of those actively opposing the tsarist regime in the nineteenth century, promoted a realist, people-centered approach to

---

1. For a politico-literary analysis, see Drozd, *Chernyshevskii's "What Is to Be Done?"*

2. For a brief analysis of Russian populism and its continuities with populist politics in the nineteenth, twentieth, and twenty-first centuries, see my article "Populism as Plebeian Politics."

politics that nevertheless proved incapable of producing institutional proposals to empower the people within the political system.

In this time of crisis, in which the legitimacy of representative institutions is rapidly eroding, choosing a path of organization and institutionalization of popular power seems the only long-term solution to disable the oligarchization of political power. However, the same way that it is necessary to move away from vanguard-party solutions to domination, it is also essential to shed any traces of idealist thinking in regard to the self-organizing power of atomized peoples living in contemporary consumer societies. Without proper institutionalization, the power of the *many* vis-à-vis the powerful *few* is bound to be ephemeral and most likely too weak to achieve the structural reforms that are needed to reverse the process of increasing oligarchization of power and the consequent oppression of contemporary plebeians.

Writing also in revolutionary times, Rosa Luxemburg proposed a solution to this question of strategy, which she laid out in her pamphlet *What Does the Spartacus League Want?*, and which seems the best one in terms of its realism and long-term emancipatory capabilities: the revolutionary party's main task must be to support the organization in councils of the workers—the many—and to enforce their expressed will. Establishing councils is a revolutionary act that needs to be enabled but not controlled by the vanguard party. For a revolutionary process to be really emancipatory and produce a framework in which freedom can dwell, it needs to materialize the autonomous self-emancipation of the people in political institutions. To achieve equal liberty, the many need to perform their own emancipation *in* action, and therefore the institutionalization of equal access to political action—which according to Arendt can be experienced only collectively in the realm of appearances—is the proper end of revolution. The first decision of the revolutionary party that seizes control of political power must be to limit its power by recognizing the supreme authority of the assembled many. This act of self-limitation, similar to the ones performed by founders of republics in antiquity, would inaugurate a new political regime in which the many, not the selected few, have final decision-making power.

Even if the birth of the assembled many as new collective sovereign subject, the *people-as-network*, is in itself revolutionary, the means by which this revolutionary end can be achieved are not necessarily part of an outright revolutionary process, but this end could be accomplished through the procedures already in place in our political systems. In a republic in which political leadership still has legitimacy, a new prince à la Machiavelli could campaign on the need to institutionalize popular power to realize the promise of democracy and keep government in check, become elected to the highest place of power, and establish, by decree, autonomous plebeian institutions through which the *many* can assemble to pass judgment on ruling elites. For the decisions reached in this network of plebeian assemblies to be binding, inaugurating with it a mixed order, the exiting constitution would need to be amended. However, if formal amendment procedures are not conducive to a constituent process, a majority decision in the network of local plebeian assemblies should have enough authority to initiate the process and at the same time constitute itself as sovereign subject. This new institutional plebeian power as ultimate guarantor of liberty would inaugurate a new regime form: a plebeian republic.

In the case that systemic corruption has taken hold of representative institutions and has undermined the legitimacy of elections to the point that a "new prince" might not be an option for a refounding, the only power with enough authority to lead structural reforms would be the one exerted by the assembled many themselves. Even if a constituent process from below, without the support of virtuous leadership and the legal power of the executive branch to institutionalize plebeian assemblies, would be extremely difficult to pull off, self-constitution and plebeian new beginnings are certainly not impossible. I hope my proposed blueprint for institutionalizing the power of the many contributes to guiding "prudent and able" leaders, revolutionary vanguards, and commonsense people in how to establish a plebeian republic capable of escaping the cycle of corruption and guaranteeing freedom from oligarchic domination to the common people.

Abensour, Miguel. *Democracy against the State: Marx and the Machiavellian Moment*. Translated by Max Blechman and Martin Breaugh. Malden, MA: Polity, 2011.

———. "Savage Democracy and Principle of Anarchy." *Philosophy and Social Criticism* 28, no. 6 (2002): 703–26.

Ackerman, Bruce. *We the People: Foundations*. Cambridge, MA: Belknap Press of Harvard University Press, 1993.

Althusser, Louis. *Écrit Philosophiques et Politiques I*. Paris: Librairie générale francaise, 1999.

———. *Machiavelli and Us*. Translated by François Matheron. London: Verso, 2000.

Aquinas. *Summa Theologica*. Vol. 2, part 1, first section. New York: Cosimo, 2007.

Arato, Andrew. "Forms of Constitution Making and Theories of Democracy." *Cardozo Law Review* 17 (1996): 191–231.

Arato, Andrew, and Jean Cohen. "Banishing the Sovereign? Internal and External Sovereignty in Arendt." *Constellations* 16 (2009): 307–30.

Arendt, Hannah. *Between Past and Future: Six Exercises in Political Thought*. New York: Meridian Books, 1969.

———. *Crises of the Republic*. New York: Harcourt, 1972.

———. "A Heroine of Revolution." *New York Review of Books*, October 6, 1966. https://www .nybooks.com/articles/1966/10/06/a-heroine-of-revolution/.

———. *The Human Condition*. Chicago: University of Chicago Press, 1998.

———. *The Life of the Mind*. New York: Harcourt, 1977.

———. *On Revolution*. New York: Penguin Books, 2006.

———. *The Origins of Totalitarianism*. New York: Harcourt, 1985.

Aristotle. *Metaphysics*. Vols. 1–9. Cambridge, MA: Harvard University Press, 1933.

———. *Nicomachean Ethics*. Indianapolis: Hackett, 1999.

———. "On the Constitution of Athens." In *Aristotle and Xenophon on Democracy and Oligarchy*, edited by J. M. Moore, 147–207. Berkeley: University of California Press, 1983.

———. *Physics*. Vols. 1–4. Cambridge, MA: Harvard University Press, 1957.

———. *Politics*. Translated by Ernest Barker. New York: Oxford University Press, 1958.

Arrow, K. J. *The Limits of Social Organization*. New York: Norton, 1974.

Aslanidis, Paris. "Populism as a Collective Action Master Frame for Transnational Mobilization." *Sociological Forum* 33 (2018): 443–64.

Baker, K. M. *Condorcet: From Natural Philosophy to Social Mathematics*. Chicago: University of Chicago Press, 1975.

Barcham, Manuhuia, Barry Hindess, and Peter Larmour, eds. *Corruption: Expanding the Focus.* Acton: Australian National University Press, 2012.

Bargu, Banu. "Machiavelli after Althusser." In *The Radical Machiavelli: Politics, Philosophy and Language,* edited by Filippo Del Lucchese, Fabio Frosini, and Vittorio Morfino, 420–39. Boston: Brill, 2015.

Barthas, Jérémie. "Il pensiero costituzionale di Machiavelli e la funzione tribunizia nella Firenze del Rinascimento." In *Il Laboratorio del Rinascimento,* edited by L. Tanzini, 239–55. Firenze: Le Lettere, 2016.

———. *L'argent n'est pas le nerf de la guerre: Essai sur une prétendue erreur de Machiavel.* Rome: École française de Rome, 2011.

———. "Machiavelli in Political Thought from the Age of Revolutions to the Present." In *The Cambridge Companion to Machiavelli,* edited by John M. Najemy, 265–66. Cambridge: Cambridge University Press, 2010.

———. "Machiavelli, the Republic, and the Financial Crisis." In *Machiavelli on Liberty and Conflict,* edited by David Johnston, Nadia Urbinati, and Camila Vergara, 257–79. Chicago: University of Chicago Press, 2017.

Beard, Charles. *An Economic Interpretation of the Constitution of the United States.* Mineola, NY: Dover Publications, 2004.

Benhabib, Sheyla. *The Reluctant Modernism of Hannah Arendt.* New York: Rowman and Littlefield, 2003.

Berlin, Isaiah. "Two Concepts of Liberty." In *Four Essays on Liberty,* 118–72. Oxford: Oxford University Press, 1969.

Billias, George A. *American Constitutionalism Heard Round the World, 1776–1989: A Global Perspective.* New York: New York University Press, 2016.

Blättler, Sidonia, and Irene M. Marti. "Rosa Luxemburg and Hannah Arendt: Against the Destruction of Political Spheres of Freedom." *Hypatia* 20, no. 2 (Spring 2005): 88–101.

Blythe, James M. *Ideal Government and the Mixed Constitution in the Middle Ages.* Princeton, NJ: Princeton University Press, 1992.

Bomhoff, Jacco. *Balancing Constitutional Rights: The Origins and Meanings of Postwar Legal Discourse.* Cambridge: Cambridge University Press, 2013.

Bonadeo, Alfredo. *Corruption, Conflict and Power in the Works and Times of Niccolò Machiavelli.* Berkeley: University of California Press, 1973.

Breaugh, Martin. *The Plebeian Experience: A Discontinuous History of Political Freedom.* New York: Columbia University Press, 2016.

Brudney, K. M. "Machiavelli on Social Classes and Class Conflict." *Political Theory* 12 (1984): 507–19.

Canovan, Margaret. *Hannah Arendt: A Reinterpretation of Her Political Thought.* Cambridge: Cambridge University Press, 1993.

Carpenter, Edward W., and Charles F. Morehouse. *The History of the Town of Amherst, Massachusetts: Published in Two Parts.* Amherst, MA: Carpenter and Morehouse, 1900.

Carrese, Paul. *The Cloaking of Power: Montesquieu, Blackstone, and the Rise of Judicial Activism.* Chicago: University of Chicago Press, 2010.

Carson, John. *The Measure of Merit: Talents, Intelligence, and Inequality in the French and American Republics, 1750–1940.* Princeton, NJ: Princeton University Press, 2007.

Castiglione, Dario. "The Political Theory of the Constitution." *Political Studies* 44, no. 3 (1996): 417–35.

Ceva, Emanuela, and Maria Paola Ferrett. "Political Corruption." *Philosophy Compass* 12, no. 12 (2017): 1–10.

Charles I, king of England. *His Majesties Answer to the Nineteen Propositions of Both Houses of Parliament.* https://www.constitution.org/eng/nineteen_propositions_1642.html.

Chernyshevsky, Nikolay. *What Is to Be Done?* Translated by Michael R. Katz. Ithaca, NY: Cornell University Press, 1989.

Cicero. *"On the Commonwealth" and "On the Laws."* New York: Cambridge University Press, 2009.

———. *Pro Rabirio Perduellionis Reo Oratio Ad Quirites.* Cambridge: Cambridge University Press, 1882.

Cohen, G. A. *Karl Marx's Theory of History: A Defense.* Princeton, NJ: Princeton University Press, 2000.

Cohen, Joshua. "Deliberative Democracy and Democratic Legitimacy." In *The Good Polity,* edited by A. Hamlin and P. Pettit, 17–34. Oxford: Blackwell, 1989.

Cohler, Anne M. *Montesquieu's Comparative Politics and the Spirit of American Constitutionalism.* Manhattan: University of Kansas Press, 1988.

Collins, Hugh. "Roberto Unger and the Critical Legal Studies Movement." *Journal of Law and Society* 14, no. 4 (1987): 387–410.

Condorcet, Nicolas de. *Adresse à l'Assemblée Nationale, sur les conditions d'éligibilité. Oeuvres,* vol. 10, 79–91. Paris: Firmin Didot Frères, 1847.

———. "Sur le sens du mot révolutionnaire." *Oeuvres,* vol. 18, 4–26. Paris: Firmin Didot Frères, 1847.

———. *Cinco memorias sobre la instrucción pública y otros escritos.* Madrid: Ediciones Morata, 1994.

Condorcet: Foundations of Social Choice and Political Theory. Edited by Iain McLean and Fiona Hewitt. Cheltenham: Elgar, 2007.

Condorcet: Political Writings. Edited by Steven Lukes and Nadia Urbinati. Cambridge: Cambridge University Press, 2012.

Condorcet Studies. Edited by Leonora C. Rosenfield. Atlantic Highlands, NJ: Humanities, 1984.

Constant, Benjamin. "The Liberty of the Ancients Compared with That of the Moderns." In *Political Writings,* 309–28. Cambridge: Cambridge University Press, 1988.

Corruption Perceptions Report 2016. Transparency International. https://www.transparency.org/news/feature/corruption_perceptions_index_2016.

Cotton, James. "James Harrington and Thomas Hobbes." *Journal of the History of Ideas* 42, no. 3 (July–September 1981): 407–21.

A Critical Dictionary of the French Revolution. Edited by François Furet and Mona Ozouf. Cambridge, MA.: Belknap Press of Harvard University Press, 1989.

Crook, Malcolm. "The Persistence of the Ancien Régime in France: The Estates General of 1789 and the Origins of the Revolutionary Electoral System." *Parliaments, Estates and Representation* 13, no. 1 (1993): 29–40.

Dalotel, Alain, Alain Faure, and Jean-Claude Freiermuth. *Aux origines de la Commune.* Paris: François Maspero, 1980.

Dautry, Jean, and Lucien Scheler. *Le Comité Central Républicain des vingt arrondissements de Paris*. Paris: Éditions Sociales, 1960.

Day, James, and Mortimer Chambers. *Aristotle's History of Athenian Democracy*. Berkeley: University of California Press, 1962.

de Dijn, Annelien. "On Political Liberty: Montesquieu's Missing Manuscript." *Political Theory* 39, no. 2 (April 2011): 181–204.

DeLeon, Peter. *Thinking about Political Corruption*. New York: Routledge, 1993.

Del Lucchese, Filippo. "Machiavelli and Constituent Power: The Revolutionary Foundation of Modern Political Thought." *European Journal of Political Theory* 16, no. 1 (2017): 3–23.

Democracy Index 2016. Economist Intelligence Unit. https://www.eiu.com/public/topical _report.aspx?campaignid=DemocracyIndex2016.

Dionysius. *The Roman Antiquities of Dionysius of Halicarnassus*. Translated by Earnest Cary. Cambridge, MA: Harvard University Press, 1937.

Dobel, Patrick. "The Corruption of a State." *American Political Science Review* 72, no. 3 (September 1978): 958–73.

Drozd, Andrew M. *Chernyshevskii's "What Is to Be Done?": A Reevaluation*. Evanston, IL: Northwestern University Press, 2001.

Dunayevskaya, Raya. *Rosa Luxemburg, Women's Liberation and Marx's Philosophy of Revolution*. Chicago: University of Illinois Press, 1991.

Elster, Jon. "Constitution-Making and Violence." *Journal of Legal Analysis* 4, no. 1 (Spring 2012): 7–39.

The English Levellers. Cambridge: Cambridge University Press, 1998.

The Essential Rosa Luxemburg: "Reform or Revolution" and "The Mass Strike." Edited by Helen Scott. Chicago: Haymarket Books, 2008.

Evgeny Pashukanis: Selected Writings. Edited by Piers Beirne and Robert Sharlet. London: Academic, 1980.

Federici, Silvia. *Caliban and the Witch: Women, the Body and Primitive Accumulation*. New York: Autonomedia, 2004.

Fine, Robert. *Democracy and the Rule of Law: Liberal Ideals and Marxist Critiques*. London: Pluto, 1984.

Fink, Z. S. "Venice and English Political Thought in the Seventeenth Century." *Modern Philology* 38, no. 2 (November 1940): 155–72.

Foucault, Michel. *Power/Knowledge: Selected Interviews and Other Writings*. Edited by C. Gordon. New York: Pantheon Books, 1980.

Fritz, Kurt. *The Theory of the Mixed Constitution in Antiquity: A Critical Analysis of Polybius' Political Ideas*. New York: Columbia University Press, 1954.

Gädeke, Dorothea. "Does a Mugger Dominate? Episodic Power and the Structural Dimension of Domination." *Journal of Political Philosophy*, 28.2 (2020), 199–221.

Gaille, Marie. "What Does a 'Conjuncture-Embedded' Reflection Mean? The Legacy of Althusser's Machiavelli to Contemporary Political Theory." In *Machiavelli on Liberty and Conflict*, edited by David Johnston, Nadia Urbinati, and Camila Vergara, 399–413. Chicago: University of Chicago Press, 2017.

Gardbaum, Stephen. "The 'Horizontal Effect' of Constitutional Rights." *Michigan Law Review* 102, no. 3 (2003): 387–459.

Gardiner, Samuel. *The Constitutional Documents of the Puritan Revolution, 1625–1660*. Oxford: Clarendon, 1962.

Geras, Norman. *The Legacy of Rosa Luxemburg*. New York: Verso, 2015.

Geuna, Marco. "Extraordinary Accidents in the Life of Republics: Machiavelli and Dictatorial Authority." In *Machiavelli on Liberty and Conflict*, edited by David Johnston, Nadia Urbinati, and Camila Vergara, 280–306. Chicago: University of Chicago Press, 2017.

Giannotti, Donato. "Della repubblica de' Viniziani." In *Opere politiche*, edited by Furio Diaz, 43–58. Milan: Marzorati, 1974.

Goldoni, Marco, and Michael A. Wilkinson. "The Material Constitution." *Modern Law Review* 81 (2018): 567–97.

Gourgouris, Stathis. *The Perils of the One*. New York: Columbia University Press, 2019.

Green, Jeffrey. *The Shadow of Unfairness: A Plebeian Theory of Liberal Democracy*. New York: Oxford University Press, 2016.

Guicciardini, Francesco. *Dialogue on the Government of Florence*. Edited by Alison Brown. Cambridge: Cambridge University Press, 1994.

Hamilton, Alexander, James Madison, and John Jay. *The Federalist Papers*. Edited by Clinton Rossiter. New York: Signet Classics, 2003.

Hamilton, Lawrence. *Freedom Is Power: Liberty through Political Representation*. Cambridge: Cambridge University Press, 2016.

Hankins, James. "Machiavelli, Civic Humanism, and the Humanist Politics of Virtue." *Italian Culture* 32, no. 2 (September 2014): 98–109.

Hansen, Mogens H. *The Athenian Democracy in the Age of Demosthenes: Structure, Principles, and Ideology*. London: Bristol Classical, 2001.

Harrington, James. *"The Commonwealth of Oceana" and "A System of Politics."* Edited by J.G.A. Pocock. Cambridge: Cambridge University Press, 2003.

———. *The First Book Containing a Full Answer to All Such Objections as Have hitherto Bin Made against Oceana*. London, 1700. In *The "Oceana" of James Harrington and His Other Works*, edited by Jihn Toland. Old English Books Online. https://quod.lib.umich.edu/cgi/t/text/text-idx?c=eebo;idno=A45618.0001.001.

———. *The Political Works of James Harrington*. Edited by J.G.A. Pocock. Cambridge: Cambridge University Press, 2010.

Harris, W. V. *War and Imperialism in Republican Rome, 327–70 B.C.* Oxford: Clarendon, 1979.

Head, Michael. *Pashukanis: A Critical Reappraisal*. New York: Routledge, 2008.

Heidenheimer, Arnold, ed. *Political Corruption*. New York: Routledge, 2017.

Heywood, Paul, ed. *Political Corruption*. Oxford: Blackwell, 1997.

Hill, Lisa, and Bruce Buchan. *An Intellectual History of Political Corruption*. Hampshire: Palgrave Macmillan, 2014.

Hobbes, Thomas. *Leviathan*. Edited by David Johnston. New York: W. W. Norton, 2020.

Holmes, Stephen. "Precommitment and the Paradox of Democracy." In *Constitutionalism and Democracy*, edited by Jon Elster and Rune Slagstad, 195–240. Cambridge: Cambridge University Press, 1988.

Htun, Mala. "Is Gender Like Ethnicity? The Political Representation of Identity Groups." *Perspectives on Politics* 2, no. 3 (September 2004): 439–58.

Hudis, Peter. *Marx's Concept of the Alternative to Capitalism*. Chicago: Haymarket, 2013.

Isaac, Jeffrey. "Oases in the Desert: Hannah Arendt on Democratic Politics, *American Political Science Review* 88, no. 1 (March 1994): 156–68.

Jefferson, Thomas. *Political Writings*. New York: Cambridge, 1999.

Jensen, Merrill. *The Making of the American Constitution*. Princeton, NJ: Van Nostrand, 1964.

John Adams, Works. Vol. 6. Edited by C. F. Adams. Boston: Little and Brown, 1850–56.

Johnson, Martin Philip. *Paradise of Association*. Ann Arbor: University of Michigan Press, 1997.

Johnston, Michael. *Syndromes of Corruption: Wealth, Power, and Democracy*. Cambridge: Cambridge University Press, 2010.

Jones, Peter Murray. *The Peasantry in the French Revolution*. Cambridge: Cambridge University Press, 1988.

Judde de Larivière, Claire, and Rosa M. Salzberg. "Le peuple est la cite: L'idée de popolo et la condition des popolani à Venise (XVᵉ–XVIᵉ siècles)." *Annales: Histoire, Sciences Sociales* 68, no. 4 (2013): 1113–40.

Kalyvas, Andreas. "Constituent Power." In *Political Concepts: A Critical Lexicon*. https://www.politicalconcepts.org/constituentpower/.

———. *Democracy and the Politics of the Extraordinary: Max Weber, Carl Schmitt, and Hannah Arendt*. Cambridge: Cambridge University Press, 2009.

Kelsen, Hans. *Das Problem der Souveränität und die Theorie des Völkerrechts: Beitrag zu Einer Reinen Rechtslehre*. Tubingen: J.C.B. Mohr, Paul Siebeck, 1920.

Kennedy, Duncan. "Form and Substance in Private Law Adjudication." *Harvard Law Review* 89, no. 8 (June 1976): 1685–778.

King, Margaret L. *Venetian Humanism in an Age of Patrician Dominance*. Princeton, NJ: Princeton University Press, 1986.

Krause, Sharon. "The Spirit of Separate Powers in Montesquieu." *Review of Politics* 62, no. 2 (Spring 2000): 231–65.

Lahtinen, Mikko. *Politics and Philosophy: Niccolò Machiavelli and Louis Althusser's Aleatory Materialism*. Chicago: Haymarket Books, 2011.

Leipold, Bruno. "Marx's Social Republic: Radical Republicanism and the Political Institutions of Socialism." In *Radical Republicanism: Recovering the Tradition's Popular Heritage*, edited by Karma Nabulsi, Stuart White, and Bruno Leipold, 172–93. Oxford: Oxford University Press, 2020.

Lenin, V. I. *Collected Works*. Vol. 1. New York: Verso, 2017.

———. *Collected Works*. Vol. 10. Moscow: Foreign Languages, 1965.

———. *Collected Works*. Vol. 25. Moscow: Foreign Languages, 1972.

———. *What Is to Be Done? Burning Questions of Our Movement*. New York: International, 1929.

Lenowitz, Jeffrey. "'A Trust That Cannot be Delegated': The Invention of Ratification Referenda." *American Political Science Review* 109, no. 4 (2016): 803–16.

Lessig, Lawrence. "Foreword: 'Institutional Corruption' Defined." *Journal of Law, Medicine and Ethics* 41, no. 3 (2013): 553–55.

———. *Republic, Lost: How Money Corrupts Congress—and a Plan to Stop It*. New York: Twelve Hachette, 2011.

Levitsky, Steven, and Daniel Ziblatt. *How Democracies Die*. New York: Crown, 2018.

Lintott, Andrew. *The Constitution of the Roman Republic*. Oxford: Oxford University Press, 2015.

Livy. *The History of Rome*. Vol. 1. Translated by George Baker. London: Jones, 1834.

Locke, John. *Political Writings*. Edited by David Wootton. Cambridge, MA: Hackett, 2003.

Lutz, Donald S. "The Relative Influence of European Thinkers of Late Eighteenth-Century American Political Thought." *American Political Science Review* 78 (1984): 189–97.

Machiavelli Chief Works and Others. Vols. 1, 2, and 3. Translated by Allan Gilbert. Durham, NC: Duke University Press, 1989.

Machiavelli on Liberty and Conflict. Edited by David Johnston, Nadia Urbinati, and Camila Vergara. Chicago: University of Chicago Press, 2017.

Madison, James. "Speech Proposing the Bill of Rights." June 8, 1789. https://www.let.rug.nl/usa /documents/1786-1800/madison-speech-proposing-the-bill-of-rights-june-8-1789.php.

———. *The Virginia Report of 1799–1800, Touching the Alien and Sedition Laws*. Richmond: J. W. Randolph, 1850.

Maher, Amanda. "What Skinner Misses about Machiavelli's Freedom: Inequality, Corruption, and the Institutional Origins of Civic Virtue." *Journal of Politics* 78, no. 4 (2016): 1003–15.

Main, Jackson T. *The Antifederalists: Critics of the Constitution, 1781–1788*. Chapel Hill: University of North Carolina Press, 2004.

Manin, Bernard. *The Principles of Representative Government*. Cambridge: Cambridge University Press, 2010.

Mansbridge, Jane. *Beyond Adversary Democracy*. New York: Basic Books, 1980.

Markell, Patchen. "The Experience of Action." In *Thinking in Dark Times: The Legacy of Hannah Arendt*, edited by Robert Berkowitz, J. Katz, and T. Keenan, 5–102. New York: Fordham University Press, 2010.

———. "The Rule of the People: Arendt, Archê, and Democracy." *American Political Science Review* 100, no. 1 (2006): 1–14.

Marx, Karl. "The German Ideology." In *The Marx-Engels Reader*, edited by Robert C. Tucker, 146–200. New York: Norton, 1978.

The Marx-Engels Reader. Edited by Robert C. Tucker. New York: Norton, 1978.

Mayer, Arno. *The Furies: Violence and Terror in the French and Russian Revolutions*. Princeton, NJ: Princeton University Press, 2013.

McCormick, John. "Democracy, Plutocracy and the Populist Cry of Pain." John Cabot University Rome Political Theory Colloquium, 2018.

———. "'Keep the Public Rich, but the Citizens Poor': Economic and Political Inequality in Constitutions, Ancient and Modern." *Cardozo Law Review* 34, no. 3 (2013): 879–92.

———. "Machiavelli against Republicanism: On the Cambridge School's "Guicciardinian Moments." *Political Theory* 31, no. 5 (2003): 615–43.

———. *Machiavellian Democracy*. Cambridge: Cambridge University Press, 2011.

———. "Machiavellian Democracy in the Good Society." *Good Society* 21, no. 1 (2012): 90–117.

———. "Machiavelli's Inglorious Tyrants: On Agathocles, Scipio and Unmerited Glory." *History of Political Thought* 36, no. 1 (2015): 29–52.

Meader, Lewis H. "The Council of Censors." *Pennsylvania Magazine of History and Biography* 22, no. 3 (1898): 265–300.

Mendle, Michael. *Dangerous Positions: Mixed Government, the Estates of the Realm and the Making of the Answer to the XIX Propositions*. Tuscaloosa: University of Alabama Press, 1985.

Merrill, Elmer T. "The Attitude of Ancient Rome toward Religion and Religious Cults." *Classical Journal* 15, no. 4 (1920): 196–215.

Michels, Robert. *Political Parties: A Sociological Study of the Oligarchical Tendencies of Modern Democracy*. New York: Dover, 1959.

Miéville, China. *Between Equal Rights: A Marxist Theory of International Law*. London: Pluto, 2006.

Mill, J. S. *Considerations on Representative Government*. London: Saville and Edwards, Printers, 1861.

Millar, Fergus. *The Crowd in Rome in the Late Republic*. Ann Arbor: University of Michigan Press, 2005.

Mintz, Max M. "Condorcet's Reconsideration of America as a Model for Europe." *Journal of the Early Republic* 11, no. 4 (Winter 1991): 493–506.

Mitchell, Allan. *Revolution in Bavaria, 1918–1919: The Eisner Regime and the Soviet Republic*. Princeton, NJ: Princeton University Press, 1965.

Montesquieu. *The Spirit of the Laws*. Cambridge: Cambridge University Press, 1989.

Mortati, Constantino. *Constitución en sentido material*. Madrid: Centro de Estudios Políticos y Constitucionales, 2000.

Mouffe, Chantal. "Deliberative Democracy or Agonistic Pluralism?" *Social Research* 66, no. 3 (1999): 745–58.

Muldoon, James. "Arendt's Revolutionary Constitutionalism: Between Constituent Power and Constitutional Form." *Constellations* 23, no. 4 (2016): 596–607.

———. "The Origins of Hannah Arendt's Council System." *History of Political Thought* 37, no. 4 (2016): 761–89.

Mungiu-Pippidi, Alina. *The Quest for Good Governance: How Societies Develop Control of Corruption*. Cambridge: Cambridge University Press, 2015.

Najemy, John M. "Guild Republicanism in Trecento Florence: The Successes and Ultimate Failure of Corporate Politics." *American Historical Review* 84, no. 1 (February 1979): 53–71.

———. *A History of Florence: 1200–1575*. Oxford: Wiley-Blackwell, 2006.

Negri, Antonio. *Insurgencies: Constituent Power and the Modern State*. Minneapolis: University of Minnesota Press, 2009.

Nettl, John Peter. *Rosa Luxemburg*. Vol. 2. London: Oxford University Press, 1966.

Ober, Josiah. *Democracy and Knowledge: Innovation and Learning in Classical Athens*. Princeton, NJ: Princeton University Press, 2010.

———. *Demopolis: Democracy before Liberalism in Theory and Practice*. Cambridge: Cambridge University Press, 2018.

———. *Mass and Elite in Democratic Athens: Rhetoric, Ideology, and the Power of the People*. Princeton, NJ: Princeton University Press, 1989.

Olson, Mancur. *The Logic of Collective Action: Public Goods and the Theory of Groups*. Cambridge, MA: Harvard University Press, 2012.

Paine, Thomas. *Rights of Man*. New York: Penguin Books, 1985.

Palti, Elias J. "On the Thesis of the Essential Contestability of Concepts, and 19th Century Latin American Intellectual History." In *Redescriptions: Yearbook of Political Thought and Conceptual History*, edited by Kari Palonen, Pasiu Ihalainen, and Tuija Pulkkinen, 113–34. Münster: LIT Verlag, 2005.

Pashukanis, Evgeny. *The General Theory of Law and Marxism*. London: Routledge, 2017.

Pasquino, Pasquale. "Classifying Constitutions: Preliminary Conceptual Analysis." *Cardozo Law Review* 34, no. 3 (2013): 999–1020.

———. "Machiavelli and Aristotle: The Anatomies of the City." *History of European Ideas* 35 (2009): 397–407.

Pedullà, Gabriele. *Machiavelli in Tumult: The Discourses on Livy and the Origins of Political Conflictualism*. New York: Cambridge University Press, 2019.

Peltonen, Markku. "Citizenship and Republicanism in Elizabethan England." In *Republicanism: A Shared European Heritage*, vol 1., edited by Martin van Gelderen and Quentin Skinner, 85–106. Cambridge: Cambridge University Press, 2004.

Peters, F. E. *Greek Philosophical Terms: A Historical Lexicon*. New York: New York University Press, 1974.

Pettit, Philip. *On the People's Terms: A Republican Theory and Model of Democracy*. Cambridge: Cambridge University Press, 2014.

———. *A Theory of Freedom: From the Psychology to the Politics of Agency*. Cambridge, MA: Polity, 2001.

———. *Republicanism: A Theory of Freedom and Government*. Oxford: Oxford University Press, 1999.

Philp, Mark. "Defining Political Corruption." In *Political Corruption*, edited by Arnold Heidenheimer, 17–29. New York: Routledge, 2015.

Pierson, Paul. "Big, Slow-Moving, and . . . Invisible: Macrosocial Processes in the Study of Comparative Politics." In *Comparative Historical Analysis in the Social Sciences*, edited by James Mahoney and Dietrich Rueschemeyer, 77–207. New York: Cambridge University Press, 2003.

Plato. *Laws*. Cambridge, MA: Harvard University Press, 1984.

———. *The Republic*. New York: Cambridge University Press, 2008.

———. *Timaeus*. Indianapolis: Bobbs-Merrill, 1959.

Plutarch. "Life of Tiberius and Caius Gracchi." In *Plutarch's Lives: A Selection*, translated by Thomas North, 163–207. Cambridge: Cambridge University Press, 2014.

Pocock, J.G.A. (John). "The Classical Theory of Deference." *American Historical Review* 81, no. 3 (June 1976): 516–23.

———. *The Machiavellian Moment*. Princeton, NJ: Princeton University Press, 1975.

Polybius. *The Histories*. Translated by Robin Waterfield. Oxford: Oxford University Press, 2010.

Popkin, Richard H. "Condorcet, Abolitionist." In *Condorcet Studies*, edited by Leonora C. Rosenfield, 35–47. Atlantic Highlands, NJ: Humanities, 1984.

Przeworski, Adam. *Democracy and the Market: Political and Economic Reforms in Eastern Europe and Latin America*. Cambridge: Cambridge University Press, 1991.

———. "Minimalist Conception of Democracy: A Defense." In *Democracy's Values*, edited by Ian Shapiro and Casiano Hacker-Cordón, 23–55. Cambridge: Cambridge University Press, 1999.

The Radical Machiavelli: Politics, Philosophy and Language, edited by Filippo Del Lucchese, Fabio Frosini, and Vittorio Morfino. New York: Brill, 2015.

Rahe, Paul. "Machiavelli and the Modern Tyrant." In *Machiavelli on Liberty and Conflict*, edited by David Johnston, Nadia Urbinati, and Camila Vergara, 207–31. Chicago: University of Chicago Press, 2017.

———. *Republics Ancient and Modern*. Vol. 2. Chapel Hill: University of North Carolina Press, 1994.

———. *Soft Despotism, Democracy's Drift: Montesquieu, Rousseau, Tocqueville, and the Modern Prospect*. New Haven, CT: Yale University Press, 2009.

Rana, Aziz. *The Two Faces of American Freedom*. Cambridge, MA: Harvard University Press, 2010.

Rancière, Jacques. *Disagreement: Politics and Philosophy*. Minneapolis: University of Minnesota Press, 1998.

———. *Dissensus: On Politics and Aesthetics*. London: Continuum, 2010.

Rasmussen, Dennis. "Adam Smith on What Is Wrong with Economic Inequality." *American Political Science Review* 110, no. 2 (2016): 342–52.

The Records of the Federal Convention of 1787. Edited by Max Farrand. New Haven, CT: Yale University Press, 2008.

Republicanism: A Shared European Heritage. Vol 1. Edited by Martin van Gelderen and Quentin Skinner. Cambridge: Cambridge University Press, 2004.

Riklin, Alois. "Division of Power 'Avant La Lettre': Donato Giannotti (1534)." *History of Political Thought* 29, no. 2 (Summer 2008): 257–72.

The Rosa Luxemburg Reader. Edited by Peter Hudis and Kevin Anderson. New York: Monthly Review Press, 2004.

Rosanvallon, Pierre. *Counter-democracy: Politics in an Age of Distrust*. Cambridge: Cambridge University Press, 2013.

Rose-Ackerman, Susan, and Bonnie J. Palifka. *Corruption and Government: Causes, Consequences, and Reform*. Cambridge: Cambridge University Press, 2016.

Rosenkranz, Nicholas Quinn. "Condorcet and the Constitution: A Response to 'The Law of Other States.'" In "Symposium on Global Constitutionalism," special issue, *Stanford Law Review* 59, no. 5 (March 2007): 1281–308.

Ross, Kristin. *The Emergence of Social Space*. London: Verso, 2008.

Rothstein, Bo. *The Quality of Government: Corruption, Social Trust, and Inequality in International Perspective*. Chicago: University of Chicago Press, 2011.

Rousseau, Jean-Jacques. *The Social Contract and Discourses*. London: J. M. Dent, 1993.

Rubinstein, Nicolai, and Sarah-Louise Raillard. "The Early Years of Florence's Grand Council (1494–1499)." *Revue française de science politique* (English edition) 64, no. 6 (2014): 99–127.

Saez, Immanuel, and Thomas Piketty. "Income Inequality in the United States, 1913–1998." *Quarterly Journal of Economics* 118, no. 1 (2003 [2015]): 1–39. http://eml.berkeley.edu/~saez/.

Saffon, Maria Paula, and Nadia Urbinati. "Procedural Democracy, the Bulwark of Equal Liberty." *Political Theory* 41, no. 3 (2013): 441–81.

Salvadori, Massimo. *Karl Kautsky and the Socialist Revolution 1880–1938*. London: Verso, 1990.

Schapiro, Salwyn. *Condorcet and the Rise of Liberalism*. New York: Octagon Books, 1963.

Schofield, Norman. *Architects of Political Change: Constitutional Quandaries and Social Choice Theory*. New York: Cambridge University Press, 2006.

Schumpeter, Joseph. *Capitalism, Socialism, and Democracy*. New York: Harper and Brothers, 1950.

Scott, James. *Domination and the Arts of Resistance: Hidden Transcripts*. New Haven, CT: Yale University Press, 1990.

Scott, Jonathan. "Classical Republicanism in Seventeenth-Century England and the Netherlands." In *Republicanism: A Shared Heritage*, vol. 1, 61–82. Cambridge: Cambridge University Press, 2002.

Shklar, J. N. "Hannah Arendt as Pariah." In *Political Thought and Political Thinkers*, 362–75. Chicago: University of Chicago Press, 1998.

Shoikhedbrod, Igor. "Estranged Bedfellows: Why Pashukanis Still Charms Legal Formalists." *Legal Form: A Forum for Marxist Analysis of Law*, June 15, 2018. https://legalform.blog/2018/06/15/estranged-bedfellows-why-pashukanis-still-charms-legal-formalists-igor-shoikhedbrod/.

Simplicius. *Commentary on Aristotle's Physics*. Ithaca, NY: Cornell University Press, 1992.

Skinner, Quentin. *The Foundations of Modern Political Thought*. Vol. 1. Cambridge: Cambridge University Press, 1978.

———. *Hobbes and Republican Liberty*. Cambridge: Cambridge University Press, 2008.

———. *Liberty before Liberalism*. Cambridge: Cambridge University Press, 1998.

———. "Machiavelli on the Maintenance of Liberty." *Politics* 18 (1983): 3–15.

———. "Meaning and Understanding in the History of Ideas." *History and Theory* 8 (1969): 3–53.

———. "The Republican Ideal of Political Liberty." In *Machiavelli and Republicanism*, edited by Gisela Bock, 293–309. Cambridge: Cambridge University Press, 1990.

Slobodian, Quinn. *Globalists: The End of Empire and the Birth of Neoliberalism*. Cambridge, MA: Harvard University Press, 2018.

Smith, Graham. "Machiavellian Democracy, Differentiated Citizenship, and Civic Unity." *Good Society* 20, no. 2 (2011): 240–48.

Smith, Graham, and David Owen. "Machiavellian Democratic Innovations: McCormick's People's Tribunate." *Good Society* 20, no. 2 (2011): 203–15.

Sparling, Robert. "Political Corruption and the Concept of Dependence in Republican Thought." *Political Theory* 41, no. 4 (2013): 618–47.

Sparling, Robert. "The Concept of Corruption in J.G.A. Pocock's *The Machiavellian Moment*." *History of European Ideas* 43, no. 2 (2017): 156–70.

Spitz, Jean Fabien. "Is Structural Domination a Coherent Concept?" Paper delivered at the 3rd Biennial of Ideas in Politics, "Republicanism in the History of Political Philosophy and Today." Prague, Check Republic, November 4, 2017.

Stepan, Alfred, and Juan J. Linz. "Comparative Perspectives on Inequality and the Quality of Democracy in the United States." *Perspectives on Politics* 9, no. 4 (December 2011): 841–56.

Tamboukou, Maria. "Imagining and Living the Revolution: An Arendtian Reading of Rosa Luxemburg's Letters and Writings." *Feminist Review* 106 (2014): 27–42.

Taylor, Keeanga-Yamahtta. *Race for Profit: How Banks and the Real Estate Industry Undermined Black Homeownership*. Chapel Hill: University of North Carolina Press, 2019.

Teachout, Zephyr. *Corruption in America: From Benjamin Franklin's Snuff Box to Citizens United*. Cambridge, MA: Harvard University Press, 2014.

Tenney, Frank. *An Economic History of Rome*. New York: Cosimo Classics, 2005.

Teubner, Gunther. *Constitutional Fragments: Societal Constitutionalism and Globalization*. Oxford: Oxford University Press, 2014.

Thompson, Dennis. *Ethics in Congress: From Individual to Institutional Corruption*. Washington, DC: Brookings Institution, 1995.

———. "Two Concepts of Corruption: Making Electoral Campaigns Safe for Democracy." *George Washington Law Review* 73 (2005): 1036–69.

Thornhill, C. J. *A Sociology of Constitutions: Constitutions and State Legitimacy in Historical-Sociological Perspective*. Cambridge: Cambridge University Press, 2013.

Thucydides. *History of the Peloponnesian War*. London: Penguin Books, 1972.

Timpanaro, Sebastiano. *On Materialism*. London: Verso, 1980.

Torres, Sebastián. "Tempo e politica: Una lettura materialista di Machiavelli." In *The Radical Machiavelli: Politics, Philosophy and Language*, edited by Filippo Del Lucchese, Fabio Frosini, and Vittorio Morfino, 174–89. Boston: Brill, 2015.

Tromp, G. W. *The Idea of Historical Recurrence in Western Thought: From Antiquity to the Reformation*. Berkeley: University of California Press, 1979.

Tuck, Richard. *Philosophy and Government: 1572–1651*. Cambridge: Cambridge University Press, 2011.

———. *The Sleeping Sovereign: The Invention of Modern Democracy*. Cambridge: Cambridge University Press, 2016.

Tushnet, Mark. "The Issue of State Action/Horizontal Effect in Comparative Constitutional Law." *International Journal of Constitutional Law* 1, no. 1 (January 2003): 79–98.

Unger, Roberto. *The Critical Legal Studies Movement*. Cambridge, MA: Harvard University Press, 1986.

———. *Democracy Realized: The Progressive Alternative*. New York: Verso, 1998.

Urbinati, Nadia. "Condorcet's Democratic Theory of Representative Government." *European Journal of Political Theory* 3, no. 1 (2004): 53–75.

———. *Representative Democracy: Principles and Genealogy*. Chicago: University of Chicago Press, 2008.

Vatter, Miguel. *Between Form and Matter: Machiavelli's Theory of Freedom*. New York: Fordham University Press, 2014.

———. "Machiavelli after Marx: The Self-Overcoming of Marxism in the Late Althusser." *Theory and Event* 7, no. 4 (2005). muse.jhu.edu/article/244122.

———. "Neoliberalism and Republicanism: Economic Rule of Law and Law as Concrete Order (*Nomos*)." In *The SAGE Handbook of Neoliberalism*, edited by Damien Cahill, Melinda Cooper, Martijn Konings, and David Primrose, 370–83. London: Sage, 2018.

———. "The Quarrel between Populism and Republicanism: Machiavelli and the Antinomies of Plebeian Politics." *Contemporary Political Theory* 11, no. 3 (2012): 242–63.

Vergara, Camila. Machiavelli's "Republican Constituent Power," In *Machiavelli's Discourses on Livy. New Readings*, edited by Diogo Pires Aurelio and Andre Santos Campos. Brill, forthcoming.

———. "Lenin and the Materialist Critique of Law." In *The Futures of Lenin*, edited by Alla Ivanchikov and Robert Maclean. State University of New York Press, forthcoming.

———. "Populism as Plebeian Politics: Inequality, Domination, and Popular Empowerment." *Journal of Political Philosophy* 28.2 (2020), 222–46.

Vile, M.J.C. *Constitutionalism and the Separation of Powers*. Oxford: Clarendon, 1967.

Viroli, Maurizio. "Machiavelli and the Republican Idea of Politics." In *Machiavelli and Republicanism*, edited by Gisela Bock, Quentin Skinner, and Maurizio Viroli. Cambridge: Cambridge University Press, 1990.

Vishnia, Rachel Feig. *State, Society, and Popular Leaders in Mid-republican Rome, 241–167 BC*. London: Routledge, 1996.

Vollrath, Ernst. "Rosa Luxemburg's Theory of Revolution." *Social Research* 40, no. 1 (Spring 1973): 83–109.

Ward, Julie. "Two Conceptions of *Physis* in Aristotle's Ethics and Politics." *Asia International Forum*, June 4, 2010. http://www.siue.edu/EASTASIA/Ward_022503.htm.

West, Thomas G. *Vindicating the Founders: Race, Sex, Class, and Justice in the Origins of America.* Lanham, MD: Rowman and Littlefield, 2001.

Winter, Yves. *Machiavelli and the Orders of Violence.* Cambridge: Cambridge University Press, 2018.

———. "Plebeian Politics: Machiavelli and the Ciompi Uprising." *Political Theory* 40, no. 6 (2012): 739–43.

Wirszubski, Chaim. *Libertas as a Political Idea at Rome during the Late Republic and Early Principate.* New York: Cambridge University Press, 2007.

Wolff, Edward N. "Household Wealth Trends in the United States, 1962 to 2016: Has Middle Class Wealth Recovered?" *NBER*, Working Paper No. 24085, November 2017.

Worden, Blair. "Republicanism, Regicide and Republic: The English Experience." In *Republicanism: A Shared European Heritage*, vol 1, edited by Martin van Gelderen and Quentin Skinner, 307–28. Cambridge: Cambridge University Press, 2004.

Young, Alfred F., Gary B. Nash, and Ray Raphael. *Revolutionary Founders: Rebels, Radicals, and Reformers in the Making of the Nation.* New York: Vintage Books, 2012.

Young-Bruehl, Elisabeth. *Hannah Arendt: For Love of the World.* London: Yale University Press, 2004.

Zerilli, Linda. "'We Feel Our Freedom': Imagination and Judgment in the Thought of Hannah Arendt." *Political Theory* 33, no. 2 (April 2005): 158–88.

Zetterberg, Pär. "Do Gender Quotas Foster Women's Political Engagement? Lessons from Latin America." *Political Research Quarterly* 62, no. 4 (December 2009): 715–30.

Zinn, Howard, ed. *The People Speak: American Voices, Some Famous, Some Little Known.* New York: HarperCollins, 2004.

INDEX

Ackerman, Bruce, 104–5

Adams, Abigail, 82

Adams, John, 81, 130, 149ft25

Agrarian Law, 50, 60, 128

Althusser, Louis, 102n2, 128, 224

ambition, 52, 68–75, 93, 126, 138, 141, 152

America. *See* United States

anarchy, 19, 52, 63

Anaxagoras, 16

Anaximander, 16

anti-oligarchic, 5, 8, 108–13, 121, 133, 137, 141, 232

Aquinas, Thomas, 26

Arendt, Hannah, 3, 7–10, 45, 109, 112, 145n4, 184–215, 241–42, 245–46, 266

Areopagus, 17, 21

aristocracy/aristocratic, 17–21, 24, 46–53, 57, 60, 66–74, 79, 86–92, 107–8, 126, 145, 188, 226

Aristotle, 2, 5, 16, 18n24, 19–26, 32, 38, 43, 107, 130n19, 187–89, 192, 246

assembly: in ancient Athens, 16–17, 20–21; cantonal, 4n9; local, 5, 10, 148, 151–52, 156–57, 212–13, 245–46, 252–64; primary, 8, 111, 146–47, 152–67, 245; in Rome, 30–31; in Venice, 62–63

Athens, 16–17, 20–21, 31, 52, 61, 233

Augustine, 26, 55

authority, 7, 10, 19–20, 24–27, 44, 47–54, 59, 63, 66–67, 78, 94, 97

Barthas, Jérémie, 27, 131

Beard, Charles, 198

Bernstein, Eduard, 170, 173

Bill of Rights, 93, 141, 209

Boule, 247

bourgeois: dictatorship, 178; law, 117; revolution, 171–73, 182; state, 176–77, 180

Breaugh, Martin, 9, 219–20, 222, 224

Brutus, sons of, 141

capital punishment, 50, 233–34

capitalism/capitalist, 35, 41, 109, 113, 116–21, 144, 169–76, 179, 182–83, 189, 206

censor/censorial, 3–5, 47, 62n90, 93, 141, 146–47, 150–52, 159–66, 214–15, 243, 249n10, 256

Chernyshevsky, Nikolay, 265

Chile, 1, 2n6, 41n121, 242, 243n1

Cicero, 2, 6, 26–28, 34, 45, 51–55, 59–60, 71–72, 101, 126, 206, 221

Ciompi Revolt, 139

civil war, 53, 55, 57, 174, 210

Cleisthenes, 16

clientelism, 37

commerce, 33, 68–75, 78–79, 83, 84n175, 90

Committees of Correspondence, 78, 112

conciliar system, 236–37

Condorcet, Nicolas de, 3, 7–10, 45, 103n9, 109–12, 144–67, 188, 192, 241–42, 245–49

conflict/tumults: and constituent power, 138–40; and corruption, 111–12; and elitist republicanism, 7, 53, 64, 107; of interest, 78, 81, 113, 117–20, 151, 183, 197–98, 212; and plebeian constitutionalism, 109, 127; as productive of liberty, 8, 27, 33, 103, 108–10, 126–30, 139, 148, 169, 213, 224–25, 232n53, 236, 242, 247n7

A NOTE ON THE TYPE

This book has been composed in Arno, an Old-style serif typeface in the classic Venetian tradition, designed by Robert Slimbach at Adobe.

CPSIA information can be obtained
at www.ICGtesting.com
Printed in the USA
JSHW040215080422
24733JS00006B/6